Psychological Development
and Early Childhood

This publication forms part of an Open University course ED209 *Child Development*. Details of this and other Open University courses can be obtained from the Student Registration and Enquiry Service, The Open University, PO Box 625, Milton Keynes, MK7 6YG, United Kingdom: tel. +44 (0)1908 653231, email general-enquiries@open.ac.uk

Alternatively, you may visit the Open University website at http://www.open.ac.uk where you can learn more about the wide range of courses and packs offered at all levels by The Open University.

To purchase a selection of Open University course materials visit http://www.ouw.co.uk, or contact Open University Worldwide, Michael Young Building, Walton Hall, Milton Keynes MK7 6AA, United Kingdom for a brochure. tel. +44 (0)1908 858785; fax +44 (0)1908 858787; email ouwenq@open.ac.uk

Psychological Development and Early Childhood

John Oates, Clare Wood and Andrew Grayson

The Open University

Blackwell
Publishing

First published 2005 by Blackwell Publishing Ltd in association with The Open University
Reprinted 2009

The Open University
Walton Hall, Milton Keynes
MK7 6AA

Blackwell Publishing Ltd:

350 Main Street, Malden, MA 02148-5020, USA
9600 Garsington Road, Oxford OX4 2DQ, UK
550 Swanston Street, Carlton, Victoria 3053, Australia

For further information on Blackwell Publishing please visit our website:
www.blackwellpublishing.com

Library of Congress Cataloguing in Publication Data has been applied for.
A catalogue record for this title is available from the British Library.

Edited, designed and typeset by The Open University.

Printed in the United Kingdom by TJ International Ltd, Padstow.

ISBN 13: 978-1-4051-1693-0 (paperback)

ISBN 10: 1-4051-1693-5 (paperback)
1.2

The paper used in this publication contains pulp sourced from forests independently
certified to the Forest Stewardship Council (FSC) principles and criteria. Chain of
custody certification allows the pulp from these forests to be tracked to the end
use (see www.fsc-uk.org).

Contents

Foreword

Creating a textbook like this cannot be done without the collaborative efforts of many people as well as the contributing authors. As editors of the book as a whole, we have valued immensely the knowledge and understanding that has been so ably provided by the consultant authors of the chapters, Emma Flynn, Kieron Sheehy, Alan Slater, Jim Stevenson, Martin Woodhead, Mark Norrish and Nigel Wilson, as well as those in the Child Development course team. Our critical readers, Brenda Clayton, Sandy George, Rebecca Johnson, Wendy Lawrenson, Janet Thelander, Malou Spier, Sandy Banks, Donald Bennett, Linda Castle, Joanne Dawson, Sally Gallagher and Krysia Potten, provided much useful encouragement and constructive critique, and Iris Rowbotham helped throughout to manage the project efficiently. Bridgette Jones and Julia Brennan gave us outstanding support in editing the text, greatly improving the clarity of presentation. Stephanie Withers' speed and precision in turning our drafts into electronic copy was admirable throughout, and we would also like to thank Jonathan Davies and Sian Lewis, the designers; Roy Lawrance, Victoria Eves and Janis Gilbert, our illustrators; and Nikki Tolcher our compositor. Last, but not least, our External Assessor, Alyson Davies of the University of Surrey for her comments on the chapter drafts.

John Oates

Clare Wood

Andrew Grayson

Introduction

John Oates, Clare Wood and Andrew Grayson

This book is about the foundations of development in two senses; first, it focuses on the early months and years of children's lives because so much of what goes on during this period is considered by psychologists to be of significance for development throughout childhood, as well as worthy of study in its own right. Secondly, it is about the theoretical foundations of research into child development and gives an introduction to the main influences on the ways in which psychologists have investigated the development of children.

These two aspects are not quite as separate as they may seem at first sight. Theories about child development affect how children are viewed, and they affect the sorts of questions to which researchers seek to find answers. Everyone has ideas and theories about children's development and the influences on it, if only because we were all children ourselves once, and we will have given at least some thought to how our early experiences have influenced what we are. For this reason, the book starts, in Chapter 1, with an examination of a range of different images of children and childhood. An important aim of this chapter is to begin the process of examining our most basic assumptions about child development. This leads to a consideration in Chapter 2 of four influential theories of child development which, in different ways, reflect the questions asked more generally about what the potential influences on development might be.

Psychologists realize that there may be many different and equally appropriate ways of 'bringing up children', and that there may be no absolute yardstick of the 'normal course of development' against which to assess any particular set of practices and beliefs. Rather, the authors of these chapters share a view that child development should be treated as an expression of cultural expectations. In this way of thinking about child development, what a child comes to be is largely a matter of what is appropriate for the culture in which they develop. Through those who care for them, children are exposed to ways of thinking, behaving and feeling that contain all sorts of implicit ideas about what it is to be a person within a particular culture.

Are children then merely passive recipients of the influences of their environments? Our answer to this is a definite 'no', and this book aims to show how the most appropriate model of child development needs to recognize that children are active agents in their own development, in other words, that a transactional relationship holds between children and their environments. Children influence what happens to them just as they are influenced by their experiences.

Chapter 3 examines the links between what we know of the physical development of infants' senses, a fascinating story in itself, with the way in which their senses seem to be particularly well-matched to their social worlds. The chapter also stresses the cognitive work of constructing mental representations of the world with which infants have to engage. In Chapter 4, infant cognition is further examined by reviewing research into how infants come to see the world as made up of objects that have identity and permanence, a theme that is revisited in the final chapter of the book.

In Chapter 5, the transactional view of child development comes to the fore again, as the authors examine the complex issues surrounding the differences that are seen, even from birth, in the way individual babies behave. While the extent to which these are genetically determined remains an open question, this chapter argues that development rests not only on these individual differences, but also on how children's environments match them and, indeed, are influenced by them.

In Chapter 6, biological influences on child development are considered. The idea is discussed that evolution has prepared children for a level of adaptability, primarily through their prodigious ability to learn, which far transcends the abilities of any other species. The contribution that genetics makes to our understanding of child development has moved beyond notions of simple determination to the view that our biological inheritance equips us with the potential to be many different sorts of people.

The book concludes with a chapter which brings together some of the ideas of developmental theory and research as they apply to the relationships between babies and those who care for them. These first relationships can be seen as the context within which each child comes to be a unique, human individual, with their own skills, thoughts, feelings and ways of being.

Chapter 1
Children and development

Martin Woodhead

Contents

Learning outcomes

After you have studied this chapter you should be able to:

1   consider the significance of diverse ways of thinking about children, including the idea that children are developing;
2   describe the origins of developmental research in terms of the social and economic context of Western societies and the emergence of scientific approaches;
3   analyse some key concepts involved in developmental research, drawing on examples from different aspects of development;
4   discuss historical ideas about how development occurs, especially the significance of 'nature' and 'nurture';
5   evaluate the relevance of theories about children's development in global cultural contexts, especially the relative importance attached to work, play and learning.

1   Introduction: a right to development

Social attitudes towards children have changed dramatically in recent decades, notably through the influence of the United Nations Convention on the Rights of the Child (UNCRC, 1989), with its strong emphasis on children's rights to be respected and to be consulted about matters that affect them. One hundred and ninety one countries have ratified the UNCRC, making this the most significant international human rights instrument designed to promote children's well-being. The UNCRC draws heavily on the principle that children have a right to development, for example, 'States Parties shall ensure to the maximum extent possible the survival and *development* of the child'. (UNCRC, 1989, Article 6, my emphasis).

The UNCRC was built on many decades of international activity with the goal of improving the treatment and well-being of the world's children. For example, the earliest attempt to codify children's rights declared 'The child must be given the means requisite for its *normal development*, materially, morally and spiritually' (Geneva Declaration of the Rights of the Child, 1924, Article 1, my emphasis). Indeed, recognizing that children are growing and developing was one of the main justifications for a separate UN Convention on the *Rights of the Child*, over and above the 1948 UN Declaration of *Human Rights*. Children are understood as being different in important ways from adults and requiring special provisions. They are seen as more vulnerable and inexperienced, and in many ways dependent on adults who will protect them from harm and promote their development (Burr and Montgomery, 2003).

The UNCRC (1989) includes over 40 articles covering a wide range of children's rights. Concepts of development run throughout the Convention. For example,

Article 27 affirms children's right to provision of a standard of living '... adequate for the child's physical, mental, spiritual, moral and social development'. Article 32 is about protecting children from '... any work that is likely to be hazardous or to interfere with the child's education, or to be harmful to the child's health or physical, mental, spiritual, moral or social development'.

This book is concerned with scientific questions about children's development which have been investigated using a variety of methods: carrying out observations and experiments, constructing theories and testing hypotheses about how children develop, and evaluating major influences on the process of development. Starting with the UNCRC is a reminder that children's development is not just a subject for scientific study. The importance of understanding children's development is widely recognized – for parents, teachers, health visitors, paediatricians, psychologists, social workers, lawyers, policy makers and others who work with, or are responsible for children and young people. Promoting children's development has also become fundamental to the framing and interpretation of international law – and not just in the Western societies where so much of the research has been conducted.

This chapter will introduce you to the study of child development. Early sections will outline the historical context within which developmental theory and research has become so significant. It will examine the concept of 'development', and summarize some of the ways children can be described as 'developing'. The scientific study of children's development originated within Western societies, but the influence of developmental ideas is now widespread. The chapter concludes by outlining some of the challenges of applying child development research and theory in global contexts.

Summary of Section 1

- The United Nations Convention on the Rights of the Child (UNCRC, 1989) is designed to promote children's well-being throughout the world.
- The idea that children are developing and that their development must be protected and promoted is central to articles of the Convention.

2   Images of childhood

Within any one culture, people's ideas of what childhood is and what a child is may vary according to their occupation, gender, ethnicity, and, of course, their own experiences and inclinations. This section begins by asking you to think about your own and other people's ideas about children and childhood.

Activity 1

Allow about
45 minutes

What is a child?

This activity will stimulate your thoughts about different ways of understanding children, as a starting point for introducing the concept of child development.

1   When you think of children, what ideas come to mind? Initially, concentrate on visual images of children – how they look, what they are doing and the feelings they evoke in you. Make a note of three contrasting images of children that occur to you, either from personal experiences or images in the media.

2   Now explore some ways in which childhood has changed. For example, think about what it was like for your parents or carers when they were young. Were their experiences of childhood different from the experiences of children today? Next, think about your own memories and then think about children growing up today. Some areas of change might relate to home, school or starting work, clothing, games and pastimes, deference to authority, or differences between boys and girls.

3   Finally, think about your personal beliefs about children, and about how they should be treated at different ages. For example, in relation to care, the importance of play and learning, how much freedom they should be allowed or the role of discipline. You may find these proverbs a useful starting point:

'Children are the wealth of the nation' (proverb – Tanzania)

'Children are innocent like angels; they can't do any harm' (proverb – Pakistan)

'A tree should be bent while it is still young' (proverb – South Africa)

'The egg should not be smarter than the duck' (proverb – Vietnam)

'It is the young trees that make the forest thick' (proverb – Uganda)

(Cited in Kirby and Woodhead, 2003, p. 234)

If you can, ask someone else about (1), (2) and (3) and compare your ideas.

Comment

While carrying out this activity, you may have found that you have very definite ideas about children and childhood. You may also have become aware of the sources of these views; for example, memories of your own childhood, experiences with your own children or with the children of others, your parents' or grandparents' views, the views of your community, information in books and other media or religious belief. If you were able to talk to someone else for this activity you may have found a wide range of views and you may also be aware of the way these ideas have changed over time. For example, during the early decades of the twentieth century, parents were urged to feed their new babies according to a strict timetable and not to pick them up when they cried, which may seem unthinkable to new parents nowadays.

Figure 1
What is a child?

If people think about children differently, are behaving differently with children, and consider children themselves are behaving differently, does this mean children are fundamentally different or is it more that people's ideas about childhood have changed?

2.1 Children and childhood

One way to make sense of the huge range of images, beliefs and experiences associated with children is to distinguish between the young people called 'children' and the phase in their lives conventionally known as 'childhood'. You may be able to recall vividly features of your childhood with difficult as well as happy moments. But childhood is not just about personal experiences. Childhood is an important social category which defines children's activities and experiences: for example, in England they must receive education until they reach 16, but they may not vote in elections until they are 18. 'Childhood' also defines children's role and status, and it is closely linked to beliefs about their needs, rights, vulnerabilities and competencies. Children's experiences of childhood are not simply an expression of the fact that they are young, growing and learning. Their childhood is shaped by the circumstances in which they grow up, and by the beliefs and attitudes of those who influence them. This distinction between children and childhood has been summed up by James and Prout:

> The immaturity of children is a biological fact but the ways in which that immaturity is understood is a fact of culture ... childhood is ... *constructed and reconstructed* both *for and by* children.

> (James and Prout, 1997, p. 7, my emphasis)

The final phrase of this quotation contains two other important ideas about childhood. Describing childhood as 'constructed and reconstructed' draws attention to its variable and changing character. Childhood has been understood in very different ways at different periods in Western history. Differences are marked both within and between societies, for example according to children's gender, ethnicity or social and economic background. One illustration of the 'constructed and reconstructed' status of childhood is seen in changes in law, as for example when school-leaving ages in England were raised to 14 in 1918, to 15 in 1936 and to 16 in 1973. Meanwhile voting ages in England were lowered from 21 to 18 in 1970. Each of these changes generated debate about children's needs and capacities at various ages although the fact that children were considered capable of voting earlier, but were required to stay on at school longer, suggests that children's needs and capacities were not the only considerations affecting these changes in policy. In fact, legal definitions often appear inconsistent and are frequently contested.

Describing childhood as constructed both 'for and by' children raises the issue of children's own role in shaping their childhoods. Children's experiences are powerfully influenced by adults in terms of the laws, regulations, curricula and practices that shape their lives at home, in schools, hospitals and playgrounds, as well as the influence of individual parents, teachers and others. But children are not always under the direct influence of adults, especially when they are playing with others or sharing in peer culture (Kehily and Swann, 2003). And even when children are with adults, they shape these adults as well as being shaped by them. They negotiate their daily lives, their rights, responsibilities, activities and the choices available about what they do, although how far these choices are possible depends on their circumstances (see Box 1).

Figure 2   Children negotiate their daily lives with adults.

BOX I

Children on childhood

Brian (8 years, USA)

'I'm a child because, if I was a baby I would be still small. And, and now I'm a child because I'm not a baby any more. Because I'm, I'm grown up.'

Joshua (8 years, South Africa)

'A child is like a little person who's learning how to be ... moulded into adult.'

Sophie (12 years, USA)

'I think I am kind of a child. But I'm kind of more getting out of my child stage and more into my like older stage ... I think I'll be an adult when I get my bat mitzvah. I'll feel more grown up.'

Yassir and Yamin (14 years, Bangladesh)

'I think an adult is somebody who has passed school. And we're still young so that's why we are a child ... There are less worries being a child. And we would have to be a lot more responsible when we are an adult.'

Assanda (15 years, South Africa)

'Ever since I joined Molo Songololo [a youth organization] I've kind of changed, in the way that I have – what can I call it? – I have grown into myself, you understand, because now I've been given a chance to express my views: what I think ... how I live and how I would express myself as a child.'

Maya (about 15 years, Bangladesh, on being a mother)

'There are more responsibilities as a wife and mother but I don't feel like an adult. I feel I'm a young girl. I don't feel like I'm a grown-up.'

Source: Stainton Rogers, 2003, pp. 7–8.

Whatever the context, you can see from Box 1 that children construct their own personal understandings of what it means to be a child. In all these senses then, children need to be understood not just as passive victims of circumstance but as 'social actors' with beliefs and ideas of their own.

Summary of Section 2

- Ideas and beliefs about children vary according to people's age, gender, social background and values and according to the time and place in which they are living.
- Definitions of childhood vary between societies and at different periods of history and are illustrated by laws that define when childhood ends.
- Although adults play a powerful role in defining children's experiences of childhood, children are also 'social actors' who have ideas and beliefs of their own.

3   Childhood as development

It is important to recognize that the idea that children are different from adults – and especially that they are developing physically and psychologically – has become a powerful framework for thinking about (or constructing) childhood. This section briefly sketches the historical background to child development, tracing how children's lives increasingly became differentiated from the world of adults, how greater attention was given to children's distinctive characteristics and needs and how 'child development' became a recognized field for research. My aim is to illustrate how developmental approaches emerged as a dominant paradigm for thinking about childhood and planning for children's well-being in Western industrial societies. Different accounts of the history of childhood could be offered for other cultural traditions. My reason for concentrating on Western societies is because scientific approaches to child development originated in these contexts and these approaches are now globally influential.

3.1   Origins of child study in Western societies

The 'discovery' of childhood?

One of the most hotly debated issues in the history of childhood has been whether childhood is itself a recent invention. The historian Philippe Ariès argued that in Western Europe during the Middle Ages (up to about the end of the fifteenth century) children were regarded as miniature adults, with all the intellect and personality that this implies. He scrutinized medieval pictures and diaries, and found no distinction between children and adults as they shared similar leisure activities and often the same type of work. Ariès, however, pointed out that:

> this is not to suggest that children were neglected, forsaken or despised. The idea of childhood is not to be confused with affection for children; it corresponds to an awareness of the particular nature of childhood, that particular nature which distinguishes the child from the adult, even the young adult. In medieval society this awareness was lacking. That is why, as soon as the child could live without the constant solicitude of his mother, his nanny or his cradle rocker, he belonged to adult society.
>
> (Ariès, 1962, p. 125)

After the fifteenth century, however, children were increasingly depicted as different from adults, and Ariès argued that this was due to the emergence of a new image of children which stressed their special nature and needs.

Other historians (notably Shahar, 1990) have rejected both Ariès's views and the methods he used to gather evidence for them. They criticized him for depending too heavily on very limited sources (the diaries, letters and pictures to be found only in literate, aristocratic homes) and for drawing conclusions about medieval childhood *in general*. It was felt that these sources presented a selective picture because the poorest children were rarely painted or written about, despite comprising the majority of children.

The useful child

There is a long tradition of the children of the poor playing a functional role in contributing to the family income by working either inside or outside the home. In this sense children are seen as 'useful'. Back in the Middle Ages, children as young as 5 or 6 did important chores for their parents and, from the sixteenth century, were often encouraged (or forced) to leave the family by the age of 9 or 10 to work as servants for wealthier families or to be apprenticed to a trade.

With industrialization in the eighteenth and nineteenth centuries, a new demand for child labour was created, and many children were forced to work for long hours, in mines, workshops and factories. Social reformers began to question whether labouring long hours from an early age would harm children's growing bodies. They began to recognize the potential of carrying out systematic studies to monitor how far these early deprivations might be affecting children's development.

Gradually, the concerns of the reformers began to impact on the working conditions of children. In Britain, the Factory Act of 1833 signified the beginning of legal protection of children from exploitation and was linked to the rise of schools for factory children. The worst forms of child exploitation were gradually eliminated, partly through factory reform but also through the influence of trade unions and economic changes during the nineteenth century which made some forms of child labour redundant. Childhood was increasingly seen as a time for play and education for all children, not just for a privileged minority. Initiating children into work as 'useful' children became less of a priority. As the age for starting full-time work was delayed, so childhood was increasingly understood as a more extended phase of dependency, development and learning. Even so, work continued to play a significant, if less central role in children's lives throughout the later nineteenth and twentieth centuries. And the 'useful child' has become a controversial image during the first decade of the twenty-first century especially in the context of global concern about large numbers of the world's children engaged in child labour (Cunningham, 2003).

The school child

The Factory Act of 1833 established half-time schools which allowed children to work and attend school. But in the 1840s, a large proportion of children never went to school, and if they did, they left by the age of 10 or 11. The situation was very different by the end of the nineteenth century in Britain. The school became central to images of 'a normal' childhood. Attending school was no longer a privilege (Hendrick, 1990) and all children were expected to spend a significant part of their day in a classroom. By going to school, children's lives were now separated from domestic life at home and from the adult world of work. School became an institution dedicated to shaping the minds, behaviour and morals of the young. Education dominated the management of children's waking hours, not just through the hours spent in classrooms but through 'home' work, the growth of 'after school' activities and the importance attached to 'parental involvement'. Most important, children's performance on school tests and examinations increasingly shaped their future economic and social prospects (Mackinnon, 2003).

Industrialization, urbanization and mass schooling also set new challenges for those responsible for protecting children's welfare, and promoting their learning. Increasingly, children were being treated as a group with distinctive needs and they were organized into groups according to their age. For example, teachers needed to know what to expect of children in their classrooms, what kinds of instruction were appropriate for different age groups and how best to assess children's progress. They also wanted tools that could enable them to sort and select children according to their abilities and potential.

In this section I have briefly traced how the changing roles of children in the economy, the growth of schooling and changing social attitudes towards their needs and well-being combined to generate demand for systematic knowledge about children's growth and development at different ages and stages. These social trends affecting industrial societies during the nineteenth and early twentieth centuries created a climate within which child development became recognized as an important subject of study. But there were also more scholarly reasons why children's development increasingly became recognized as an important subject for scientific study.

3.2 Evolution and the study of development

The Industrial Revolution that so powerfully shaped the lives of children in Western societies also coincided with a revolution in the biological sciences, notably the theory of evolution proposed by Charles Darwin (1809–82). Darwin radically altered ideas about development, of species, of societies and of human beings. His evolutionary theory (set out in his book *Origin of Species*, 1859) challenged beliefs about creation and the relationship of humans to other species. It also focused attention on the significance of immaturity in young humans. The study of human childhoods posed some interesting questions for scientific investigation. For example:

- Why does the human species, in many ways the most complex and sophisticated on earth, give birth to offspring that are so helpless and dependent for care and nurturance over such a long period?
- What is the extended period of human childhood for?
- How do young humans develop from infancy to maturity?
- Is it possible to discover a natural pattern of human development?

At that time, some evolutionists believed that by observing the sequence of changes that occur in human development, the theory that human beings evolved from lower species could be confirmed.

Scientists' acceptance of Darwin's thesis that human beings have evolved from species that developed earlier fundamentally changed the way people thought about children. Instead of imperfect adults to be seen and not heard children came to be viewed as scientifically interesting because their behavior provided evidence that human beings are related to other species. It became fashionable, for example, to compare the behavior of

children to the behavior of higher primates to see if individual children went through a 'chimpanzee stage' similar to the one through which the human species was thought to have evolved ...
(Cole and Cole, 1996, pp. 5–7).

This so-called 'recapitulation theory' of development was soon discredited amongst the scientific community, but basic evolutionary principles have become widely accepted. Darwin did not just revolutionize theoretical ideas about the young of the human species. He made his own contribution to the new science of child study, drawing on principles of observation and experimentation that were already well established in the natural sciences. As a young parent in London during the 1840s, Darwin kept a detailed daily record of his infant son William (nicknamed Doddy). Towards the end of his life, Darwin returned to this diary and wrote an article for the journal *Mind* (published in 1877) outlining his observations. Some brief extracts are in Box 2.

As you read Darwin's account, notice the following:

- the impersonal way Darwin approaches the task of recording his son's development, especially the way he links his observations to the baby's age;
- the way he uses simple experiments to try to find out what his son feels and understands;
- the questions that seem to be guiding Darwin's enquiry, especially about how far observed behaviours are the expression of 'instinct' or shaped by experience and learning;
- the way he compares his son's development with another species as well as with his daughter's development.

BOX 2

Darwin's account of his Son's development

... During the first seven days various reflex actions, namely sneezing, hickuping, yawning, stretching and of course sucking and screaming, were well performed by my infant. On the seventh day, I touched the naked sole of his foot with a bit of paper, and he jerked it away, curling at the same time his toes, like a much older child when tickled.

... At this time, though so early, it seemed clear to me that a warm soft hand applied to his face excited a wish to suck. This must be considered as a reflex or an instinctive action, for it is impossible to believe that experience and association with the touch of his mother's breast could so soon have come into play ...

... It was difficult to decide at how early an age anger was felt; on his eighth day he frowned and wrinkled the skin round his eyes before a crying fit, but this may have been due to pain or distress, and not to anger. When about ten weeks old, he was given some rather cold milk and he kept a slight frown on his forehead all the time that he was sucking, so that he looked like a grown-up person made cross from being compelled to do something which he did not like. When nearly four months old, and perhaps much earlier, there could be no doubt, from the manner in which the blood gushed into his whole face and scalp, that he easily got into a violent passion ... When eleven months old, if a wrong plaything was given him, he would push it away and beat it; I presume that

Figure 3 Charles Darwin pictured with his son Doddy.

the beating was an instinctive sign of anger, like the snapping of the jaws by a young crocodile just out of the egg, and not that he imagined he could hurt the plaything. When two years and three months old, he became a great adept at throwing books or sticks &c., at anyone who offended him; and so it was with some of my other sons. On the other hand, I could never see a trace of such aptitude in my infant daughters; and this makes me think that a tendency to throw objects is inherited by boys...

... The first sign of moral sense was noticed at the age of nearly 13 months: I said 'Doddy (his nickname) won't give poor papa a kiss, – naughty Doddy.' These words, without doubt, made him feel slightly uncomfortable; and at last when I had returned to my chair, he protruded his lips as a sign that he was ready to kiss me; and he then shook his hand in an angry manner until I came and received his kiss. Nearly the same little scene recurred in a few days, and the reconciliation seemed to give him so much satisfaction, that several times afterwards he pretended to be angry and slapped me, and then insisted on giving me a kiss. ...When 2 years and 3 months old, he gave his last bit of gingerbread to his little sister, and then cried out with high self-approbation 'Oh kind Doddy, kind Doddy.' Two months later, he became extremely sensitive to ridicule, and was so suspicious that he often thought people who were laughing and talking together were laughing at him. A little later (2 years and 7 months old) I met him coming out of the dining room with his eyes unnaturally bright, and an odd unnatural or affected manner, so that I went into the room to see who was there, and found that he had been taking pounded sugar, which he had been told not to do. As he had never been in any way punished, his odd manner certainly was not due to fear, and I suppose it was pleasurable excitement struggling with conscience. A fortnight afterwards, I met him coming out of the same room, and he was eyeing his pinafore which he had carefully rolled up: and again his manner was so odd that I determined to see what was within his pinafore, notwithstanding that he said there was nothing and repeatedly commanded me to 'go away' and I found it stained with pickle-juice; so that here was carefully planned deceit. As this child was educated solely by working on his good feelings, he soon became as truthful, open, and tender, as anyone could desire [...]

Source: Darwin, 1877, pp. 285–94.

G. Stanley Hall (1846–1924) was one of the new breed of child researchers who was greatly influenced by Darwin's theories and scientific approach. He believed that 'infancy, childhood and youth are three bunches of keys to unlock the past history of the race' (quoted in Cleverley and Phillips, 1976, p. 42). Hall became an advocate for basing child-rearing on scientific principles and offered some of the earliest accounts of adolescence as a distinctive life stage. Around the same time James Sully established Child Psychology as a recognized subject at London University. In his book, *Studies of Childhood* (1895) Sully confirmed his vision for the new science:

> Ours is a scientific age, and science has cast its inquisitive eye on the infant ... we can now speak of the beginning of a careful and methodical investigation of child-nature, by men trained in scientific observation.
>
> (Sully, 1895, pp. 3–4)

Evidence of what is 'normal' or 'typical' became a standard to judge which children were 'subnormal' or 'retarded', not just in physical and motor development, but also in intellectual development. One of the first 'intelligence tests' was published in 1905 by Alfred Binet and Theodore Simon in Paris, as a direct response to a French Ministry of Public Instruction request for a method to objectively identify low ability children within the public school system. In due course, the new professions of 'clinical psychologist' and 'educational psychologist' began to apply these and other techniques to assess children, offer therapies, classify them according to their aptitudes and offer advice on their placement in normal or special schools.

In all these ways, developmental psychology was emerging as a new, scientific way of understanding children, linked to a powerful set of institutions and professional practices that would shape their lives.

The emphasis on objective scientific enquiry became a hallmark of child development research throughout the twentieth century. As one textbook author wrote:

> Developmental psychology today is a truly objective science ... Today a developmentalist determines the adequacy of a theory by deriving hypotheses and conducting research to see whether the theory can predict the observations he or she has made. There is no room for subjective bias in evaluating ideas; theories of human development are only as good as their ability to account for the important aspects of children's growth and development.
>
> (Shaffer, 1993, p. 38)

However, you should note that many areas of developmental research that adopt a strict scientific approach have more recently been criticized for the tendency to treat children as objects of scientific enquiry, rather than as participants with their own perspectives on the topics concerned (Woodhead and Faulkner, 2000; Alderson and Morrow, 2004).

Summary of Section 3

- Some historians have argued that childhood is a recent invention, signalled when children began to be represented as different from adults in paintings and literature, after the end of the fifteenth century for example.
- In Western societies, early industrialization created a huge demand for child labour, which led social reformers to question its impact on children's well-being.
- The growth of universal schooling marked a shift in beliefs and expectations about children. Childhood became more clearly differentiated from the adult world of work.
- Interest in scientific studies of children's development was also shaped by new theories about human evolution, illustrated by Darwin's studies of his own son.
- Early scientific theories about children offered valuable knowledge and tools to guide the growing numbers of professionals concerned with children's psychological development, their care and education.

4   What is development?

Earlier sections have outlined the context within which studies of child development became an established and valued field of scientific enquiry. This section looks in more detail at what it means to describe children as developing by looking at the features of this way of 'constructing childhood'.

Activity 2

Allow about 30 minutes

The concept of development

This activity will help you explore the concept of development in relation to children.

1   What does the word 'development' suggest to you? Think about the significance of saying someone or something is 'undeveloped', 'developing' or 'developed'?

2   Next think about what it means to describe children as 'developing'. Make a list of some of the ways that they develop, from birth onwards. You may find it easier to draw up parallel lists for different aspects of development: physical, mental, emotional and social.

3   Finally, think about why children grow up. What causes children to develop physically as well as in their capacities for thinking, moral judgement and independent living? Do you see development mainly as a biological process of maturation, or as a process of learning and teaching, or as a combination of the two?

Comment

Development is a widely used term in everyday language. Gardeners enjoy watching seeds develop into plants; managers construct a development plan for their company; linguists study the way languages develop; rich nations offer aid to developing countries; students learn to develop an argument in their essays. In each case, development is concerned with change, with a strong sense that these changes follow an ordered plan and that the outcome will be a more advanced, complex or sophisticated level of organization. The same applies to using the word 'development' in relation to children. Development is about progressing, physically and psychologically, from dependent immaturity towards more mature competence and adulthood. Botanical metaphors have been especially influential, wherein a child's development, like a plant's, is seen as a process of naturally unfolding. As Mussen *et al.*, put it: '... these changes usually result in new improved ways of reacting – that is in behaviour that is healthier, more organised, more complex, more competent or more efficient' (Mussen *et al.*, 1984, p. 7).

A major goal of developmental research has been to describe and explain these processes of growth and change. A first task was to attempt to identify normal, universal processes, as well as to identify deviations from the norm. Researchers began to ask what a 'typical 3 month old' or a 'typical 3 year old' or a 'typical 13 year old' can do. They tried to identify the ages at which most children, for example, begin to walk, talk, or become capable of logical reasoning. Trying to identify universal patterns of this sort was consistent with the belief that developmental processes are rule-governed and that these rules can be discovered by scientific methods. Although differences between children are of course recognized in contemporary studies of children, the emphasis of much developmental research has been on what children have in common by identifying 'normal' patterns of development, rather than on what is unique to individuals or to specific cultures. The use of the singular noun 'child' in textbooks on 'child development' sums up this approach to studying children and childhood.

4.1 What develops?

This section, looks at some examples of a developmental approach and introduces the concept of 'stages of development'. The clearest examples of development relate to physical growth and maturation. Humans grow from the moment of conception through to achieving adult height at around the age of 20. But this process of growth is not regular. It follows a distinctive pattern with rapid growth during the early years, and again around puberty. For example, by the end of the first year, a typical infant has achieved three times his or her birth weight. The increase in weight and height continues through the first few years, but then the rate of growth slows down until around puberty when there is another growth spurt (which begins earlier for girls than for boys) triggered by the release of growth hormones.

Activity 3   *Key developmental themes*

Allow about
15 minutes

This activity uses two examples of development to introduce some key developmental themes.

Study Figures 4 and 5 carefully. Figure 4 is about physical growth which is based on measurements of height and weight for girls and boys. Figure 5 illustrates changes in physical mobility during the first 2 years of life when young children are learning to sit up, crawl, stand and walk. What conclusions do you draw about the patterns of development in each case? Is there any other information that you feel is missing or that you would like to know?

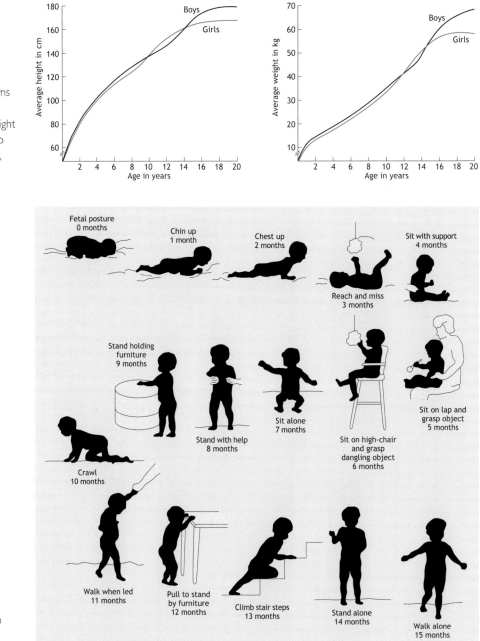

Figure 4
Normal patterns of growth in height and weight from infancy to maturity (Berk, 1989, p. 177).

Figure 5
The visible sequence of motor development (adapted from Shirley, 1933).

Comment

Figure 4 shows typical patterns of human growth and offers a simple illustration of the 'normative' approach discussed earlier. It does not tell us about any particular child's growth but about girls and boys in general. The aim is to identify patterns of change shared in common by all 'normal' children (the average or mean), as well as the 'normal' range of variation. The researcher might also carry out separate analyses showing how patterns of growth and change vary between different groups, for example related to ethnicity or social class. Or they might use the 'norms' in Figure 4 to assess the 'developmental delay' of children living in extreme poverty or lacking basic nutrition.

Many of the same developmental principles also apply to Figure 5. This is also a generalized, normative account of development, represented through a series of sketches. But there is an important difference between Figures 4 and 5. The changes taking place in children's physical mobility could not readily be plotted on a graph like increases in height. Also, the shift from sitting to standing to walking is much more dramatic and involves a completely new set of skills. One way to make sense of this difference is by asking: how far are these examples of development *continuous* or *discontinuous*?

With these distinctions in mind, look again at Figures 4 and 5. Figure 4 suggests ways in which children's physical growth is a continuous process of change. These changes are usually gradual and incremental. By contrast Figure 5 suggests discontinuous changes are taking place. The idea that some kinds of development are about discontinuous change introduces another key developmental idea: that there are 'stages' of development. Figure 5 suggests growth in mobility follows a fairly predictable sequence, but it seems to be marked off into quite separate phases. While each new achievement builds on the skills of the last, new neural and muscular systems have to be co-ordinated, for example, when children first coordinate their limbs in crawling, or first pull themselves up to a standing posture. Equally, each stage (sitting, crawling, standing, etc.) can be seen as a developmental plateau during which children are able to consolidate skills and prepare for the next major transition. These changes in physical mobility also have psychological consequences, opening up new possibilities for activities, relationships and learning. Babies who can sit unsupported, look around and play with a toy are at a very different stage from newborns, not yet able to lift their head. Toddlers who begin to crawl no longer have to wait for experiences to come to them – they can seek them out.

Figures 4 and 5 offer helpful summaries of development, but they also draw attention to some of the limitations of a normative approach. While it may be important to compare an individual child against developmental norms, these norms are less useful for understanding an individual child's development in depth. For example, Figure 5 tells us very little about the variety of ways children may achieve these transitions (e.g. children who favour 'bottom shuffling' over crawling), nor about the aids they use (e.g. items of furniture), nor about the impact of cultural differences (e.g. extent of carrying and holding young children), nor about the impact of technologies (baby slings, strollers, car seats, baby bouncers, etc.), nor about how much support and encouragement they receive, nor about different ways children who are physically or psychologically disabled may tackle these milestones.

What about other aspects of development? How far do developmental principles apply to children's social and emotional relationships, their capacities for communication, thinking and moral reasoning, social understanding and sense of self? In your answer to Activity 2, you may have noted that babies are totally dependent on others (parents or other carers) during the early years. They normally establish strong emotional attachments to those that care for them and they can find separations distressing, especially from about 9 months old. You may also have noted that early relationships are transformed once children learn to communicate through spoken language. You may have wondered about the significance of the so-called 'terrible-twos' when toddlers often seem to go through a difficult stage as they start asserting their new found sense of self. You may have noted children's growing understanding, their ability to recognize dangers, make moral judgements and offer reasoned arguments. Then there are the changes in children's social relationships, especially friendships, that typically increase in importance during the preschool and school years. Finally, you may have noted the social and emotional changes associated with puberty and adolescence and the ways young people's personal identities shift as they make the transition towards becoming an adult. The question is: how far do developmental principles apply to all these changes too? Is it possible to identify patterns of development that apply to all children?

This question has been widely debated, as will become clear in the chapters that follow. Some theorists have proposed that there are distinct stages for children's intellectual, language, emotional, social or moral development. Other theorists have been critical of stage theories, for example, arguing that it is misleading to think about children's psychological development in the same way as their physical development. These debates connect with the next major question: how does development occur?

4.2 How does development occur?

One of the major goals of developmental research has been to explain patterns of development, using scientific methods to find out what drives processes of growth and change from embryo to baby to toddler to child to adolescent to young adult, and so on. Some theories emphasize natural processes of maturation where a genetically encoded development plan unfolds. These are referred to as 'nativist' theories of development. In contrast, 'environmentalist' theories emphasize the influences of learning and experience. You may also find the contrast between nativist and environmentalist approaches expressed through a distinction between 'nature and nurture', 'biology and experience', or 'heredity and environment'. As noted earlier, many aspects of motor development may be maturational (such as the progression from sitting to crawling to walking). But the importance of maturation is less clear for psychological, intellectual, linguistic, emotional or social development. Numerous theories have attempted to explain the influence of learning on development. Some emphasize individual experiences, while others place greater emphasis on social and cultural processes through which children are introduced to ways of thinking and behaving that are valued within a specific community.

These attempts to understand what causes development are not only of theoretical interest. They have practical consequences. For example, parents want to know how a genetic condition (e.g. Down Syndrome) is likely to affect their child's development; social workers want to know how they can help a child who has suffered emotional trauma; and policy-makers want to know how to implement the articles of the UNCRC.

Activity 4   A natural or a social and cultural process?

Allow about
5 minutes

This activity takes a simple example to illustrate why claiming something is 'natural' is not straightforward.

Goldblatt (2000) offers a useful way to start thinking about the contrast between nativist and environmentalist approaches by asking whether his desk is natural. As you read his analysis, ask the same question about children – how far is their development driven by natural processes and how far shaped by growing up within a society?

> Let us assume that trees count as *natural*. But are the products we make from trees natural? The desk on which this was written is made of MDF. This is basically wood-chips pulped down and remoulded into items of furniture. The wood probably came from a tree specially planted to provide timber for the furniture industry. It was cut in a particular way using sophisticated techniques, transported to a factory, underwent the pulping process, was remoulded into various parts and constructed into desk-like shape and then painted. Is my desk a natural product or is it a product of human society?
>
> (Goldblatt, 2000, p. 8)

Comment

At first you may have thought that a newborn baby is a product of nature, but you may then have had second thoughts. The development of the foetus is strongly shaped by where a mother is living, the quality of her diet, support received from a partner, pressures of work, access to health care, as well as medical interventions. There is also evidence that the baby is capable of simple learning, even before birth. Following birth we have seen there are regularities in children's growth and development that may appear to be governed by maturation. But learning may have a major role in other areas. Society doesn't pulp and remould children like wood – but children's ways of communicating, thinking and behaving have been shaped by many years of nurture, teaching and training. As noted in Section 1, children's experiences vary dramatically in different societies and periods in history. Any number of social and cultural factors affects development.

Importantly, too, children also affect their own development by evoking responses from others and by making their own choices. They are not passive, but are active agents, affecting the environment in which they develop.

Trying to understand the role of maturation and learning has been the starting point for some of the most contentious theoretical debates in developmental psychology. Many of these theoretical debates were being argued long before developmental psychology became an established field of scientific research. In fact, it is very helpful to recognize the ways contemporary theoretical models have a history in generations of philosophical and popular debate. This section outlines four major lines of argument: development as control and discipline, development as natural stages, development as experience and development as interaction.

Development as control and discipline

Since the fourth century AD, the religious doctrine of original sin has seen children as inherently sinful. Children were believed to be born with original sin and therefore had to be disciplined in order to be saved. Christianity was and is often ambivalent about the nature of the child – the newborn can be seen as sweet, pure and innocent, and at the same time both sinful and susceptible to corruption. This ambivalence was exemplified by the Puritans in the sixteenth and seventeenth centuries, who were greatly devoted to their children but also sometimes punished them harshly in order to make them 'good' and obedient. They believed that children had to learn obedience to God through obedience to their parents.

The English philosopher Thomas Hobbes (1588–1679) elaborated on this view of children's natural tendency towards expressing dangerous impulses which need to be curbed through discipline and strict training. This view was famously expressed by Susanna Wesley in a letter to her son John Wesley (founder of Methodism) in 1732. She wrote:

> Break their will betimes: begin this great work before they can run alone, before they can speak plain, or perhaps speak at all … make him do as he is bid, if you whip him ten times running to effect it … Break his will now and his soul will live, and he will probably bless you to all eternity.

> (S. Wesley, quoted in Montgomery, 2003, p. 63).

These views were also expressed in the early nineteenth century, as for example in Hannah More's writings on child-rearing. More argued that it was 'a fundamental error to consider children as innocent beings, whose little weaknesses may, perhaps, want some correction, rather than as beings who bring into the world a corrupt nature and evil dispositions, which it should be the great end of education to rectify' (quoted in Hendrick, 1990, p. 39). More recently, the theories of Sigmund Freud (1856–1939) also build on views about the power of children's nature. Put simply, he argued that the infant is driven by instinctual impulses (or 'id'). Freud argued that these are only regulated by the development of conscience (or 'super-ego'), through parental control becoming internalized.

Development as natural stages

In summarizing the Puritan view of children as naturally sinful, I noted the tension with the opposing idea of children as naturally innocent. This view found clearest expression in the writings of the French philosopher Jean-Jacques Rousseau (1712–78). Like Hobbes, he emphasized the role of *nature*, or internal forces, on development. But he saw nature as a positive rather than a negative force. Children are 'noble savages', according to Rousseau, with a natural sense of right and wrong. The child is inherently good, born with the potential to develop reason and moral judgement. He asserted that society has a corrupting rather than a positive influence. Rousseau also stressed that children are different from adults. He is often credited as offering the first truly developmental account of childhood, through his emphasis on maturation and stages of development. In the book *Emile, or On Education* (1762), Rousseau applied his thinking to practical questions about how children should be reared. He proposed an 'Age of Nature' that lasts from birth to 12 years of age, when children's natural innocence should be respected: they should be free 'to jump, play and run all day' (Rousseau, 1762, 1979, p. 107).

Rousseau's belief in the importance of respecting children's natural development illustrates the close linkages between developmental theories and pedagogical principles. The German originator of the kindergarten movement, Friedrich Froebel, also emphasized natural stages of development:

> The child, the boy, man, indeed, should know no other endeavor but to be at every stage of development wholly what this stage calls for. Then will each successive stage spring like a new shoot from a healthy bud; and, at each successive stage, he will with the same endeavour again accomplish the requirements of this stage: for only the adequate development of man at each preceding stage can effect and bring about adequate development at each succeeding later stage.

> (Froebel, 1885, p. 30)

The idea of natural stages of development has been very influential and widely taken up as a scientific basis for prescribing what counts as 'developmentally appropriate' practice, especially the balance of play and teaching within early years education (Woodhead, 1998).

Development as experience

John Locke (1632–1704) was an English philosopher and physician who challenged the image of children being born either naturally 'sinful' or naturally 'innocent'. Locke's position is often described as 'empiricist', by contrast with the 'rationalist' views of the Greek philosopher Plato (350 BC). Plato had argued that knowledge is not derived from experience but comes about through a process of rational discourse or logical deduction that reveals to us the knowledge we are born with. Locke by contrast, proposed that at birth the child is a *'tabula rasa'* ('blank slate' in Latin) that is written on by experience, by interaction with people and the environment. He believed that children are born with the potential to develop into mature human beings, and he recognized individual differences in

Empiricism
The belief, associated with the seventeenth to eighteenth century philosophers Locke, Berkeley and Hume, that all knowledge comes from experience.

Rationalism
An approach to human learning originally associated with Plato, which proposes that learning is based not so much on actual experience but on revealing to ourselves knowledge which we already have, and indeed are born with.

intelligence and temperament. But he rejected the notion (which stemmed from Plato) that they are born with knowledge, or that their ways of thinking and behaving are the expression of a natural state of being. According to Locke it is experience that shapes the child for good or ill. He set out these ideas in the *Essay Concerning Human Understanding* (1690). He saw parents as tutors with responsibility for providing the right environment and education to mould children's thinking towards capacities for rational understanding and for making sound moral judgements. Locke stressed the importance of the principles of association (links between old and new knowledge), imitation and repetition. In his emphasis on the crucial role of experience, Locke rejected the emphasis on the inner forces of children's *nature*. He saw *nurture*, or external forces, as the driving force in development. The legacy of Locke's views can still be found in contemporary debates about the erosion of parents' moral authority and teaching, and in the failures of schools to ensure children are taught basic skills required for modern living.

Development as interaction

Seeing 'development as interaction' involves trying to reconcile the influence of both nature and nurture, by showing how maturational processes link into social processes of learning. Psychologists who take this position acknowledge a debt to the German philosopher Immanuel Kant (1724–1804). Kant rejected the 'rationalist' notion of innate knowledge. He also rejected the 'empiricist' notion that knowledge is derived solely from the environment. Although Kant agreed with Locke that experience is crucial for learning, he argued that knowledge could not arise from what people took in through their senses alone. Kant suggested a synthesis (a merging) of the two opposed viewpoints of rationalism and empiricism. Basically, he proposed that we are born with certain mental structures that help us to interpret input from our senses in particular ways. He called these mental structures categories of understanding. By themselves, they cannot give us knowledge and it is only through interaction with the environment that these structures order and organize experience. Furthermore, there is an active role for individuals as organizers of experience: no longer are they seen either as passively receiving sensory stimuli (as in empiricism), or passively following some biological programme (as in rationalism or nativism). The major mechanism for development is the continuous, two-way interaction between the child and the environment. In this view, both nature and nurture play an important role in development.

Most contemporary theories of development recognize the active roles of children in their own development. Children affect how their caregivers behave towards them, they make choices about their own lives, and, as they get older, increasingly select their own environments. This is much more than a simple interaction of nature and nurture, and developmental researchers are now attempting to capture this two-way complexity of cause and effect in what are sometimes called 'transactional models' of development.

Figure 6 Social interaction is crucial for psychological development.

In this section we have outlined four historical views on development. Many modern theories about development build on these fundamental ideas about children's nature and the role of the environment. For example, *behaviourist* approaches emphasize the way environments shape children's behaviour towards desirable outcomes. *Social learning* theories emphasize learning by experience, especially through imitation. The child's own role in their development is recognized in *constructivist* theories, such as Piaget's stage theory. Interactions between the child and their environment are also emphasized by *social constructivist theories*. Social constructivist theories ask about young children's guided induction into particular settings, sets of relationships and ways of thinking. They see development as involving social processes of communication, teaching and learning, not just the individual child interacting with their environment.

You will be studying these major theories of development in the next chapter. But it is worth bearing in mind that competing theories about development can also be found in more everyday attempts to make sense of children.

Activity 5   *Everyday views of development*

Allow about
10 minutes

This activity explores the ways in which theories of development are expressed in everyday accounts of children.

The four quotations below come from research interviews carried out with 24 women from middle income communities in south-east England during the 1980s. Study the quotations and consider how far they seem to reflect the four models of development outlined in this section: development, as 'control and discipline'; as 'natural stages'; as 'experience'; or as 'interaction'.

Parent 1:

'Children are different. They're loveable little things ... you just think they're the most wonderful things that's come on earth'

Parent 2:

'(If) you just give into them all the time ... they just push you and push you and push you, until they're doing the most awful outrageous things'

Parent 3:

Our children are what we make them. If we give them proper loving care and firm guidance they'll become happy and well integrated members of society. If we don't ...well we've only ourselves to blame'

Parent 4:

'I wouldn't say they have equal voting rights to us, there's not quite a democracy, we do tend to have the casting vote if it comes to a tie, but we certainly do listen to them ...'

(Source: Ribbens, 1994, pp. 60–78)

Comment

The quotations from Parents 2 and 3 seem closest to the views on development outlined above (emphasizing 'control and discipline' and 'experience' respectively). Parent 1's image of children hints at natural stages as well as Rousseau's idea of the innocent child. Parent 4's view is harder to place. It certainly implies 'interaction' in that parents are seen as listening as well as teaching. But it also conveys a much more recent set of ideas about the balance of power between children and adults, the rights of children to make choices and express an opinion. These examples are a reminder that ideas about children's nature, development and treatment are not static.

Summary of Section 4

- Development is about rule-governed patterns of change towards a more advanced level of organization.
- A major emphasis of early developmental research was on identifying normal patterns of physical and psychological development.
- Studies of physical growth and physical mobility illustrate basic developmental issues, especially how far changes are continuous or discontinuous and introduce the idea of developmental stages.
- Questions about what causes children to develop are expressed through debates about biology and experience or heredity and environment.
- Contemporary developmental theories can often be traced to long-standing philosophical debates, for example about development as natural stages, learning and experience, interactions, or control and discipline.

5 Child development and global childhoods

In the introduction to this chapter I noted that promoting children's development is a global goal, expressed through the UNCRC. Developmental research has a great deal to offer, but there are also many challenges to be faced in the implementation of children's right to development.

As you have seen, the scientific study of child development has its roots in Western ideas about children's nature and needs and the emphasis of much traditional developmental research has been on identifying normal, universal processes. Yet the vast majority of child development researchers are located within economically rich, Western societies and their studies have mostly been about children growing up in these same societies. Recall that the study of children's development was established during a period of major social reform affecting children in industrial societies, especially the growth of universal schooling.

There have been exceptions to this concentration on Western childhoods, and there is an important tradition of cross-cultural research. But the overall imbalances in research and theory present a challenge for the study of children's development. Consider how far current knowledge offers a scientific account of universal features of childhood, and how far it reflects particular kinds of childhood as experienced by a minority of the world's children. For example, one of the basic assumptions of child development research is that children develop an autonomous sense of self. Anthropologists have long pointed out that this is a dangerous assumption to make:

> The Western conception of the person as a bounded, unique, more or less integrated motivational and cognitive universe, a dynamic centre of awareness, emotion, judgement, and action organized into a distinctive whole and set contrastively both against other such wholes and against its social and natural background, is, however incorrigible it may seem to us, a rather peculiar idea within the context of the world's cultures.

(Geertz quoted in Golberger and Veroff, 1995, p. 29)

One of the most comprehensive studies of child development in different cultures was conducted during the 1970s by a research team led by Beatrice and John Whiting. The team studied childhood in six cultures (the Gusii of Nyasongo, Kenya; the Mixtecans of Juxtlahuaca, Mexico; the Baco of Tarong, Philippines; the Hokan of Taira, Okinawa; the Rajputh of Khalapur, India; and North Americans of 'Orchard Town', USA). These studies, known as the Six Cultures Project, provided some of the first systematic and detailed recordings of children's behaviour in different cultures and provided a wealth of information on children's work, play and social interaction, as well as on how adults regarded children (Whiting and Whiting, 1975).

In every culture, there are customary ideas and expectations about the nature, capacities and proper behaviour of children. In some cultures, babies and small children are characterized in terms of incapacities where they are considered unable to reason, unaware, fragile, unable to learn, and so on. For instance, the Six Cultures Project found that parents in the 1970s in the Philippines believed maturation is slow and cannot be hurried (children do not have 'sense' until the age of 4) and individuals differ in the way they mature. In Khalapur, India, young children were thought of as passive and much like one another, requiring mainly protection and physical care. Among the Gusii of Kenya, however, great emphasis was placed on training in early life, mainly training for work and responsibility. Gusii infants were weaned by the age of 2, and after that were considered capable of being trained. By the age of 6 and 7, they assumed many adult responsibilities. Similarly, in Khalapur, girls learned to do most of the tasks done by older women from the age of 9 or 10; gathering and drying berries, and making mats, baskets and clothing (Whiting and Whiting, 1975).

Western approaches to child development have generally assumed that young children learn through play, that school is a major influence on development, and that children only acquire adult responsibilities as they leave school and begin work, normally during the late teen years. The Six Cultures Project helped to challenge these assumptions, drawing attention to societies where (at that time) children 'normally' took on responsibilities from an early age and where working was perceived as at least as significant as playing. This does not mean that children did not play. In traditional African cultures, for example, children's games were many and varied, but play was dominated by imitation of adult activities. They played at mother and baby, at marriage, at holding tribunals and at performing rites. They hunted small animals, built miniature huts and villages, and musical instruments (Erny, 1981). According to Jomo Kenyatta, who was Prime Minister of Kenya, 'games are, in fact, nothing more or less than a rehearsal prior to the performance of the activities which are the serious business of all members of the Gikuyu tribe' (Kenyatta, 1938).

Figure 7
Work or play?

Reading

At this point you should turn to the end of this chapter and read the Reading, 'Work, play and learning in the lives of young children' at the end of this chapter. This reading reconsiders conventional assumptions about the balance between work, play and learning in the development of young children and draws on a number of cultural examples. The reading also introduces the concept of 'developmental niche' to help you understand these cultural dimensions of development. This reading may seem to be more about the conditions in which children develop and about the significance attached to their activities, rather than about their development as such. In the reading the case is made for recognizing that the value and meaning attached to children's activities and developing skills is part and parcel of the developmental process. The example of children's motor development (as discussed in Section 4.1) is used in order to show that even those aspects of development that are apparently universal may be culturally patterned in a variety of ways. More generally, the reading draws attention to the ways that 'taken for granted' knowledge about children's development may be an expression of cultural beliefs and expectations of particular societies at particular points in their history.

Summary of Section 5

- Child development theories have mainly originated from within Western societies but they have been applied globally to children in diverse societies and cultures.
- A major challenge for contemporary developmental research is to encompass cultural diversities in children's circumstances, experiences and expectations for development.
- These themes are illustrated by examining the place of work, play and learning in the lives of young children, drawing on the concept of a developmental niche.

6   Conclusion

This chapter has emphasized the respects in which children's development is a social and cultural as well as a biological process. This is important because as societies become not only culturally diverse but also more interconnected, psychological theories are required that fully acknowledge the influence of social context, both within and across cultures. You have been encouraged to recognize a range of different, often competing, ideas and beliefs about children, especially about how children develop. There are two major reasons for this. First, you need to be aware of the variety of views on children, so that you can spot the influences of these views in different theories that you encounter. Secondly, you need to understand that theories about children's development are themselves culturally located which then shapes the questions that researchers ask about children, the methods they use and the concepts they employ to interpret their findings.

In these ways you are encouraged to think critically about the theories and research you encounter in later chapters of this book. This includes reflecting on the core concept of 'child development' as a framework for studying children. For example, how far do generalized accounts of normal development increase our understanding of children? Are there respects in which the scientific, developmental paradigm can actually be a barrier to knowing about children?

Trying to achieve a better understanding about children's 'development' has generally been seen as a positive, progressive way of thinking about children. Scientific knowledge about children's 'development' has contributed significantly to changes in the care and treatment of children at home, in nurseries, schools, hospitals, etc. (e.g. Schaffer, 1998). But some childhood theorists have also been critical of the core concept of 'development' as reinforcing power relationships between adults, who are assumed to be 'developed', and children who are still 'developing' (James *et al.,* 1998). From a developmental perspective, childhood is a journey to mature, rational, responsible, autonomous, adult competence. Since theories of development mostly concentrate on the childhood years, they can give the impression that attaining adulthood is the 'end-point' of development, which is misleading for a number of reasons, not least because this exaggerates the links between a person's chronological age and their maturity, personal autonomy and wisdom. Studying children's development within a lifespan perspective helps in part to overcome this problem.

But critics draw attention to other limitations of some types of developmental research as an approach to understanding children. For example, how often do developmental researchers invite children to talk about their experiences of childhood and their views on being children? Until recently, children played only a very minor role in the study of childhood. This may seem a paradox, but child research has been done by adults and it largely reflects adults' interests and priorities rather than those of children, even though the underlying motive may be to protect children's interests and promote their well-being. So, the study of children has been dominated by adult theories and preconceptions about children and human nature. Where children have been asked to express their beliefs and ideas, these have been interpreted in relation to developmental theories, e.g. about stages of development, rather than being treated as important in their own right. Social attitudes towards children have changed dramatically in recent decades, not least through the influence of the UNCRC, with its strong emphasis on children's rights to be respected and consulted about matters that affect them. As a result, some approaches to child research that were common in the past are now considered ethically unacceptable, and increasing attention is being paid to understanding children's own perspectives on their childhood, including their development.

References

Alderson, P. and Morrow, V. (2004) *Ethics, Research and Consulting with Children and Young People*, London, Barnardo's.

Ariès, P. (1962) *Centuries of Childhood*, Harmondsworth, Penguin.

Berk, L. E. (1994) *Child Development*, 3rd edn, Massachusetts, Allyn and Bacon.

Burr, R. and Montgomery, H. (2003) 'Children and Rights', in Woodhead, M. and Montgomery, H. (eds) *Understanding Childhood: an interdisciplinary approach*, Chichester, Wiley/Open University.

Cleverly, J. and Phillips, D. C. (1976) *From Locke to Spock: influential models of the child in modern Western thought*, Melbourne, Melbourne University Press.

Cole, M. and Cole, S. (1996, 3rd edn) *The Development of Children*, New York, Scientific American.

Cunningham, H. (2003) 'Children's Changing lives from 1800 to 2000', in Maybin, J. and Woodhead, M. (eds) *Childhoods in Context*, Chichester, Wiley/Open University.

Darwin, C. R. (1877) 'A biographical sketch of an infant', in Kessen, W. (ed.) (1965) *The Child*, New York, Wiley.

Erny, P. (1981) *The Child and his Environment in Black Africa: an essay on traditional education*, Milton Keynes, Open University Press.

Froebel, F. (1885) *The Education of Man*, New York, A. Lovell and Co.

Geneva Declaration of the Rights of the Child (1924) League of Nations O. J. Spec. Supp. 21, at 43 (1924) [online]. Available from http://www1.umn.edu/humanrts/instree/childrights.html [accessed 10 January 2005].

Goldberger, N. R, and Veroff, J. B. (1995) *The Culture and Psychology Handbook*, New York, New York University Press.

Goldblatt, D. (2000) *'Work Book 2', DD100 An Introduction to the Social Sciences: Understanding Social Change*, Milton Keynes, The Open University.

Hendrick, H. (1990) 'Constructions and reconstructions of British childhood: an interpretive survey, 1800 to the present', in James, A. and Prout, A. (eds) *Constructing and Reconstructing Childhood: contemporary issues in the sociological study of childhood*, London, Falmer Press.

James A, and Prout, A. (eds) (1997) *Constructing and Reconstructing Childhood: contemporary issues in the sociological study of childhood*, London, Falmer Press.

James, A. Jenks, C. and Prout, A. (1998) *Theorizing Childhood*, Cambridge, Polity Press.

Kehily, M. and Swann, J. (eds) (2003) *Children's Cultural Worlds*, Chichester, Wiley/Open University.

Kenyatta, J. (1938) *Facing Mount Kenya: the tribal life of the Gikuyu*, London, Secker and Warburg.

Kirby, P. and Woodhead, M. (2003) 'Children's Participation in Society', in Montgomery, H., Burr, R. and Woodhead, M. (eds) *Changing Childhoods, Local and Global*, Chichester, Wiley/Open University.

Mackinnon, D. (2003) 'Children and School', in Maybin, J. and Woodhead, M. (eds) *Childhoods in Context*, Chichester, Wiley/Open University.

Montgomery, H. (2003) 'Childhood in Time and Place' in Woodhead, M. and Montgomery, H. (eds) *Understanding Childhood: an interdisciplinary approach*, Chichester, Wiley/Open University.

Mussen, P. H., Conger, J. J. and Kaga, J. (1984) *Child Development and Personality*, New York, Harper and Row.

Ribbens, J. (1994) 'Mothers' images of children and their implications for maternal response', in Brannen, J. and O'Brien, M. (eds) *Childhood and Parenthood: proceedings of ISA Committee for Family Research Conference on Children and Families*, London, University of London Institute of Education.

Rousseau, J. J. (1979) *Emile, or on Education*, translated by Allan Bloom, New York, Basic Books (first published 1762).

Shaffer, D. R. (1993) *Developmental Psychology*, 3rd edn, Pacific Grove, CA, Brooks/Cole.

Schaffer, H. R. (1998) *Making Decisions about children: psychological questions and answers*, 2nd edn, Oxford, Blackwell.

Shahar, S. (1990) *Childhood in the Middle Ages*, London, Routledge.

Shirley, M. M. (1933) *The First Two Years – A Study of Twenty-five Babies*, vol. 2, *Intellectual Development*, Minneapolis, University of Minnesota Press.

Stainton Rogers, W. (2003) 'What is a Child?', in Woodhead, M. and Montgomery, H. *Understanding childhood: an interdisciplinary approach*, Chichester, Wiley/Open University.

Sully, J. (1895) *Studies of Childhood*, New York, Appleton.

United Nations Convention on the Rights of the Child (UNCRC) (1989) United Nations General Assesmbly Resolution 44/25 of 20 November 1989 [online]. Available from http://www.unhchr.ch/html/menu3/b/k2crc.htm [accessed 10 January 2005].

Whiting, B. B. and Whiting, J. W. M. (1975) *Children of Six Cultures: a psycho-cultural analysis*, Cambridge, MA, Harvard University Press.

Woodhead, M. (1998) "Quality' in early childhood programmes – a contextually, appropriate approach', *International Journal of Early Years Education,* vol. 6, pp. 5–13.

Woodhead, M. (2002) 'Work, play and learning in the lives of young children', in Miller, L., Drury, R. and Campbell, R. (eds) *Exploring Early Years Education and Care*, London, David Fulton.

Woodhead, M. and Faulkner, D. (2000) 'Subjects, objects or participants: dilemmas of psychological research with children', in Christensen, P. and James, A. (eds) *Conducting Research with Children*, London, Falmer Press.

Reading

Work, play and learning in the lives of young children

Martin Woodhead

'Play is the child's work', so early childhood experts sometimes claim (following Susan Isaacs, 1929). Their concerns are often about the kinds of learning and teaching that are appropriate for young children and especially about the value of play. For example, in Britain there's been an ongoing debate about when children should start school (Woodhead 1989), as well as about what curriculum is appropriate, especially for four-year-olds (Miller *et al.* 2002). But I also want to ask about young children 'working' in a more conventional sense, in economic activity.

The place of work in young children's lives

Few young children work in contemporary Britain, in the literal sense of paid employment, with the possible exception of the babies and toddlers recruited to appear on TV, in films and especially in advertising – everything from nappies to mineral water! But it is meaningful to talk about work in the sense of young children's contributions to the household and community – however modest, immature and playful. And work isn't just playful for most of the world's children, especially during the middle and later years of childhood.

The world's children do many different kinds of work, including household chores, agricultural work, fishing, market portering, street trading, shoe-shining, mining, craft workshops and engineering, rubbish picking, domestic work, and prostitution (Woodhead 1999a). Most public attention is rightly focused on the exploitative and hazardous kinds of child labour, mostly in the poorest countries of the world. One unfortunate consequence can be that the more moderate kinds of work done by the vast majority of children is overlooked. It is also widely assumed that school is now a universal experience of childhood. But it is estimated that about one fifth of the world's children never go to school (Watkins 2000). Finally, school is not an alternative to work for most of the world's children, many of whom combine work with school. They have to work to support their families, and sometimes to help pay some of the costs of going to school (Boyden *et al.* 1998).

To get an impression of the significance of children's economic contribution Hoffman *et al.* (1987) asked parents in eight countries about the value they placed on their children: 75 per cent of Thai parents, 71 per cent of parents on the Philippines, 54 per cent in Turkey referred to children's value as contributors to the family income, compared with only 6 per cent of US parents. Parents in the USA were much more likely to refer to the emotional significance of having children, the stimulation and fun involved (see also Zelizer 1985).

In a similar study carried out in Cameroon, West Africa, parents valued children for their ability to do domestic chores (56 per cent), and run errands (30 per cent) (Nsamenang and Lamb 1993). In these poor, mainly rural economies, young children are not just playful dependants, who are growing and learning towards some future goal of mature competence when they are ready to enter the workforce. They are an essential, trainable, economic resource, contributing now, and even more so as they get older.

Cross-cultural studies of young children's work

These statistics are about children in general. What about the youngest children – where do they fit in? Samantha Punch carried out a detailed study of children's work in Churquiales, a small rural community in southern Bolivia. By three or four years old, children were already fetching water, collecting firewood, going on errands, feeding ducks and chickens, scaring birds from crops, picking peas and beans, peeling maize stalks and harvesting peaches. As children got older they progressed onto more complex, physically demanding and responsible tasks. Through observation and questioning, Punch drew up a list of what might be called 'key stages in the curriculum' for work among these rural children. A summary of some of the tasks expected of each age group is given in Table 1.

Table 1   Children's work in a rural community in Bolivia

Domestic work	Agricultural tasks	Animal care
3–5 years: Fetching water, collecting firewood, running errands	4–6 years: Picking vegetables, harvesting peaches, peeling maize stalks	3–6 years: Feeding ducks and chickens, scaring birds from crops
6–7 years: Bed making, cleaning and sweeping, peeling potatoes, washing dishes	7–9 years: Sowing seeds, watering crops, weeding, harvesting maize	7–9 years: Looking after pigs, milking and feeding goats, and cows, plucking a chicken
8–9 years: Lighting fire and simple food preparation; looking after younger siblings	10–12 years: Preparing ground for planting, hoeing, fertilising, harvesting potatoes	10–13 years: Harnessing oxen for ploughing, killing a chicken for eating, skinning a pig
10/11+ years: Washing clothes, making main meals, including bread, shopping for household	13–14 years: Ploughing, clearing forest land, storing maize	14+ years: Loading up a donkey securely, taking cattle to forest pastures, killing a goat or pig

Source: Adapted from Punch (2001: 811–12)

Punch concludes:

> Even from an early age children carry out some tasks independently and they should not be seen purely as helpers but active contributors in their own right. Their unpaid work not only benefits the household ... but also increases their sense of autonomy, enabling them to gain skills and competencies useful for their individual independence. (2001: 818)

In other societies, expectations of work may be very different. In some traditional communities, children may be apprenticed to learn a particular trade from an early age, which becomes the main focus for their daily lives and their learning. For example, in certain communities in Bangladesh, young boys are regularly engaged in learning hand embroidering in small workshops (Woodhead 1999a).

From a Western perspective, child work is viewed as a potential threat to children's welfare and development. The expression 'child labour' is frequently used, which has connotations of exploitation and harm. From his research among the Abaluyia of Kenya, Weisner (1989) notes that parents may hold a quite contrary view. Children's work is seen as valuable, not just in preparing them for their adult roles, but serving an essential function as a form of emotional and social support, integrating children into a family and community network that places high value on interdependence and interconnectedness. The absence of a productive economic function for young family members in industrialised societies has its own repercussions:

> Western children do not begin to learn the occupational competencies they will need as adults until late adolescence or early adulthood, and often are not prepared for adult responsibilities until about the same time. This continuity may contribute to feelings of alienation and aimlessness experienced by many adolescents and described by many social scientists. (Tietjen 1989: 406)

Are early childhoods in Europe and North America work-free?

Clearly, the role of children in economically advanced societies, such as in Europe and North America, is very different from Bolivia, Kenya or the Philippines. But are early childhoods in the West quite so 'work-free' as these contrasts suggest? Dominant discourses of early childhood development emphasise the early years as a period of dependency and playful innocence (Woodhead 1999b). Research that has looked more closely at children's social lives tells a slightly different story.

A study by Harriet Rheingold carried out in the USA, confirms very young children's enthusiasm to contribute to domestic tasks, even in societies with a culture of childhood which emphasises children's playfulness. She observed mothers carrying out domestic chores with their toddlers present, e.g. laying the table, sweeping the floor, tidying newspapers:

> All the children, even those as young as 18 months of age, promptly and for the most part without direction participated in some everyday housekeeping tasks performed by adults ... In declaring their intentions to carry out contributing behaviors and in promptly leaving a task on its completion, as well as in verbalizing the accomplishment of the goal – behaviors that increased with age – they showed an awareness of themselves as working jointly with adults to a recognised end. (Rheingold 1982: 122–3)

In short, most young children's activities are interpreted within the dominant discourse of 'play' and 'learning'. From the children's point of view they are experienced as attempts to contribute, as small examples of 'work'.

Developmental niches for work, play and learning

The concept of 'developmental niche' provides a useful framework for exploring how universal features of children's development are culturally patterned in diverse ways. Originally proposed by Super and Harkness (1986) in order to make sense of cross-cultural comparisons between communities in Kenya and the USA, the 'developmental niche' draws attention to three components of children's environment:

1. *The physical and social settings they inhabit.* This includes who they live with (in terms of family patterns, peer groups, etc.); the space, organisation and resources in their domestic, play, school and work environments; and the basic schedules of eating, sleeping, studying, working, etc.

2. *The culturally regulated customs and child-rearing practices.* This includes the way parents and others arrange child care and education, the way they relate to the child, instruct them, train them or play with them, their approach to discipline and punishment, etc.

3. *The beliefs or 'ethnotheories' of parents, or others.* This includes goals and priorities for children's development and socialisation, and beliefs or discourses about how they can best be achieved, and indeed how far they are able to influence their children's future.

One of the strengths of this framework is that it recognises the power of cultural beliefs, and discourses in shaping the ways young children's development is understood, which in turn informs the ways they are treated, the skills they learn and their emerging identity. Take motor development, for example. At first sight this might seem a universal developmental process, with young children increasing their skills in eye–hand co-ordination, physical competence, strength and mobility. Motor development also has social purposes. The way these emergent skills become integrated in children's development depends on how the young child's initiatives are patterned within the developmental niche – followed-up, given content, meaning and purpose. In Western contexts, motor co-ordination is practised through grasping rattles, playing with 'activity centres', assembling Lego blocks, laying out Brio trains or dressing Barbie dolls. Mobility is marked by learning to sit on trikes, and push trucks, although free exploration is constrained by the dangers of the street and traffic, and increasingly institutionalised within a specialised nursery or kindergarten environment (Singer 1992). In non-industrial niches these skills are practised through play with natural objects, everyday household items or tools. Among the poorest communities in South Asia some families survive by breaking bricks for use as aggregate in house and road building. A brick-chipper's child may start to practise hitting bricks with a small hammer, at an age when other children are hitting wooden or plastic pegs into a block of holes, with equal enthusiasm. The following comment is from a girl in Bangladesh thinking back to her earliest experiences, sitting alongside her mother surrounded by the piles of bricks: 'When I was a child, I used to cry for a hammer. So my mother bought me a hammer and I started breaking bricks'

(Woodhead 1998: 35). In this case, it is hard to separate the study of children's work, play and learning from moral questions about children's rights to be protected from harm. Brick breaking is a hazardous job for any child (or indeed adult) to be doing, monotonous, dusty and without protective clothing.

Another example of cultural patterning within the development niche is less controversial – an everyday observation I once made of a three-year-old girl carrying a miniature watering can around the garden. In suburban England (where I made that observation) the child's enthusiasm for watering the plants is likely to be seen as a playful activity, an activity of shared fun with her father. Not too much attention would have been paid to whether the water landed on a clump of dandelions or on the prize dahlias. Transpose the activity to rural Bolivia. According to Samantha Punch's research, a young child's involvement in watering the crops would also be treated with a degree of indulgence, with older siblings and parents praising the child's efforts. The difference is that the child's initial attempts at plant watering are the beginnings of acquiring the skills and responsibility to contribute to productive agriculture, which is crucial to the economic life of the community. Finally, transpose the same activity to a nursery class, where the child pouring water will probably be seen as evidence of practicing co-ordination skills as well as exploring the properties of liquids.

Lessons for early childhood

Most research and debate about early childhood takes place in economically rich Western societies in Europe, North America and Australasia. A major focus of debate is on children's play and learning, and this is also the subject of most research. Setting these early childhood issues in an historical as well as cross-cultural context draws attention to other claims for early childhood, related to children's current contribution and future economic activity. Through the examples in this chapter, I have drawn attention to ways that universal features of early development are channelled differently according to context, in terms of cultural priorities for children's work, play and learning. Set in a broad global context, early childhoods in economically advanced societies represent a rather specialised developmental niche, within which discourses about children's dependency, play and learning dominate, to the exclusion of any concept of work. I have tried to show that work – in the broad sense of contributing to household, family and community – has been important and continues to be so for many of the world's children.

References for Reading

Boyden, J., Ling, B. and Myers, W. (1998) *What Works for Working Children*. Stockholm: Radda Barnen.

Hoffman, L. W. (1987) 'The value of children to parents and child rearing patterns', in Kagitcibasi, C. (ed.) *Growth and Progress in Cross-cultural Psychology*. Berwyn: Swets N. America Inc.

Issacs, S. (1929) *The Nursery Years*. London: Routledge and Kegan Paul.

Miller, L., Soler, J. and Woodhead, M. (eds) 'Shaping early childhood education' in Maybin, J. and Woodhend, M. (eds) *Childhoods in Context*. Chicester: John Wiley.

Nsamenang, A. B. and Lamb, M. E. (1993) 'The acquisition of socio-cognitive competence by Nso children in the Bamenda grassfields of Northwest Cameroon', *International Journal of Behavioural Development* **16** (3), 429–41.

Punch, S. (2001) 'Household division of labour: generation, gender, birth order and sibling composition', *Work, Employment and Society* **15** (4), 803–23.

Rheingold, H. (1982) 'Little children's participation in the work of adults, a nascent pro-social behaviour', *Child Development* **53**, 114–25.

Singer, E. (1992) *Childcare and the Psychology of Development*. London: Routledge.

Super, C. and Harkness, S. (1986) 'The developmental niche: a conceptualisation at the interface of child and culture', *International Journal of Behavioural Development* **9**, 545–69.

Tietjen, A. M. (1989) 'The ecology of children's social support networks', in Belle, D. (ed.) *Children's Social Networks and Social Supports*. New York: John Wiley.

Watkins, K. (2000) *The Oxfam Education Report*. Oxford: Oxfam.

Weisner, T. S. (1989) 'Cultural and universal aspects of social support for children: evidence from the Abaluyia of Kenya', in Belle, D. (ed.) *Children's Social Networks and Social Supports*. New York: John Wiley.

Woodhead, M. (1989) 'School starts at five ... or four years old? The rationale for changing admission policies in England and Wales', *Journal of Education Policy* **4** (1), 1–21.

Woodhead, M. (1998) *Children's perspectives on their working lives*. Stockholm: Radda Barnen (Save the Children Sweden).

Woodhead, M. (1999a) 'Combating child labour: listen to what the children say', *Childhood* **6** (1), 27–49.

Woodhead, M. (1999b) 'Reconstructing developmental psychology: some first steps', *Children and Society* **13** (1), 3–19.

Zelizer, V. A. (1985) *Pricing the Priceless Child: The Changing Social Value of Children*. New York: Basic Books.

Source: Woodhead, M. (2002) 'Work, play and learning in the lives of young children', in Miller, L., Drury, R. and Campbell, R.(eds) *Exploring Early Years Education and Care*, London, David Fulton.

(This is a shortened and revised version of the original chapter.)

Chapter 2
Theories of development

John Oates, Kieron Sheehy and Clare Wood

Contents

Learning outcomes

After you have studied this chapter you should be able to:
1 describe the key features of behaviourist, social learning, constructivist and social constructivist theories of development;
2 evaluate critically these four theories;
3 illustrate their application to practical issues in child development.

1 Introduction

The previous chapter illustrated how ideas about children and their development have varied across different periods of history and cultural contexts. Four contrasting, commonly held views of how children develop were identified:
- development as discipline;
- development as natural stages;
- development as experience; and
- development as interaction.

Developmental psychology, as a field of enquiry devoted to understanding how children's minds and behaviour change over the lifespan, has produced theories of child development that have been empirically tested and that can be applied to real concerns and issues. Such theories 'formalize' lay beliefs to some extent, but also in some cases challenge our everyday assumptions.

This chapter introduces four theories, which are outlined in this section. These theories are sometimes referred to as 'grand theories' in the sense that they offer general explanations of child development as a whole, rather than just certain areas. It should be noted that they are not the only theories of child development that exist, but these four have been and continue to be especially influential, underpinning much contemporary theory and research.

The first of these theories, explored in Section 2, is *behaviourism*, also commonly referred to as *learning theory*. This approach sees child development arising from specific forms of learning, based on the idea of the child as a passive recipient of environmental influences that shape behaviour. The generic term for the process of learning as defined by behaviourism is *conditioning*, which emphasizes how external factors, such as reward and punishment, affect behaviour. In the 1950s and 1960s, this was the dominant model in psychology, and research with both humans and animals testified to the power of this approach in explaining some aspects of learning.

Section 3 considers *social learning theory*, which challenged behaviourism by recognizing that children can learn by simply observing someone else. This emerged in the 1960s, supported by research that showed how aggressive behaviour was often imitated by children who observed others engaging in it. The social learning model thus recognized the more active part that a child can play in learning from their environment. It also stressed the significance of 'role models' in children's development.

Section 4 explores the most ambitious theory of child development put forward to date which was also developed during the first half of the twentieth century: Jean Piaget's stage theory. Contrasting with behaviourist views, this saw children as independent agents in their own learning, and more important than the influences of parents and teachers. It described in detail a series of four successive stages through which all children were believed to progress. This theory, also described as a form of *constructivism*, because Piaget saw children as having to construct their understanding of the world for themselves, prompted a massive volume of research activity, which continues today.

Finally, Section 5 of the chapter turns to another theory that also sees children as active participants in their own development, but in addition stresses the roles that other people and the culture the child grows up in play in fostering development. S*ocial constructivism* also contrasts with social learning theory, as it argues that the key to learning and development lies in social interaction, rather than in mere social observation.

From these brief descriptions it is already apparent that some of these theories have aspects in common, but all of them differ in important respects, and make contrasting claims about what kinds of things will affect children's development. By the end of the chapter we hope that you will understand the strengths and limitations of each approach, rather than seeing one as 'right' and all the others as 'wrong'.

BOX 1

Evaluating theories

As a student you need to develop your own views on theories that you are introduced to. Questions you might ask yourself include:

Does this theory offer a more complete explanation of the topic under consideration than other theories in the area?

Does it have the same limitations as other theories in this area?

Are the terms used in the theory well defined, such that it is possible to investigate them in the context of a research study?

Is it based on sound empirical research? Are the studies that support the theory problematic in some way?

Has it subsequently been extended by other researchers or otherwise resulted in further research in that topic?

Can its principles be applied to everyday questions about children's development and be used to address 'problems' in this area?

Summary of Section 1

- Theories produced by developmental psychologists have the potential to inform everyday discussions of children's behaviour and development.
- 'Grand theories' attempt to explain the general processes that underlie children's development and behaviour. Four of the most important are behaviourism, social learning theory, constructivism and social constructivism.

2 Behaviourism

Behaviourism was an approach driven by an attempt to treat psychology as an objective science. To do this, behaviourists focused only on directly observable, measurable events and behaviours. Consequently, they rejected theorizing about 'mental events' to explain why we do the things we do. The behaviourist approach considered how the environments that people live in influence their behaviour. Learning was defined as any relatively permanent change in behaviour produced by environmental events. The process of learning was referred to as 'conditioning' and two forms of conditioning were identified: classical conditioning, and operant conditioning

SG

Classical conditioning
The learning of an association between a reflex behaviour and a previously unrelated environmental stimulus.

2.1 Classical conditioning

Ivan Pavlov (1849–1936) was a Russian neurophysiologist who studied the physiology of digestion. During this research he noticed that hungry dogs would salivate at the mere sight of the attendant who brought the food. He used this seemingly minor observation to develop his theory of classical conditioning (see Box 2).

Extinction
The decline of a learned association between a stimulus and a behavioural response, as a result of the conditioned stimulus no longer being consistently paired with the presence of an unconditioned stimulus.

BOX 2

Classical conditioning

In Figure 1 you can see how, to begin with, food (the unconditioned stimulus) elicits salivation (the unconditioned response). This is a 'reflex' response; it is unlearned and 'built-in' to the nervous system, like knee-jerking if the knee is tapped, or eye-blinking to a puff of air. The ringing of a bell at this point in time has no effect on salivation. Next the bell is regularly rung just prior to the food being presented. After a period of time the bell alone will elicit the salivation reflex in the absence of food. The bell has now become a conditioned stimulus and the salivation a conditioned response. This association can be weakened if the bell (conditioned stimulus) is regularly presented without the food (unconditioned stimulus). This process is called extinction.

Before conditioning

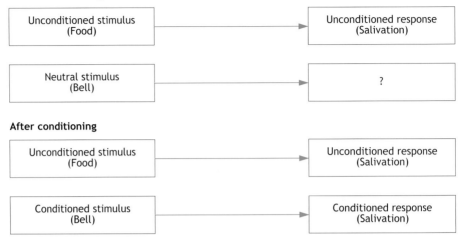

After conditioning

Figure 1 Classical conditioning.

An example of how classical conditioning has been applied to understanding children's behaviour is found in the work of American psychologist John B. Watson (1878–1958). Watson gave the behaviourist school its name in his publication 'Psychology as the behaviourist views it' (1913). His belief in the power of the environment to influence development led him to make the following statement:

> Give me a dozen healthy infants, well-formed, and my own specified world to bring them up in and I'll guarantee to take any one at random and train him to become any type of specialist I might select—doctor, lawyer, artist, merchant, chief, and yes, even beggar-man and thief, regardless of his talents, penchants, tendencies, abilities, vocations, and race of his ancestors.
>
> (Watson, 1924, p. 104)

This reflects the behaviourist viewpoint that not only can behaviour be explained by examining the environment, but that by changing the environment the person's behaviour can be altered.

Watson's particular interest was the study of emotions. Together with Rayner he conducted an experiment into the conditioning of fear with an 11-month-old infant Albert B., more commonly known as 'Little Albert' (Watson, 1924).

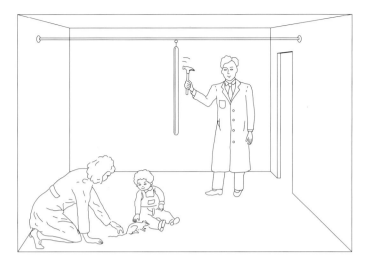

Figure 2 Little Albert and the white rat (from Swenson, 1980).

When initially presented with a white rat, Albert showed no fear. Subsequently, the rat was shown to him four times. Each time a metal bar was 'clanged' behind Albert's head. On the fifth presentation the rat was shown but without the noisy 'clang'. Although there was no noise, Albert still whimpered and moved away. He had learned to associate fear with the presence of rats through the process of classical conditioning. This response generalized to other previously neutral stimuli that were similar to the rat and which he previously had liked. He now also showed fear of furry toys, a fur coat and a Father Christmas mask. It should be noted that this study pre-dated ethical concerns about the potential of research to impact negatively on an individual's well-being.

Classical conditioning can only be used to re-train reflex behaviours (like crying when frightened or salivating when smelling food) and lead the individual to produce them in response to a new environmental stimulus. However, what if a behaviourist needed a child to produce a response that was not a part of his or her repertoire of reflex behaviours? In this instance, operant conditioning would be used.

2.2 Operant conditioning

According to behaviourism, all behaviour is learned and maintained by its consequences. B. F. Skinner (1905–1990) devised apparatus and methods for studying these effects. Figure 3 shows a 'Skinner Box' designed for use with a rat. The early behaviourists often examined animal learning and then extrapolated it to human learning. This was because they proposed that the fundamental principles of learning underpin the learning of all species.

Generalization
When other neutral stimuli are sufficiently similar to a conditioned stimulus to elicit the conditioned response.

Reflex
An instinctive, uncontrolled reaction to a given stimulus, such as salivating when presented with food.

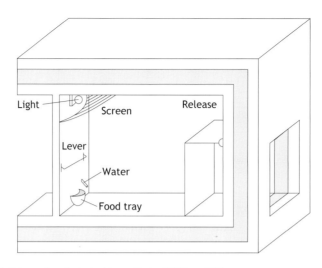

Figure 3   A Skinner Box (adapted from Crain, 2000, p. 179).

The animal in the box can choose to behave in a variety of ways. The box contains a lever that delivers a food pellet when pressed. Initially, while moving about in the box the animal discovers by accident that when the lever is pressed, food appears. Over time the rate at which the lever is pressed by the animal increases, and other behaviours decrease by comparison. This suggests that the animal has learned to associate pressing the lever with the appearance of food. In Skinner's terminology, the lever-pressing behaviour was reinforced, that is, the consequences of pressing the lever made lever pressing more likely to occur in the future. When the lever pressing resulted in an unpleasant experience, such as an electric shock, then lever-pressing behaviour would occur less often. This is an example of punishment. The important point to remember is that reinforcement always refers to something that *increases* the frequency of a given behaviour, whereas punishment always refers to something that *reduces* the frequency of a given behaviour. 'Punishment' is therefore used here as a technical term with a precise meaning that differs from its everyday meaning.

Reinforcement has both positive and negative forms. The terms 'positive' and 'negative' refer to the presentation or removal of an environmental stimulus. So, for example, 'positive reinforcement' refers to the *presentation* of a stimulus that increases the occurrence of a behaviour. 'Negative reinforcement' refers to an increase in a behaviour following the *removal* of an unpleasant ('aversive') stimuli (e.g. if a child increases the frequency of 'room-cleaning behaviour' because it results in the removal of parental disapproval).

Punishment can take one of three forms. 'Positive punishment' refers to the presentation of an unpleasant stimulus that will decrease the occurrence of the behaviour it follows. 'Time-out' is where a child is isolated from a reinforcing stimulus in their environment, with the aim of producing a decrease in the target behaviour. Finally, 'response cost' is where a penalty is applied every time an undesired behaviour is produced, again resulting in a decrease in that behaviour. The penalty, may be, for example, the removal of 'tokens' – items that are valued by the person, such as reward stickers or money. Table 1 summarizes reinforcement and punishment.

Punishment
An environmental stimulus that results in a decrease in a given behaviour.

Reinforcement
An environmental stimulus that results in an increase in a given behaviour.

Table I   Reinforcement and punishment

Reinforcement		
Positive reinforcement	Positive stimulus presented	Behaviour increases
Negative reinforcement	Aversive stimulus removed	Behaviour increases
Punishment		
Positive punishment	Aversive stimulus presented	Behaviour decreases
Time-out	Isolation from reinforcer	Behaviour decreases
Response cost	For example token removed	Behaviour decreases

Extinction burst
A period of increased production of a previously reinforced behaviour following the withdrawal of that reinforcement.

As with classical conditioning, extinction can occur if the behaviour is no longer reinforced. However, it should be noted that extinction is usually preceded by an extinction burst.

▼

Activity I

Allow about 5 minutes

Understanding punishment and reinforcement terms

This activity will help you to understand the meaning of the different types of reinforcement and punishment.

Read each statement below and identify which ones are examples of (a) positive reinforcement, (b) negative reinforcement, (c) positive punishment, (d) time-out and (e) response cost.

1   Getting burned when touching a hot pan, and never doing it again.

2   Getting a gold star for neat handwriting, and increasing your attempts to write neatly.

3   Watching your parents walk away when you are having a tantrum, and eventually calming down to run after them.

4   Stopping hitting your brother after you have a favourite toy taken away every time you hit him.

5   Having not had the opportunity to eat all day, you are eating a large chocolate bar, and then stop having eaten three-quarters of it.

Comment

The important thing to note in all these examples is what happened to the person's behaviour in relation to the environmental change, as it is *the actual effect on behaviour* that defines something as reinforcing or punishing. So, being burned in (1) is an example of positive punishment, as the presence of the burning sensation reduced the future incidence of the behaviour. (2) is an example of a positive reinforcement, as being given the star increased the production of neat writing. (3) is an example of time-out: the removal of parental attention resulted in reduced tantrum behaviour. (4) is an example of response cost – the favourite toy is systematically removed every time the undesired behaviour was produced. (5) is an example of negative reinforcement. Your hunger (an aversive stimulus) is removed by eating three-quarters of the chocolate bar.

▲

However, ideally we should consider all these behaviours over time. For example, in (5) if your *future* consumption of chocolate *decreased*, then your 'chocolate-eating behaviour' was punished (eating three-quarters of a bar of chocolate may have made you feel unwell). If this behaviour *increased* in future then it was reinforced – either negatively (by reducing hunger) or positively (because you love chocolate!). This highlights one of the difficulties in identifying reinforcers and punishers in practice: they are defined by their outcomes, which may vary from individual to individual. For example, what is 'reinforcing' for one person may be 'aversive' for another.

Schedule of reinforcement
The frequency and/or regularity of a given reinforcement or punishment in a setting.

In addition to reinforcement and punishment, Skinner examined the effect that different schedules of reinforcement have on the production of a behaviour: does it matter if a reward or punishment is not presented *every* time a behaviour is produced? Of particular significance is the predictability of the environment: the more unpredictable the pattern of reinforcement or punishment, the more resilient the behaviour will be to extinction. Consider the example of a child who has learned to expect a gold star every time she produces good work; as soon as the stars stop appearing she will quickly become de-motivated. However, if she learns that she *occasionally* gets gold stars for good work, she will be more likely to sustain good work in the expectation that she will, eventually, get a star again.

2.3 Use of punishment: spare the rod?

One issue, introduced in Chapter 1, about which there is regular debate, concerns the use of 'punishment' to control children's behaviour. Behaviourism might, at first glance, appear to offer support for using punishment to reduce undesirable behaviour. For example, imagine that a father and his daughter are out shopping and the child steals a bar of chocolate and eats some of it whilst her father is distracted. He then sees her and shouts at her. In operant terms the stealing event is followed by an aversive response. This suggests that the stealing behaviour will occur less often in the future. However, one also needs to consider the *contingency* of the events. Before the father scolded the child, she had already eaten some of the chocolate. Consequently, eating the chocolate is likely to have been a contingent positive reinforcement, and perhaps the child's hunger may have also been reduced (a contingent negative reinforcement). Both of these immediate consequences increase the likelihood that the child will steal again (Huesmann *et al.*, 2003).

Contingency
Two events are said to be contingent on one another if the presence of one event *immediately* results in the occurrence of the other.

Behaviourist research has shown that for punishment to be effective, it must be immediate (contingent), severe and consistently applied (Klein, 1996). However, outside of the laboratory, it is virtually impossible to achieve such aims: adults cannot supervise the behaviour of children continually and be in a position to intervene immediately with appropriate punishment every time a child misbehaves. In the absence of these conditions, punishment as a means of behavioural control is, at best, short lived. Even Skinner (1938) found that punishment can only temporarily suppress a behaviour in a specific context, not eliminate it. Furthermore, in terms of classical conditioning, the child might associate the aversive response (shouting) with the person delivering the response, and show a conditioned fear response to her parent (see Figure 4).

There is also a risk of inappropriate association: the child who is punished for stealing in the supermarket may associate the punishment with the wrong behaviour (e.g. eating the chocolate, or visiting the supermarket).

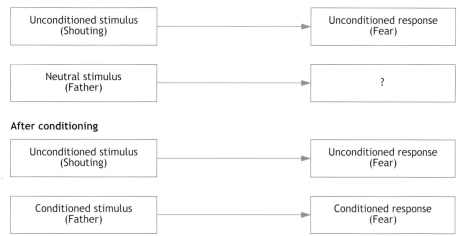

Before conditioning

| Unconditioned stimulus (Shouting) | → | Unconditioned response (Fear) |

| Neutral stimulus (Father) | → | ? |

After conditioning

| Unconditioned stimulus (Shouting) | → | Unconditioned response (Fear) |

| Conditioned stimulus (Father) | → | Conditioned response (Fear) |

Figure 4 Classical conditioning and punishment.

Punishment has been found to stimulate aggressive behaviour in some circumstances and to suppress it in others, and its long-term effects on behaviour are often not what was initially expected (Huesmann *et al.*, 2003). A range of research studies has shown that, overall, punishment can be used to successfully manage inappropriate behaviour but it also has many negative short- and long-term consequences (Gershoff, 2002). These include increased aggression, decreased quality of relationships with carers, decreased mental health, and a later increased likelihood for antisocial and criminal behaviour. However, time-out procedures have been found to be effective in controlling the extent of behaviours like tantrums in typically developing children and those with learning difficulties (Klein, 1996). Yet, it should be noted that the need for contingency and consistency would also apply to the application of such schemes.

Punishment only teaches a child what response not to make. For behaviour to change, children also need to learn what alternative behaviour is appropriate and then be reinforced for producing it. For these reasons contemporary techniques of behavioural change based on behaviourism do not use punishment, but teach appropriate behaviours and increase their frequency through reinforcement. One example of such an application is known as applied behavioural analysis (ABA).

2.4 Application: applied behavioural analysis

ABA is a method of teaching that involves breaking tasks into small, discrete 'teachable' steps. At each step appropriate behaviours are reinforced. ABA selects developmentally appropriate behaviours as teaching targets. These can range from maintaining eye contact to complex responses such as social interaction. The child is given enough support to ensure success, which is then positively reinforced by consequences that are reinforcing for that child. Gradually the amount of support and reinforcement is reduced.

Early intervention programmes for children with learning difficulties have the potential to produce positive changes in development and consequently reduce the need for later interventions. Therefore in many ABA programmes parents are trained to become the primary therapists and their children receive one-to-one tuition in their own homes. There is evidence that intervening in a child's development in this way can help children with autism to be more successful in mainstream schools (Keenan *et al.*, 2000). However, such schemes have proved difficult to foster widely because of the association with behaviourist approaches and the negative connotations associated with such ideas (Keenan, 2004). It is important to make a distinction between behaviourism as it was originally conceived, and its contemporary manifestation in behavioural analysis, which does not ignore cognitive processes during learning.

Reading

At this point you should turn to the end of this chapter and read Reading A, 'Applied behavioural analysis and autism' by Keenan (2004). He is an advocate of ABA as a means of helping the development of children with autistic spectrum disorders.

2.5 Evaluating behaviourism

As the previous section indicates, although 'classic' behaviourism is rare in contemporary explanations of child development, many of its guiding principles have been retained in some form or other in the field of learning difficulties. One of the advantages of behaviourism lies in its utility as a form of direct communication with children who are too young to speak, or who are otherwise difficult to communicate with about their behaviour. It resulted in decades of research, becoming the dominant theory in psychology during the 1950s and 1960s. Behaviourism continues to stimulate research and inform debates both in child development and psychology more generally, albeit in a modified form, as illustrated by advocates of behavioural analysis. ABA shows how operant conditioning principles relating to the reinforcement of desirable behaviour can be successfully applied.

A missing factor in 'classic' behaviourist explanations of child behaviour is the importance of children's thoughts, beliefs and interpretations of a situation. The development of appropriate social behaviour is more likely if the child understands why they are being treated in a particular way (Huesmann *et al.*, 2003). It is an oversimplification to propose that children can only learn through direct experience and contingent rewards. This does not seem to explain the vast array of things that children master in the areas of language, cognition and social behaviour. Furthermore, the section of this chapter on punishment indicated some important limitations in the application of that aspect of behaviourist theory. In particular, research has shown that children learn more from experiencing punishment than just its relationship to their own behaviour. Adults who are aggressive towards children, either verbally or physically, are modelling a behaviour and potentially signalling its acceptability as a means of affecting the behaviour of those around them. Such concerns are reflected in the ideas developed by Bandura, in his *social learning theory*.

Summary of Section 2

- Behaviourism proposes that all behaviour is learned and maintained by its consequences. It does not theorize about 'mental events'.
- Classical conditioning describes how reflex behaviours can become associated with neutral stimuli in the environment.
- Operant conditioning describes how the incidence of freely occurring behaviours can be increased or reduced as a result of the incidence of pleasant and unpleasant consequences for those behaviours, and how behaviour can be 'shaped' by the use of rewards.
- Punishment is only effective as a means of behavioural control if it is severe, contingent and consistently applied. However, even when these conditions are in place, it is only successful in temporarily suppressing a behaviour in a specific context.
- Reinforcement is used to help children with learning difficulties make progress at home and at school by using a technique known as applied behavioural analysis (ABA).

3 Social learning theory

It was clear to Canadian psychologist Albert Bandura (1924–) that not only is children's behaviour shaped by its consequences, but also that children learn by watching the behaviour of people around them. In contrast to behaviourism, Bandura's social learning theory emphasized the importance of children imitating the behaviours, emotions and attitudes of those they saw around them:

> Learning would be exceedingly laborious, not to mention hazardous, if people had to rely solely on the effects of their own actions to inform them what to do ... from observing others one forms an idea of how new behaviors are performed, and on later occasions this coded information serves as a guide for action.
>
> (Bandura, 1977, p. 22)

There are many examples of children learning complex skills by observation. For example, Guatemalan girls learn to weave 'almost exclusively by watching models. The teacher demonstrates the operations of the textile machine, while the girl simply observes. Then, when the girl feels ready, she takes over, and she usually operates it skilfully on her very first try' (Crain, 2000, p. 194).

Bandura's theory explains children's learning by considering four interrelated factors. To imitate someone a child must:

1   *Attend* to relevant aspects of the 'model' and their behaviour.
2   *Retain* what they have seen, through appropriate encoding and rehearsal.
3   *Be physically able* to reproduce the behaviour.
4   *Be motivated* to perform the new skill, through the presence of reinforcement and punishment in the observed setting.

He detailed aspects of each of these processes and demonstrated, for example, that memorizing modelled behaviour by translating what is observed into words or images produces better retention than observation alone (Bandura and Jeffery, 1972). Importantly, he acknowledged the role of observing others experiencing reinforcement and punishment, but argued that its role was in influencing which behaviours children attend to in the first place, and also in affecting children's motivation to reproduce a behaviour.

3.1 Observation and imitation of aggression

Bandura conducted a series of experimental studies into children's tendency to imitate. In these experiments pre-school children watched adult models act either non-aggressively or aggressively towards an inflatable doll called a Bobo doll. The children were subsequently observed to see to what extent they imitated what they had seen – one such study is presented in Research summary 1.

RESEARCH SUMMARY 1

Observing aggression

Bandura's study (1965) observed a group of 4-year-old children watching, on their own, a film of a man being aggressive towards the doll. The man laid the doll on its side, sat on it and punched it repeatedly on the nose. The man then raised the doll, picked up a mallet and struck the doll on the head. He then tossed the doll up in the air aggressively and kicked it about the room. This sequence of physically aggressive acts was repeated approximately three times, interspersed with aggressive comments such as, 'Sock him in the nose ...', 'Hit him down ...', 'Throw him in the air ...', 'Kick him ...', 'Pow ...', and two non-aggressive comments, 'He keeps coming back for more.' and 'He sure is a tough fella.'

There were three versions of the film which were shown to three different groups of children. These films were the same except for the endings. For the first version of the film one group of children saw the man receiving treats and praise from another adult for hitting the doll. For the second version another group saw the man being verbally and physically admonished for his behaviour and in the third version the group saw no consequences for the man's behaviour.

Having seen the film, the children went into a room containing a Bobo doll and some other toys. The children who had seen the film of the man being punished imitated much less aggression than did the children in the 'no-consequences' and the 'rewarded' groups. There was no difference in the amount of aggression produced by the 'no-consequences' and 'rewarded' groups. However, later when told that they would get a reward for doing what the man (the model) had done, all groups imitated equally. For Bandura the important point was that each group had learned the same behaviours through mere observation; observing the man being punished only affected the conditions in which they chose to perform the behaviour.

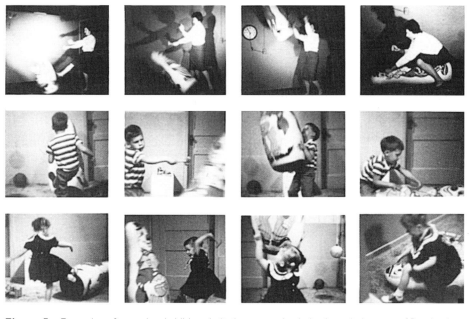

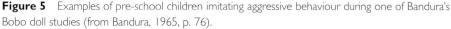

Figure 5   Examples of pre-school children imitating aggressive behaviour during one of Bandura's Bobo doll studies (from Bandura, 1965, p. 76).

3.2 Application: children and television violence

Bandura's use of filmed events prompted other researchers (Liebert *et al.*, 1977) to argue that his work had important implications for the influence that television violence may have on young children. In general, children aged 2–7 years watch television for approximately 25 hours per week, a figure that increases for older children (Roberts *et al.*, 1999). By the age of 12, the average child will have viewed over 8,000 murders (Beckman, 1997). Furthermore, children are more likely to give attention to commercials than the programmes themselves (Alexander and Morrison, 1995) and it has been estimated that approximately one-third of commercials that feature children also contain aggression (Larson, 2003). Bandura (1973) also explored the idea that televised aggression may have adverse effects on children's behaviour, and considered some of the variables that influence when a child will imitate. For example, children are more likely to copy another's behaviour if the model is similar to them in age and sex, or if the model has desirable characteristics and is seen as attractive. Reading B describes one study that considered the potential influence of filmed aggression compared to real-life aggression on children's imitative behaviour.

Reading

At this point you should turn to the end of this chapter and read Reading B, 'Learning through modeling' which is a paper written by Bandura (1973).

SG

Bandura's (1973) view was that children's learning goes through three stages: exposure, acquisition, and acceptance. They may thereby learn, through observation, to be more aggressive and less sensitive to the results of violence. This straightforward account has been disputed by others who argue that other factors intervene in the learning process, such as the family conditions within which the television is being viewed (Kytömäki, 1998). However, there is some support for Bandura's stance. Davidson (1996) reports research showing that the amount of violence children watched as 8 year olds was a better predictor of adult aggression than socioeconomic and childrearing factors.

If children's development is significantly influenced, through social learning, by their television viewing then it also has the potential to act as a positive influence. Huston *et al.* (1981) found that very young children who spent a few hours a week watching educational programmes (e.g. *Sesame Street*) had higher academic scores 3 years later than those who did not watch educational programmes. Also, children who watched many hours of entertainment programmes and cartoons had lower scores than those who watched fewer hours of such programmes.

3.3 Evaluating social learning theory

Bandura's work shows that learning can occur without the sorts of reinforcement that behaviourists see as essential, and that children are active in their learning. The sort of learning that Bandura highlighted goes further than simple mimicry. It implies that children extract general principles from what they observe. However, it does not tell us about the nature of the children's thinking or give us an insight into the processes of cognitive change occurring within the child. Moreover, it still places the emphasis on factors that are external to the child as the key influences on their developing behaviour; in this case the behaviour and experiences of people around them. To understand cognitive development a different theoretical perspective is needed, namely constructivism.

Summary of Section 3

- Social learning theory proposes that it is possible for children to learn by observing other people.
- Bandura found that pre-school children would copy aggressive behaviour modelled by another person, and that this was most likely if the model was similar to them in some way and not seem to be punished.
- Social learning research has informed the ongoing debate about television being either a positive or negative influence on young children.
- Social learning theory does not attempt to explain children's cognitive development.

4 Constructivism

Jean Piaget (1896–1980) was not primarily interested in child development, but in the nature of knowledge and how it could be seen as a form of adaptation to the environment. He described his work as genetic epistemology.

Genetic epistemology
Piaget's term for the study of the origins and development of knowledge.

He argued that individuals develop progressively more elaborate and sophisticated mental representations of the environment, based on their own actions on the environment and the consequences of these. Thus he saw cognitive development as progressive and constructive, with the child becoming increasingly competent at acting in more complex ways on the environment as a result of building up mental representations of how the world works.

Mental representation
An internalized, personal understanding of some aspect of the external world.

Piaget theorized that there is an inherent logic to the development of human knowledge that means that it is constructed by all children in the same order. This sequence was seen as emerging from the nature of human knowledge and the child's own actions. Although he saw the basic building blocks and the processes of development as universal, he saw development itself as being the child's own construction.

4.1 The origins of Piagetian theory

Piaget started his career as a biologist, interested in the processes by which organisms adapt to their environment during development. Born in Switzerland, his interest in child development began in 1920 when he worked in Alfred Binet's laboratory, helping to translate items for one of the first intelligence tests into French. Piaget became interested in the wrong answers the children gave. These 'errors' seemed to be systematic rather than random, suggesting some underlying consistencies in the children's developing mental abilities.

Piaget based many of his ideas on observations of his own children; Jacqueline, Lucienne and Laurent. One of Piaget's observations is provided in Box 3.

BOX 3

Piaget's observations of the infant Jacqueline

Jacqueline tries to grasp a celluloid duck on top of her quilt. She almost catches it, shakes herself, and the duck slides down beside her. It falls very close to her hand but behind a fold in the sheet. Jacqueline's eyes have followed the movement, she has even followed it with her outstretched hand. But as soon as the duck has disappeared—nothing more! It does not occur to her to search behind the fold of the sheet, which would be very easy to do (she twists it mechanically without searching at all). But, curiously, she again begins to stir about as she did when trying to get the duck and again glances at the top of the quilt.

I then take the duck from its hiding-place and place it near her hand three times. All three times she tries to grasp it, but when she is about to touch it I replace it very obviously under the sheet. Jacqueline immediately withdraws her hand and gives up. The second and third times I make her grasp the duck through the sheet and she shakes it for a brief moment but it does not occur to her to raise the cloth.

Then I recommence the initial experiment. The duck is on the quilt. In trying to get it she again causes it to slide behind the fold in the sheet; after having looked at this fold for a moment (it is near her hand) she turns over and sucks her thumb.

I then offer her her doll which is crying. Jacqueline laughs. I hide it behind the fold in the sheet; she whimpers. I make the doll cry; no search. I offer it to her again and put a handkerchief around it; no reaction. I make the doll cry in the handkerchief; nothing.

(Source: Piaget, 1955, pp. 36–7)

Object permanence
The understanding that objects exist when they can no longer be seen.

SG

Centration
The tendency to focus exclusively on a single aspect of a situation.

Egocentrism
An absence of any awareness of the separate existence of either other people or objects. Thus, other people's views are seen to be the same as the child's own; objects only exist when they are perceived by the child.

From such observations, Piaget reached the conclusion that infants lack an understanding of object permanence. As adults, we know that objects have a continuing existence when they are not actually in our sight; when we put something down we normally expect to find it again when we go back to the same place. Piaget proposed that all of us go through a stage when we are completely without this belief. According to Piaget, the world is totally impermanent for the young infant, and exists only when actually being perceived in some way, such that when an object is out of sight it no longer exists for the child.

This idea of 'centring' – the sense of the baby feeling herself to be the centre and the moving force of her world – runs through much of Piaget's theory, particularly the ideas of centration and egocentrism. The tendency of infants to focus or 'centre' on a single aspect of a situation illustrates the complete dominance of their own perceptions. For example, when an object disappears from their sight and they behave as if the object has ceased to exist, they are 'centring' on their own perception. Piaget called this particular sort of centring, where one's own viewpoint is dominant, 'egocentrism'.

If at first the baby sees the world only as 'fleeting tableaux', how is the concept of an enduring, permanent world formed? According to Piaget, through the experience of repeating actions and their effects, babies come to understand that actions have consequences. For example, in the earliest stages, looking away from an object causes it to 'disappear' and looking back to the same location causes it to reappear. What is happening here, according to Piaget, is that the baby is storing something in the mind about both the act (looking away and back) and its effects (disappearance and reappearance); a mental representation.

As the baby becomes able to grasp objects, the potential for this sort of learning is increased: for example, things can be moved in and out of vision. There are activities that the baby repeats again and again, taking obvious pleasure in the effects of such actions, and according to Piaget, continuing to construct mental representations. Indeed, repetitive behaviour, such as dropping objects or putting one thing in another, is a characteristic of early development. These repetitions give the child a lot of information about the properties of objects in the world. It is also as if the child has some sort of motivation to repeat continually things that she can do.

4.2 Processes of development

Schema
A representation of a sequence of actions developed as a result of a child's action on the environment.

A central concept in Piaget's theory is that of the schema. A schema is, initially, a simple sequence of behaviour like sucking, or reaching and grasping. Piaget believed that the fact of possessing a schema, such as sucking, in itself creates a motivation for its exercise and for its application to multiple objects and situations which is beyond any immediate physical need to apply it, such as for feeding.

At first, a schema such as sucking has a reflex quality about it, since it does not seem to be adapted at all to the properties of the object being sucked; the same action is evoked by a finger, a nipple or the corner of a cloth. Piaget described this sort of schema activity as assimilation, when the schema 'assimilates' different objects without adaptation.

Assimilation
The process of 'fitting' aspects of the environment into existing schemas.

We see this sort of behaviour in the child initially applying sucking in a more or less indiscriminate way to any object that can be brought to the mouth, as a means of exploring that object. It is as if sucking has a need to be exercised, at first just for itself, then on the baby's hands and later as a means of exploring objects. Piaget saw this intrinsic motivation as a primary moving force in development, keeping the child actively applying schemas to new situations as they arise.

Intrinsic motivation
The desire to spontaneously apply existing schemas to new situations.

Gradually, the action schema of sucking becomes more adaptable, more responsive to differences in objects. This introduces a third central process in Piaget's theory: accommodation. This happens when schemas are modified to match the special characteristics of objects and situations. For example, the schema of reaching for and grasping objects is, initially, predominantly assimilative: it consists of a fairly crude 'swipe and grab' in the general direction of an attractive object. As the baby grows, the schema becomes more refined and is adapted to the object's position and size: it begins to accommodate to the object.

Accommodation
The process of modifying schemas to suit the environment better.

The three processes – of intrinsic motivation, assimilation and accommodation – were central to Piaget's explanation of how development progresses. We can see how this might account for the step-by-step development of behaviour by the gradual modification of schemas, each accommodation introducing new flexibility and adaptive possibilities.

4.3 Structure and stages

Piaget's developmental processes can be described in the context of infant behaviour to show how they explain behaviour becoming more adapted, in a step-by-step way. First, the infant develops the ability to combine different schemas in order to achieve new ends. Then, the child represents schemas 'internally'; they become representations of actions ('operations'). Finally, by the age of 2 years, the child becomes capable of combining representations into sets of actions. He saw one of the goals of the first 2 years of life as being the achievement of a set of operations that are represented as a structure; not just a random collection of unconnected actions, but a co-ordinated set of possibilities for manipulating the world.

Piaget's theory described four stages of intellectual development: these are outlined in Box 4.

BOX 4

Piaget's stage theory of development

Stage 1: Sensori-motor stage (from birth to about 2 years)

Children are born with innate behavioural patterns (reflexes), which are their first means of making sense of their world. Children can take in new knowledge and experiences as far as they are consistent with their existing behaviours. Eventually they begin to generate new behaviours in response to their environment (schemas). As contact with the environment increases, they develop more elaborate patterns of behaviour. This stage ends when children are able to represent their behaviours internally.

Stage 2: Pre-operational stage (from about 2 to 6 years)

Children begin to use combinations or sequences of actions that can be carried out symbolically. For example, putting two objects together can be represented symbolically as an abstract mathematical principle (addition). However, at this stage children are only able to perform them as actions in the real world rather than to represent them symbolically.

Stage 3: Concrete operations stage (from about 6 to 12 years)

During this stage children are mastering the ability to act appropriately on their environment by using the sequences of actions they acquired in the pre operational stage. They develop the ability to generate 'rules' based on their own experiences (e.g. noticing that adding something to a group of objects always 'makes more'). Children can now manipulate their environment symbolically too, so they can imagine adding 'more' to a group of objects. They are still only able to understand the rules that they have had concrete experience of, but can now begin some mental manipulation of these concepts. What they are unable to do at this stage is use rules to anticipate something that could happen, but that they have not yet experienced.

Stage 4: Formal operations stage (from about 12 years onwards)

By this stage children can reason in a purely abstract way, without reference to concrete experience. They can tackle problems in a systematic and scientific manner and are able to generate hypotheses about the world based on their accumulated representations of it.

Each stage is, according to Piaget, marked by characteristic modes of thought. The general progression through the stages is such that thought, and consequent action, become progressively less 'centred'. Through increasing abstraction of representation, 'mental operations' become less tied to concrete realities and egocentric perceptions.

Using the word 'stage' to describe a period of development suggests that children do different things at each of these stages. This idea of stage makes it possible to describe these changes in terms of particular behaviours and ways of solving problems that appear to dominate in particular age ranges. However, it should be noted that Piaget's theory recognizes that some children develop more slowly or faster than others, and the development of an individual child may not be maintained at a constant rate. For example, illness can slow development down and, when they have recovered, children often show a spurt of 'catch-up' growth, both mentally and physically.

An implication of Piaget's theory is that there is some sort of abrupt change or discontinuity in development that establishes a boundary between one stage and the next. Indeed, if there is no such boundary implied, then it is rather dubious whether we would be justified in calling a particular period a 'stage' at all. But using the word 'stage' also often carries with it a notion of sequence, that one stage must follow another stage in a set order, or even that there is a causal relationship in which the completion of one stage is deemed a necessary condition for the transition to the next one. Piaget's stages form a necessary sequence, with no child missing out any of the stages, nor passing through them out of sequence.

So, how did Piaget determine when a child passed from one stage to the next? This was achieved by administering sets of experimental tasks, each task being linked to a core concept associated with a given stage of development. For example, pre-operational children, in Piaget's theory, are basically egocentric, centred on their own perceptions because they are still very tied to the concrete world and their actions on it. Also, because this group of children lack the ability to reflect on operations, their understanding of the world tends to focus on states, rather than on transformations. Similarly, such children are unable to comprehend points of view different from their own.

One of the concepts that Piaget suggested was absent from pre-operational children's representation of the world was conservation – the understanding that a quantity will be the same, even if its manner of presentation changes. For example, a quantity of water remains the same whether it is presented in a tall, thin glass or a short, wide glass. His conservation of liquid task involves three basic steps:

1   The child is shown two identical transparent beakers, each about two-thirds full of water. They are placed side-by-side in front of the child. The experimenter seeks the child's agreement that the quantities of water in each are the same, if necessary adding or taking away small amounts until the child is satisfied.

2   The water from one beaker is all poured into another beaker, which is either taller and narrower than the first one, or shorter and wider.
Typically, up to the age of about 6 or 7 years, children will assert, when asked, that the amount of liquid has changed. If the children are then asked why this is so, they will tend to say something like 'because it's taller'. The children's answers seem to indicate that their judgement of quantity is centred on the visual change brought about by the transformation (see Figure 6).

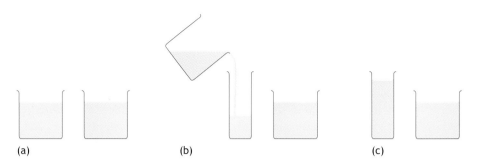

(a)   (b)   (c)

Figure 6   (a) Identical beakers of water. (b) Water is poured from one beaker to another which is either taller and narrower or shorter and wider. (c) Comparison of water levels in different sized beakers (adapted from Light and Oates, 1990).

Conservation
The understanding that a quantity remains the same, in spite of any transformation of the way in which it is presented.

Piaget considered conservation not just in relation to amounts of liquid, but also in relation to mass, volume, weight, area, length and number. For example, to assess conservation of mass, a child is shown two balls of clay and asked whether each ball has the same amount in it. When the child is satisfied that both are equal, one of the balls is rolled out into a sausage shape and placed alongside the other, untransformed, ball. Then, just as in the conservation of liquid task, the child is asked whether there is more material in the sausage shape, or less, or the same amount. A 'non-conserver' will now say that the amounts are no longer the same, as the sausage shape now has more in it.

Piaget's theory involves the child progressively becoming freed from the constraints of their own perspective and the concrete objects around them, as mental operations become more abstract. This process reaches its end-point in Piaget's final stage, when operations become wholly abstract and the child becomes able to reason purely hypothetically and systematically.

4.4 Application: discovery learning

Piaget's theory offers a rich description of a child developing a more abstract and general capacity to tackle problems in the world, in a very independent way. There is little place in Piaget's theory for teaching, and his ideas were used to support the pedagogic principles of discovery learning, in which the provision of a rich learning environment is seen as essential, rather than direct tuition. In this approach, children are given opportunities to actively explore and investigate concepts and physical events in order to build their understanding. According to the main tenets of discovery learning, teaching needs to encourage self-directed investigation rather than a potentially superficial understanding in imitation of adult performance. Piaget also stressed the need for teachers to make the learning environment appropriate to the developmental level of the child.

Socio-cognitive conflict
Exposure to conflicting ideas presented by a peer that force a child to reconsider their own understanding.

While discovery learning downplayed the significance of adults as tutors, Piaget did value *peer* contact as having the potential to foster cognitive development. That is, he suggested that such contact would expose them to other, conflicting viewpoints, which they would need to accommodate their own developing representations to; this was referred to as socio-cognitive conflict. Importantly, peer contact was believed to foster this in a way that contact with adults could not, as adults are perceived by children as having greater authority. As a result, they would be more willing to accept adult ideas without experiencing them as a personal challenge that would prompt thoughtful evaluation of the ideas being presented. Thus, this type of contact with adults was believed to hinder children's ability to appreciate other perspectives. Ironically, it was 'dominance of adults' that proved to be at the heart of one of the criticisms that have been levelled at Piaget's experimental work.

4.5 Evaluating constructivism

Piaget's theory was revolutionary in many respects. It recognized that children thought differently to adults. The view that learning is an individual and constructive process differed sharply from the prevailing climate of behaviourism when it was published. However, the experimental tasks that Piaget used to establish his theory have been subjected to criticism. Subsequent research, most notably by Donaldson (1978), has shown that under certain conditions young children are able to operate at levels above those predicted by Piagetian theory. For example, simple modifications to Piaget's conservation tasks show that many children can grasp this concept at a 'pre-operational' age (see Research summary 2).

RESEARCH SUMMARY 2

The chipped beaker

Light and colleagues (1979) studied 80 4-year-old children and tested them in pairs. Half of them completed a standard Piagetian conservation task. Two identical beakers were filled to the same level with dried pasta shapes. When the children agreed that there was the same amount of pasta in each beaker, the contents of one were poured into a wider beaker. Only 5 per cent of the children said that the amounts were still the same.

For the other half of the children the procedure was different. They were told at the outset that they were going to use the pasta shells in a competitive game. But after they had agreed that the two beakers contained the same amount of pasta, the experimenter 'noticed' that one of the beakers was dangerously chipped around the rim. He looked around and found the alternative (wider) beaker and poured the contents in, asking the children, before they started their game, whether they had the same amount of shells each. This time 70 per cent of the children judged that the quantities were equal.

Donaldson (1978) argued that young children's reasoning is more sophisticated than Piaget's research implied, that their reasoning is embedded in the social situations it occurs within, and it is this social element that may account for the results obtained by her and others. In particular, she argued that the tasks had to make 'human sense' to the children. In Light *et al.* (1979), putting the pasta into another beaker because the original one was chipped, 'makes sense' and there is no reason to suspect that the content would have changed as a result. However, in the standard version of the task, where no rationale for changing the beaker is presented, the children may assume that the adult is demonstrating it for a purpose, and guess that the reason must be to do with the question they are asked about the amount of pasta in the beakers changing. In fact, Hughes and Grieve (1980) demonstrated that both 5-year-old and 7-year-old children will actually attempt to answer bizarre questions put to them by an adult, such as 'Is milk bigger than water?' and 'Is red heavier than yellow?'. Hughes and Grieve argued that the children are simply doing what children do during much of their young lives: trying to make sense of information from a position of relative ignorance. If this idea is applied to Piaget's tasks, then it may be that many of the 'incorrect' responses Piaget noted were the result of the children trying to identify meaning in apparently meaningless tasks. When the task is given an accessible meaning, as in the work of Donaldson and others, children are able to offer more appropriate responses. Moreover, it would seem that young children's social experience, especially that of school, teaches them that it is inappropriate to ask for clarification when asked a question by an adult, no matter how bizarre. This feature of adult–child relationships was recognized by Piaget in his theory, but he failed to recognize its potential impact in a research context.

The relative lack of attention paid to the social and cultural context of child development has been a substantial criticism of Piaget's ideas. One of Piaget's critics on this point was a Russian contemporary, Lev Vygotsky. His theory of development only emerged many years after his death and he is seen as the founder of an area of developmental research known as 'social constructivism'.

Summary of Section 4

- Piaget proposed that all children pass through an ordered sequence of stages of cognitive development. This development arises through the processes of intrinsic motivation, assimilation and accommodation and equilibration.
- Children's actions on the environment are the basic building blocks of development.
- Piaget argued that children reason differently to adults, as their mental representations of the world are initially centred on their own perceptions and experiences of it. Cognitive development occurs as children become able to act on their environment in increasingly sophisticated ways. Children are therefore seen as active in constructing their understanding of the world from an initial set of innate behaviours.
- A pedagogical approach known as 'discovery learning' was developed as a result of Piaget's ideas about cognitive development. This positions the teacher as the provider of a developmentally appropriate learning environment, rather than as an active tutor.
- Piaget has been criticized for failing to recognize the importance of the social context of children's cognitive activity.

5 Social constructivism

Vygotsky (1896–1934) wrote two important books, *Mind in Society* (1978) and *Thought and Language* (1986), which were only widely published after his death. Due to state suppression, since they challenged some of the orthodox beliefs of the Soviet regime, these books took some time to come to the attention of developmental psychologists. Vygotsky came, independently, to much the same conclusions as Piaget about the constructive nature of development.

Cultural tool
A means of achieving things in the world which are acquired during development and passed on to subsequent generations. Cultural tools can be either physical (e.g. a hammer) or psychological (e.g. language) in nature.

However, he differed in the role he ascribed to the social and cultural world surrounding the child. Vygotsky's perspective was that human history is created through the construction and use of cultural tools. The inventive use of tools is what makes, and has made, humans human. Cultural tools are ways of achieving things in the world, acquired in the course of development and passed on to subsequent generations. So, for example, a hammer is a physical example of a cultural tool: it is a means of knocking sharp objects (e.g. nails) into surfaces. Its form and function are the result of generations of cultural development and adaptation. Moreover, its meaning and use is not immediately obvious to someone who has never come across a hammer before, or who has never needed to knock nails in – this information is also culturally transmitted. Each generation may adapt a hammer for its own needs or use it in new ways; a process referred to as 'appropriation'.

Not all cultural tools are physical objects: they include ways of thinking as well as ways of doing. For example, perhaps one of the most significant cultural tools people use is language, and it shares the same characteristics attributed above to the hammer: long-term cultural development, adaptation, transmission and appropriation. Vygotsky proposed that it is through social interaction that ways of thinking begin to be appropriated by children, not, as Piaget thought, by children constructing them on their own. Cognitive development takes place within a social context and is supported by it.

Activity 2   *Thinking in context*

Allow about 15 minutes

This activity will demonstrate how even adult cognition is facilitated by the social context.

Try these two puzzles and write down your answer to the first puzzle before moving on to the second.

Puzzle 1

There are four cards, labelled either A or D on one side and either 3 or 7 on the other. They are laid out like this:

| A | D | 3 | 7 |

A rule states: 'if A is on one side then there must be a 3 on the other'.

Which two cards do you need to turn over to find out if this rule is true?

Puzzle 2

As you walk into a bar you see a large sign stating that 'To drink alcohol here you must be over 18'. There are four people in the bar. You know the ages of two of them, and can see what the other two are drinking. The situation is:

Ailsa is drinking beer;

Dymphna is drinking Coke;

Maureen is 30 years old;

Lauren is 16 years old.

Which two people would you need to talk to in order to check that the 'over 18 rule' for drinking alcohol is being followed?

Once you have written down your answers, turn to the end of the chapter to check whether you are correct.

▲

The puzzles illustrate the significance of reasoning and cognitive ability being embedded in, and affected by, particular social contexts. The second puzzle is much easier than the first for most people, but the logical form of the reasoning required in both puzzles is the same. The significance of social context for Vygotsky is well illustrated by his views on the development of thought and language.

5.1 Thought and language

For Piaget the development of thought and language was dependent on underlying 'intelligence'. Language is therefore simply a reflection of mental ability: intelligence precedes language and is independent of it.

Vygotsky (1986) however, proposed that language has two functions: inner speech, used for mental reasoning, and external speech, used for communication with other people. He suggested that these two functions arise separately. That is, before the age of about 2 years, children use words purely socially, to communicate with others. Up to this point, the child's internal cognition is without language.

At around 2 years thought and language merge. The language that once accompanied social interaction is internalized to give a language for thought. This internalized language becomes a means of guiding the child's actions and thinking. As a result of internalizing 'social language', the social environment becomes embedded in children's mental reasoning:

> Every function in the child's cultural development appears twice: first, on the social level, and later, on the individual level; first, *between* people (*interpsychological*) and then *inside* the child (*intrapsychological*) ... All the higher functions [thought and language] originate as actual relations between human individuals.

> (Vygotsky, 1978, p. 57)

Between the ages of 3 and 4, children often talk to themselves. Piaget (1923) called this self talk *egocentric speech.* As children get older egocentric speech disappears and Piaget suggested this disappearance was indicative of the child becoming less egocentric. In contrast, Vygotsky (1978) identified self talk as a critical part of the child internalizing previously external social speech. Further, unlike Piaget, Vygotsky did not believe that such speech disappeared. He argued that to believe this is like believing that children stop counting when they stop using their fingers to do so.

Vygotsky argued that self talk becomes internalized and guides the child's actions. Evidence supporting this is found when children are presented with tasks of increasing difficulty, when their conscious use of self talk is seen to increase in order to guide their efforts. Moreover, this type of speech is more common in cognitively mature and socially competent children. For Vygotsky the young child is an intensely social being and self talk is a crucial process in the development of inner speech and thought. Reading C is taken from *Thought and Language* (1986), in which Vygotsky writes about the significance of self talk.

Reading

At this point you should turn to the end of this chapter and read Reading C, 'Egocentric speech' which is written by Vygotsky (1986).

5.2 Teaching and learning

Zone of proximal development (ZPD)
The difference between what a child can do unaided, and what the same child can do with the help of more able others.

Vygotsky proposed that through contact with other, more able people children appropriate new ways of thinking and doing. Indeed Vygotsky saw learning as best supported when there is a degree of inequality in skills and understanding between two people. People of different abilities working together can create what Vygotsky termed a zone of proximal development (ZPD):

> [The zone of proximal development] is the distance between the actual developmental level as determined by *independent* problem solving and the level of potential development as determined through problem solving *under adult guidance* or in collaboration with more capable peers.

(Vygotsky, 1978, p. 86, our emphases)

Scaffolding
The type of assistance offered to support learning. A key characteristic of scaffolding is that it does not simplify the task.

The support provided by a more able partner allows the less able to tackle a new task, which in turn encourages development into a new level of competence. The social interaction and situation that create the ZPD supports the child's cognition. The concept of scaffolding was developed by Wood to describe the way in which adults or more able peers can support a learner to operate in the ZPD (Wood *et al.*, 1976). The metaphor of a scaffold, which is gradually withdrawn as the learner becomes able to work with less support, stresses the significance of social support in learning and development.

Vygotsky was positive about the potential of school instruction, as he believed it 'does not preclude development but charts new paths for it' (Vygotsky, 1934, p. 152). He believed that formal instruction had the potential to enable children to disembed their thinking from social contexts and thereby foster metacognition: the ability to gain conscious insight into one's own thought processes. For example, perhaps the only way that someone is able to solve the first puzzle in Activity 2 is if they have been *taught* how to disembed the underlying principles from socially acquired reasoning. Donaldson (1978) also saw this as a key outcome of formal education.

5.3 Application: deaf-blind education

Vygotsky's ideas have been applied to the remediation of the developmental barriers encountered by a wide variety of children, most notably deaf–blind children, and those with learning difficulties. As mentioned previously, for Vygotsky, cognition is actively developed by language. Therefore the social constructivist approach sets out to develop the language abilities of these children (often through using sign language or alternative communication systems) and through this they are enabled to develop the higher order psychological skills which can then be used to manage their lower level sensory ones.

The approach begins by teaching any basic skills that the child lacks, such as feeding him or herself. This is achieved through adult support and during such tuition the adult stimulates the child's interest in aspects of the environment relevant to that task. Once the child has developed basic skills and the desire to explore their surroundings, the next task is to develop social language. At first this will be through the introduction of gestures during routine activities and the gestures used will retain some immediate similarity to the action that they represent (e.g. the gesture for food might be an action mimicking eating). These gestures are extended by 'gesture equivalents' that contain some more arbitrary movements of the hand or fingers, but that make a distinction between different related concepts (e.g. 'food', 'eating', 'to eat outdoors', etc.). This moves the child towards an increasingly symbolic form of communication. Finally, the children are taught to associate their gesture equivalents with spoken words, by touching the face and throat of their teacher while she speaks, and eventually trying to produce the same movements and sounds themselves.

5.4 Evaluating social constructivism

Vygotsky highlighted how intrinsic developmental and cultural forces interact, and as Moll concluded 'Vygotsky's primary contribution was in developing a general approach that brought education, as a fundamental human activity, fully into a theory of psychological development' (Moll, 1990, p. 15).

His focus however was largely on the cultural elements and how these became part of the child. Yet he did not consider the 'inside out' forces from the child's point of view. This is reflected in his support for school instruction. The Soviet schools for children with developmental difficulties (except deaf-blind schools) that applied his principles were run along very formal teacher-led lines. There was little room for pupils to talk to each other; the teacher was the transmitter of the cultural knowledge.

Vygotsky's model, at least as used in the Soviet Union, promoted separate special educational practices for separate identified groups of children. This would run counter to current moves toward inclusive education in which teaching styles are developing to accommodate diversity. However, in the United Kingdom Vygotsky's theories have been used to develop ideas about inclusive education (Thomas and Glenny, 2004), effective peer tutoring and to challenge static models of learning which constrain the possibilities for children's potential development.

Crain (2000) has suggested that this theory could lead to instruction focusing too much on the young child's future attainments and exerting a pressure to get her or him started on a formal curriculum and conceptual and analytical reasoning. This might ignore the young child's need to develop their 'childish' capabilities – imagination, being physically active, drawing, singing and so forth. However, one argument against such criticism is that waiting until a child is ready for instruction is waiting until the child does not need teaching. For example, the deaf–blind children discussed might *never* be ready for instruction and would therefore remain locked out of the world without the tools to access it.

Summary of Section 5

* Vygotsky saw learning as a cultural and interpersonal process that involves the acquisition of 'cultural tools' from others.
* Language is, according to Vygotsky, initially used solely for interpersonal communication. When it becomes internalized for the purposes of thought, the social environment is reflected in children's reasoning.
* Vygotsky argued that adult tuition was important as it is through contact with more able others that children are able to achieve what would otherwise be beyond them. Such experiences lead them into new levels of reasoning.
* Sensitive teaching creates a 'zone of proximal development' (ZPD) which can foster cognitive development.
* Vygotsky's ideas have been used to teach children with special educational needs, including teaching deaf-blind children how to communicate with others.
* Vygotskian-inspired approaches to tuition have been criticized for being too formal and teacher-orientated.

6 | Conclusion

At the beginning of this chapter we recalled four views of development from Chapter 1. The 'grand theories' reviewed here can be seen to capture elements of those views:

- development as discipline – behaviourism;
- development as experience – social learning theory;
- development as 'natural stages' – constructivism;
- development as interaction – social constructivism.

However, these theories have more in common with each other than such an overview suggests.

Activity 3

Allow about 15 minutes

This activity will help you to begin to think about the similarities and contrasts that exist between the four theories explored in this chapter.

Consider which of the following statements apply to each of the theories. Put a tick in the boxes to indicate the statements that apply to each theory. When you have done this, compare your table to the one provided at the end of the chapter.

	Behaviourism	Social learning theory	Constructivism	Social constructivism
The environment is important.				
Innate factors drive development.				
Experiencing consequences of behaviour affects development.				
Observing other people affects development.				
Interacting with peers can promote development.				
Interacting with adults can promote development.				
Children are active in constructing their learning.				
Development during childhood occurs in a predetermined sequence.				

What you may notice is that the theories have more in common than one might at first realize. For example, all the theories value the environment the child develops within, although they differ in the extent to which they see the environment as central and what aspects they see as of key significance. Behaviourism is perhaps the most extreme 'empiricist' position, but the environment is also seen as important in each of the others: 'environment' in the sense of other people and their behaviours (Bandura); environment as affording opportunities for exploration and therefore cognitive development (Piaget); and environment as culture and social interaction (Vygotsky). That is not to say that nativist theories of child development do not exist, but they often only explain one aspect of child development (e.g. language development), rather than offering a grand theory. Moreover, contemporary theories are less clearly identifiable as 'nature' or 'nurture', but recognize the impact of both internal and external influences on development, although some will see either the environment or innate abilities as 'driving' the development of emergent skills. You will see examples of such positions in the next chapter, in relation to sensation and perception in infancy.

SG

Answers to Activity 2

Puzzle 1

The correct response is A and 7 but most people answer A and 3. Clearly, turning the A over will enable you to check that there is a 3 on the other side of that card. You need to check that the 7 also does not have an A on the other side, as that would 'break' the rule if it did (an A must have 3 on the other side). Turning the 3 card over will not help you because the rule only states what should be on the other side of an A card; it does not insist that all 3 cards must always have an A on them. However, people often make this (logically false) assumption.

Puzzle 2

This puzzle requires exactly the same reasoning, but you are more likely to solve this one first time around. This is because the problem is embedded in a familiar social situation. The correct solution is to ask Lauren what she was drinking, and ask Ailsa her age.

Your knowledge of the social situation means that you are less likely to make the same kind of mistake that you did in Puzzle 1 – the equivalent error in this problem would be to assume that the rule 'implies' that if you are over 18 you *must* be drinking alcohol (and so you would ask Maureen what she is drinking)! In the context of this puzzle, such a suggestion is clearly illogical.

Answers to Activity 3

	Behaviourism	Social learning theory	Constructivism	Social constructivism
The environment is important.	✓	✓	✓	✓
Innate factors drive development.			✓	
Experiencing consequences of behaviour affects development.	✓		✓	✓
Observing other people affects development.		✓		✓
Interacting with peers can promote development.	✓	✓	✓	
Interacting with adults can promote development.	✓	✓		✓
Children are active in constructing their learning.		✓	✓	✓
Development during childhood occurs in a predetermined sequence.			✓	

References

Alexander, A. and Morrison, M. A. (1995) 'Electric toyland and the structures of power: an analysis of critical studies on children as consumers', *Critical Studies in Mass Communications*, vol. 12, pp. 344–53.

Bandura, A. (1965) 'Influence of models' reinforcement contingencies on the acquisition of imitative responses', *Journal of Personality and Social Psychology*, vol. 1, pp. 589–95.

Bandura, A. (1973) *Aggression: a social learning analysis*, Upper Saddle Place, NJ, Prentice Hall.

Bandura, A. (1977) *Social Learning Theory*, New York, General Learning Press.

Bandura, A. and Jeffery, R. W. (1972) 'Role of symbolic coding and rehearsal processes in observational learning', *Journal of Personality and Social Psychology*, vol. 26, pp. 122–30.

Beckman, J. (1997) *Television and Violence: what the research says about its effects on young children*, Winnetka, IL, Winnetka Alliance for Early Childhood.

Crain, W. C. (2000) *Theories of Development: concepts and applications*, Upper Saddle Place, NJ, Prentice Hall.

Davidson, J. (1996) 'Menace to society', *Rolling Stone,* 728, pp. 38–9.

Donaldson, M. (1978) *Children's Minds*, London, Fontana.

Gershoff, E. T. (2002) 'Parental corporal punishment and associated child behaviors and experiences: a meta-analytic and theoretical review', *Psychological Bulletin*, vol. 128, pp. 539–79.

Huesmann, L. R., Moise, J., Podolski, C. P. and Eron, L. D. (2003) 'Longitudinal relations between childhood exposure to media violence and adult aggression and violence: 1977–1992', *Developmental Psychology*, vol. 39, pp. 201–21.

Hughes, M. and Grieve, R. (1980) 'On asking children bizarre questions', *First Language*, vol. 1, pp. 149–60.

Huston, A. C., Wright, J. C. and Wartella, E. (1981) 'Communicating more than content: formal features of children's television programs', *Journal of Communication*, vol. 31, pp. 32–48.

Keenan, M. (2004) 'Autism in Northern Ireland: the tragedy and the shame', *The Psychologist*, vol. 17, pp. 72–5.

Keenan, M., Kerr, K. P. and Dillenberger, K. (eds) (2000) *Parents' Education as Autism Therapists*, London, Jessica Kingsley.

Klein, S. B. (1996, 3rd edn) *Learning: principles and applications*, New York, McGraw Hill.

Kytömäki, J. (1998) 'Parental control and regulation of schoolchildren's television viewing', [online]. Available from: http://www.nordicom.gu.se/reviewcontents/ncomreview/ncomreview298/kytomaki.pdf [Accessed 25 May 2004].

Larson, M. S. (2003) 'Gender, race, and aggression in television commercials that feature children', *Sex Roles: A Journal of Research*, vol. 48, pp. 67–75.

Liebert, R. M., Poulos, R. W. and Marmor, G. S. (1977, 2nd edn) *Developmental Psychology*, Upper Saddle Place, NJ, Prentice Hall.

Light, P. and Oates, J. (1990) 'The development of children's understanding', in Roth, I. (ed.) *Introduction to Psychology*, London, Erlbaum Associates/The Open University.

Light, P. H., Buckingham, N. and Robbins, H. (1979) 'The conservation task as an interactional setting', *British Journal of Educational Psychology*, vol. 49, pp. 304–10.

Moll, L. C. (1990) 'Introduction', in Moll, L. C. (ed.) *Vygotsky and Education*, pp. 1–27, Cambridge, Cambridge University Press.

Piaget, J. (1923/1926) *The Language and Thought of the Child*, London, Kegan Paul.

Piaget, J. (1936/1955) *The Child's Construction of Reality*, London, Routledge and Kegan Paul.

Roberts, D. F., Foehr, U. G., Rideout, V. J. and Brodie, M. (1999) 'Kids and media at the new millennium: a comprehensive national analysis of children's media use', Menlo Park, CA, The Henry J. Kaiser Family Foundation Report.

Sheehy, K. (2000) 'The development of cognition, moral reasoning and language', in Gupta, D. S. and Gupta, R. M. (eds) *Psychology for Psychiatrists*, pp. 79–103, London, Whurr.

Skinner, B. F. (1938) *The Behavior of Organisms*, Upper Saddle Place, NJ, Prentice Hall.

Swenson, L. C. (1980) *Theories of Learning*, Belmont, CA, Wadsworth.

Thomas, G. and Glenny, G. (2004) 'Thinking about inclusion: whose reason?', in Sheehy, K., Nind, M., Rix, J. and Simmons, K. (eds) *Ethics and Research in Inclusive Education: values into practice*, London, RoutledgeFalmer.

Vygotsky, L. S. (1934/1986) *Thought and Language*, Cambridge, MA, MIT Press.

Vygotsky, L. (1978) *Mind in Society: the development of higher psychological processes*, Cambridge, MA, Harvard University Press.

Vygotsky, L. S. (1981) 'The development of higher forms of attention in childhood', in Wertsch, J. V. (ed.), *The Concept of Activity in Soviet Psychology*, Armonk, NY, Sharpe.

Watson, J. B. (1913) 'Psychology as the behaviorist views it', *Psychological Review*, vol. 20, pp. 158–77.

Watson, J. B. (1924) *Behaviorism*, New York, Norton.

Wood, D. J., Bruner, J. S. and Ross, G. (1976) 'The role of tutoring in problem-solving', *Journal of Clinical Psychology and Psychiatry*, vol. 17, pp. 85–100.

Readings

Reading A: Applied behavioural analysis and autism

Mickey Keenan

At Colin's belated 18-months assessment the health visitor expressed a number of concerns about him. He did not respond to the hearing tests, and it was difficult to keep him in the room. The health visitor made reference to hearing loss, possible brain damage, and developmental delay. Over the next two years Colin was seen by dozens of health professionals – community medical officers, audiologists, ear, nose and throat specialists, speech therapists, psychologists, paediatricians, an occupational therapist, a physiotherapist, and several health visitors. Family life was severely disrupted because it was too much of a battle to take him visiting or shopping. Colin had been assessed as having moderate learning difficulties, and the consultant psychiatrist diagnosed him as having Asperger's syndrome and ADHD. He had very little language – only about seven or eight words. In nursery school he refused to join in story time or planned activities, preferring solitary repetitive play with toy cars, water and sand. At home he was seldom still and his parents had to lock windows and doors. He did not respond to his name and he slept little.

Now aged 11, Colin is an entirely different child. His school report describes him as 'a very good-natured boy who enjoys the company of his classmates ... a lively, enthusiastic, friendly boy who can articulate readily and most competently his needs and opinions ... [who] always listens well and absorbs the information presented'.

From being a child destined for an institution, Colin now can look forward to a happier and more fulfilled life. So how did I work with Colin's mum Lynne to achieve this remarkable transformation? I used applied behaviour analysis (ABA).

[...]

What is ABA?

[...] Cooper *et al.* (1987) defined ABA:

> ... the science in which procedures derived from the principles of behavior are systematically applied to improve socially significant behavior to a meaningful degree and to demonstrate experimentally that the procedures employed were responsible for the improvement in behavior. (p.14)

Sounds simple enough, but somehow many psychologists have got the wrong end of the stick with 'straw-person arguments which both introductory and advanced psychology books promulgate' (Guerin, 1994, p.15). These include the idea that behaviour analysis reduces everything to food and sex reinforcers, or that it discards valuable psychological ideas like the mind, the self, innate behaviours, emotions and knowledge. Spinelli (1989, p.175) believes that 'the great majority of behavioural findings tell us little of worth about ourselves' and that 'in a sense, having denied the importance of subjective data, their findings appear limited, alien, even "soul-less". Gross (1995, p.239) describes behaviourism as the study of people as natural phenomena, 'with their subjective experience, consciousness and other characteristics, which had for so long been taken as distinctive human qualities, being removed from the "universe" ', there being 'no place for these things in the behaviourist world'.

In fact, ABA certainly doesn't view people as 'black boxes'. Watts (1966) wrote extensively on Eastern philosophies, providing remarkable parallels with the philosophy of radical behaviourism (e.g. Chiesa, 1994; Keenan, 1997; O'Donohue & Ferguson, 2001). He expands on Skinner's view that the skin does not separate you from the world but connects you to it. Behavioural principles are anchored in terms that relate changes in a person to the context in which these changes are observed:

> Today, scientists are more and more aware that what things are, and what they are doing, depends on where and when they are doing it. If, then, the definition of a thing or event must include definition of its environment, we realize that any given thing goes with a given environment so intimately and inseparably that it is more difficult to draw a clear boundary between the thing and its surroundings. (Watts, 1966, pp. 67–68)

Another distinguishing feature of behaviour analysis is its emphasis on developing research methodology that monitors changes in an individual. 'Being a person' is an experience that extends across time, but research methodology taught to undergraduate students typically hides this natural facet of our humanity by focusing on data collected in snapshots, and averaged across groups of people. In effect, the individual is sacrificed on the altar of group statistics. When dealing with autism, this means that professionals are not empowered with the skills necessary to assess the effectiveness of educational programmes intended to empower the individual.

Where single-case research methodology is employed (e.g. Johnston & Pennypacker, 1993), it has enormous implications for treatment designs. In a home programme, for example, it translates into the practice of teaching a parent how to shadow the developing child to monitor very closely the changes in choreography that make up the fine detail of the child's interaction with their physical and social environment. The box [...] shows how this would be put into practice in a typical ABA curriculum [...]

Educational curriculum for a child on the autistic spectrum

Attending skills

Basic: Child sits in chair independently. Child makes eye contact in response to name.
Intermediate: Child asks 'What?' when their name is called.
Advanced: Child makes eye contact during conversation and group activities.

Imitation skills

Basic: Child imitates gross motor, fine motor, and oral motor skills and actions with
                    objects.
Intermediate: Child imitates a sequence of actions and sounds.
Advanced: Child imitates peer play.

Receptive language

Basic: Child follows one-step instructions, and identifies objects and pictures.
Intermediate: Child identifies emotions, and follows two-step instructions.
Advanced: Child follows three-step instructions, and discriminates concepts.

Expressive language

Basic: Child imitates sounds and words, and labels objects and pictures.
Intermediate: Child labels gender, and objects based on function.
Advanced: Child labels categories, and retells a story.

Pre-academic skills

Basic: Child matches identical pictures and objects. Child undresses.
Intermediate: Child initiates for bathroom, washes hands and puts on some clothes.
Advanced: Child brushes teeth, and buttons clothes.

When this choreography is in need of change, then practical steps are taken to
see if this can be achieved. Usually this involves a functional assessment that
begins by defining the problem behaviour, then identifying possible causes of the
behaviour, predicting when the problem behaviour will occur, and finally
designing effective treatment programmes (see Desrochers *et al.*, 2002). The
questions that usually arise for parents and therapists include which aspects of the
choreography to start with, and what to do next. Behaviour analysis has
developed, and continues to develop, guidelines to address these questions
(Maurice *et al.*, 1996; see also weblinks). [...]

References for Reading A

Chiesa, M. (1994). *Radical behaviorism: The philosophy and the science.* Boston: Authors Cooperative.

Cooper, J.O., Heron, T.E. & Heward, W.L. (1987). *Applied behaviour analysis.* New York: Macmillan.

Desrochers, M., Newell, M., & Coleman, S. (2002). *Functional assessment.* Retrieved 23 Oct 2003 from www.behavior.org/autism/functionalassessment/paper7.pdf

Gross, R. (1995). *Themes, issues, and debates in psychology.* London: Hodder & Stoughton Educational.

Guerin, B. (1994). *Analysing social behaviour.* Reno, NV: Context Press.

Johnston, J.M., & Pennypacker, H.S. (1993). *Readings for strategies and tactics of behavioural research.* Hillsdale, NJ.: Lawrence Erlbaum.

Keenan, M. (1997). W -ing: Teaching exercises for radical behaviourists. In K. Dillenburger, M O'Reilly & M. Keenan (Eds.) *Advances in behaviour analysis* (pp.48–80). Dublin: University College Dublin Press.

Maurice, C., Green, G., & Luce, S.C. (Eds.) (1996). *Behavioral intervention for young children with autism: A manual for parents and professionals.* Austin, TX: Pro-Ed.

O'Donohue, W. & Ferguson, K.E. (2001). *The psychology of B.F. Skinner.* London: Sage.

Spinelli, E. (1989). *The interpreted world.* London: Sage.

Watts, A. (1966). *The book: On the taboo against knowing who you are.* New York: Vintage Books.

Weblinks

Association for Behavior Analysis: www.abainternational.org
Association for Science in Autism Treatment: www.asatonline.org
Behavior Analyst Certification Board: www.bacb.com
Cambridge Center for Behavioral Studies: www.behavior.org
US Surgeon General's Report on Mental Health, Autism Section: www.surgeongeneral.gov/library/mentalhealth/chapter3/sec6.html

Source: Keenan, M. (2004) 'Autism in Northern Ireland: The tragedy and the shame', *The Psychologist,* vol. 17, pp. 72–5.

Reading B: Learning through modeling

Albert Bandura

One of the fundamental means by which new behaviors are acquired and existing patterns are modified entails modeling and vicarious processes. It is evident from informal observation that human behavior is to a large extent socially transmitted, either deliberately or inadvertently, through the behavioral examples provided by influential models [...] in many languages, "the word for 'teach' is the same as the word for 'show'.

There are several reasons why modeling influences play a paramount role in learning in everyday life. When mistakes are costly or dangerous, skillful performances can be established without needless errors by providing competent models who demonstrate how the required activities should be performed. If learning proceeded solely through direct experience, most people would never survive their formative years because mistakes often result in fatal consequences. Some complex behaviors, of course, can be produced only through the influence of models. If children had no opportunity to hear speech, for example, it would be virtually impossible to teach them the linguistic skills that constitute a language. Where certain forms of behavior can be conveyed only by social cues, modeling is an indispensable aspect of learning. Even in instances in which it is possible to establish new skills through other means, the process of acquisition can be considerably shortened by providing appropriate models.

[...]

In technologically developed societies, behavior is usually modeled in a variety of forms. Much social learning is fostered through the examples set by individuals one encounters in everyday life. People also pattern their behavior after symbolic models they read about or see in audiovisual displays. As linguistic competencies are acquired, written accounts describing the actions and success of others can serve as guides for new modes of conduct. Another influential source of social learning, at all age levels, is the abundant and diverse modeling provided in television. Both children and adults can acquire attitudes, emotional responses, and complex patterns of behavior through exposure to pictorially presented models. Indeed, comparative studies [...] have shown that people can learn equal amounts from behavioral demonstration, pictorial representation, and verbal description, provided that they convey the same amount of response information, that they are equally effective in commanding attention, and that the learners are sufficiently adept at processing information transmitted by these alternative modes of representation. [...]

One of the early analyses of observational learning of aggression (Bandura, 1962; Bandura, Ross and Ross, 1963a) examined the relative potency of aggressive models presented in different forms. Nursery school children were matched individually in terms of their interpersonal aggressiveness and assigned to one of five conditions. One group observed adult models behaving aggressively toward the plastic figure. A second group saw a film of the same models performing the same aggressive acts [...] A third group observed the model costumed as a cartoon cat enacting the same aggressive responses on the screen of a television console. This condition was included to test the notion that the more remote the models are from reality, the weaker is the tendency for children to imitate their behavior. In addition to the three modeling treatments, two control groups were included. The behavior of one group of children was measured without any prior exposure to the models to provide a baseline for the amount and form of aggression that children display in the same test situation when they have not experienced the modeling influence. It is conceivable that merely seeing the aggressive materials in the modeling situation could later increase children's use of them, quite apart from the model's actions. Therefore, in the fifth condition, the filmed models behaved in a calm, nonaggressive manner and did not handle the aggressive materials that were visibly displayed.

[...]

Results of this study show that exposure to aggressive models had two important effects on the viewers. First, it taught them new ways of aggressing. Most of the children who had observed the aggressive models later emulated their novel assaultive behavior and hostile remarks, whereas these unusual aggressive acts were rarely exhibited by children in the control groups. [...] Further analyses showed that a person displaying aggression on film was as influential in teaching distinctive forms of aggression as one exhibiting it in real life. The children were less inclined, however, to imitate the cartoon character than the real-life model.

[...] children who were exposed to the aggressive models subsequently exhibited substantially more total aggression than children in the nonaggressive model condition or the control group. Interestingly, the cartoon model served as a somewhat weaker teacher but an equally effective disinhibitor of aggression compared with the live and filmed counterparts. In addition, children who observed the nonaggressive adult displayed the restrained behavior characteristic of their model and expressed significantly less aggression than the no-model controls.

References for Reading B

Bandura, A. Social learning through imitation. In M.R. Jones (ed.), *Nebraska symposium on motivation: 1962.* Lincoln: University of Nabraska Press, 1962. pp211–69

Bandura, A., Ross, D. and Ross, S.A., Imitation of film-mediated aggressive models. *Journal of Abnormal and Social Psychology,* 1963a, **66**, 3–11.

Source: Bandura, A. (1973) 'Origins of agression', in *Agression: a social learning analysis*, pp. 68–74, Englewood Cliffs, NJ, Prentice-Hall Inc.

Reading C: Egocentric speech

Lev Vygotsky

[...]

We [...] conducted our own experiments aimed at understanding the function and fate of egocentric speech. The data obtained led us to a new comprehension of this phenomenon that differs greatly from that of Piaget. Our investigation suggests that egocentric speech does play a specific role in the child's activity.

In order to determine what causes egocentric talk, what circumstances provoke it, we organized the children's activities in much the same way Piaget did, but we added a series of frustrations and difficulties. For instance, when a child was getting ready to draw, he would suddenly find that there was no paper, or no pencil of the color he needed. In other words, by obstructing his free activity we made him face problems.

We found that in these difficult situations the coefficient of egocentric speech almost doubled, in comparison with Piaget's normal figure for the same age and also in comparison with our figure for children not facing these problems. The child would try to grasp and to remedy the situations in talking to himself: "Where's the pencil? I need a blue pencil. Never mind, I'll draw with the red one and wet it with water; it will become dark and look like blue."

In the same activities without impediments, our coefficient of egocentric talk was even slightly lower than Piaget's. It is legitimate to assume, then, that a disruption in the smooth flow of activity is an important stimulus for egocentric speech. This discovery fits in with two premises to which Piaget himself refers several times in his book. One of them is the so-called law of awareness, which was formulated by Claparède and which states that an impediment or disturbance in an automatic activity makes the author aware of this activity. The other premise is that speech is an expression of that process of becoming aware.

Indeed the above-mentioned phenomena were observed in our experiments: egocentric speech appeared when a child tries to comprehend the situation, to find a solution, or to plan a nascent activity. The older children behaved differently: they scrutinized the problem, thought (which was indicated by long pauses), and then found a solution. When asked what he was thinking about, such a child answered more in line with the "thinking aloud" of a preschooler. We thus assumed that the same mental operations that the preschooler carries out through voiced egocentric speech are already relegated to soundless inner speech in schoolchildren.

Our findings indicate that egocentric speech does not long remain a mere accompaniment to the child's activity. Besides being a means of expression and of release of tension, it soon becomes an instrument of thought in the proper sense – in seeking and planning the solution of a problem. An accident that occurred during one of our experiments provides a good illustration of one way in which egocentric speech may alter the course of an activity: A child of five-and-a-half was drawing a streetcar when the point of his pencil broke. He tried, nevertheless, to finish the circle of wheel, pressing down on the pencil very hard, but nothing showed on the paper except a deep colorless line. The child muttered to himself, "It's broken," put aside the pencil, took watercolors instead, and began drawing a *broken* streetcar after an accident, continuing to talk to himself from time to time about the change in his picture. The child's accidentally provoked egocentric utterance so manifestly affected his activity that it is impossible to mistake it for a mere by-product, an accompaniment not interfering with the melody. Our experiments showed highly complex changes in the interrelation of activity and egocentric talk. We observed how egocentric speech at first marked the end result or a turning point in an activity, then was gradually shifted toward the middle and finally to the beginning of the activity, taking on a directing, planning function and raising the child's acts to the level of purposeful behavior ...

Source: Vygotsky, L. (1986) 'Piaget's theory of the child's speech and thought', in *Thought and Language*, pp. 29–31, translated by Alex Kozulin, Cambridge, MA, MIT Press.

Chapter 3
Sensation to perception

Alan Slater and John Oates

Contents

Learning outcomes

After you have studied this chapter you should be able to:

1 describe auditory and visual perceptual processes;

2 outline the development of the auditory and visual sensory systems;

3 give an overview of the developmental constraints on infants' visual and auditory perception during the first 18 months;

4 describe the main lines of psychological research into perceptual development during the first 18 months;

5 outline the importance of cross-modal perception during infancy and beyond;

6 understand the importance of studying infants' reactions to ecologically valid stimuli.

1 Introduction

This chapter will examine the psychological development of infants in terms of the information that is made available to their developing brains by the senses. We will concentrate on vision and hearing; examining evidence on how these systems develop from birth through the first 18 months of life. The end of the chapter will consider how infants are able to integrate information from different senses.

The development of the nervous system, including its sensory pathways, is not complete at birth: although some basic 'architecture' is laid down sufficient for the system to begin to function as a whole, there is still a lot of further development to come. Indeed, the point at which the nervous system can be said to be mature lies many years ahead for the newborn child, at least as far away as early adolescence.

The implications of this sort of immaturity for the development of sensory abilities in infants are difficult to assess: to date the most fruitful line in uncovering what babies can and cannot sense has been careful and painstaking experimentation. Babies cannot tell us what they perceive. The challenge for research has been to develop methods that allow infants to demonstrate their abilities relatively unambiguously. There have been several breakthroughs in which novel techniques have opened new windows into babies' sensory worlds. This chapter will look at the most important of these methods, and discuss some of the new insights that they offer.

1.1 Infants' sensory abilities and theories of development

Most developmental theorists make assumptions about the nature of infants' experiences of the world, and these assumptions are often central to the theories they propose. For example, Piaget described the visual world of the infant as follows:

> The universe of the young baby is a world without objects, consisting only of shifting and unsubstantial 'tableaux' which appear and are then totally reabsorbed, either without returning, or reappearing in a modified or analogous form.

> (Piaget and Inhelder, 1966, p. 14)

Mental representations
The mental 'coding' of an object or experience that reflects a child's understanding of it.

According to Piaget, the 'chaos' of early perception only begins to make sense to babies as they interact with the world, through their own actions becoming linked with their perceptions. He argued that this link comes about through the effects of these actions in bringing about changes in the perceptual world. Piaget called this period of infancy the 'sensori-motor stage', because he claimed that the main developmental task for infants is to learn the links between sensation and action ('motor' means movement), as a basis for the construction of mental representations of the world, and hence thought. Piaget described the 'sensori-motor intelligence' of the infant as follows:

> It organizes reality by constructing the broad categories of action which are the schemes of the permanent object, space, time and causality, substructures of the notions that will later correspond to them. None of these categories is given at the outset, and the child's initial universe is entirely centred on his own body and action in an egocentrism as total as it is unconscious (for lack of consciousness of the self).

> (Piaget and Inhelder, 1966, p. 13)

This is an elaboration of empiricism, which you will remember is one philosophical approach to the problem of explaining how we come to experience the world, based on the belief that knowledge can only originate from experience. Piaget's theory takes empiricism as a starting point, but also adds the process of construction, by which infants actively construct knowledge through action.

In contrast, nativism proposes that the ever-changing nature of experience does not have sufficient stability to permit the formation of ideas and knowledge, and that there is already present in the mind at birth a whole range of concepts; abstract forms of knowledge that allow us to make sense of what we experience. There are at least two distinct forms of nativism that have emerged in recent years. One, known as the 'core knowledge' approach (Spelke, 1998) claims that infants emerge into the world with a basic, or 'core' knowledge about the physical world, including the world of physical objects and a basic understanding of numbers. A second view claims that infants enter the world with a representation of faces and of people as social objects (Meltzoff, 2004). This is known as the 'social knowledge' approach. We shall see an example of this position in Section 2.4.

Developmental psychologists increasingly accept that infants enter the world with at least some understanding of the world on which experience will build.

1.2 Some definitions

Sensation

Sensation is concerned with the 'interface' between the individual and the world: the signals that are generated in the sensory receptors (the retina of the eye, the cochlea of the ear, etc.) by the impact of different sorts of energy from the outside world. We know that these signals take the form of electro-chemical changes in the receptors, changes which are then transmitted by nerve fibres to the brain.

It would be wrong to think of receptors acting as cameras or microphones do; passively picking up and transmitting pictures or sounds. Eyes, in particular, are active, 'intelligent' parts of the body: they do a lot of immediate processing of the information they receive before passing on more concise electro-chemical messages to the brain. For example, by using electrodes to pick up the signals from the eye that arrive at the brain via the optic nerves, Hubel (1963) showed that a cat's retina sends signals for features of the image, like spots of light and dark, and high contrast edges having different orientations. Much the same sort of processing is done in the ear before the transmission to the brain of information about sounds.

So the information the brain has to work on to construct representations of the outside world is already pre-processed in quite sophisticated ways. The brain works to synthesize this information so that events are actually perceived as happening in the outside world.

Perception

Perception is a mental construction of the outside world: for example, your perception of the words on this page is something that your brain has 'constructed' from lots of coded electrical impulses from your eyes.

Although adults can communicate with each other about experiencing things in the world, babies cannot do this, and psychologists are still a long way from knowing whether infants experience the world in the same ways that adults do, and if they do not, when and how they do come to do so. There are several sources of evidence that suggest that their perceptual world is different from an adult's, some of which will be dealt with in this chapter.

Cognition

Cognition, or 'knowing', refers to the brain doing more than merely registering something in the world and constructing a perception of it. Cognition involves the relating of one perception to other previous perceptions. For example, you have seen most of the individual words in this text before, and so when you perceive one it carries all the meaning you have accumulated from previous encounters with that same word and so you recognize what it means. Similarly, if you see a baby apparently recognizing his or her father when he comes into the room, you are witnessing something more than the perception of another human being; you are witnessing a cognitive act, a linking of the baby's current perception with their previous perceptions of that person. However, in making this interpretation of the baby's behaviour you are making a leap from that observation to an assumption about their cognition. For instance, you do not know quite what it is that this baby is responding to: it might simply be features such as a particular combination of facial features, hairstyle and colour, or clothes. Of course, cognition is by no means as static as this. The mental representations which enter into our perceptions of the world themselves change and grow: they develop. Each new experience has the potential to modify our representations and hence what we perceive in the future.

Behaviour

The processes of cognition are hidden from direct observation, although people do experience the products of cognition as thoughts, feelings and ultimately behaviour. To find out about cognition in babies, and to begin to picture their perceptions, psychologists have to infer it from infants' behaviour. In the earlier example of visual recognition of a parent, researchers would have to rely on behaviours like smiling, cooing, holding out the arms and so on; behaviours that are not evoked by adults that the baby has not seen before. So psychologists use differences in behaviour towards different things to make a judgement about what is perceived, and what perceptions and cognition this may be associated with.

Taking this example a little further, it is worth noting that for a baby to recognize his or her father they have to be able to sense at least some of the differences between him and other male adults, so recognition has to be based on discrimination. Much of the study of the development of sensation and perception in infants has been based on using their behaviour to assess the extent to which they can tell things apart.

So the story of most research in this area is one of establishing the links between particular infant behaviours, the processes of cognition, perception and sensation and particular properties of the stimuli presented to the infant.

It is known that the sensory systems undergo considerable physical development during infancy. It therefore seems likely that the perceptions of a baby are different from those of a more physiologically mature individual. An understanding of the ways that infants' perceptions differ, such as whether particular senses are slower, or less discriminating, or whether they are different in more radical ways, is important in understanding the nature of infant experience and cognition.

This chapter is concerned mainly with the first two steps in the chain that we have outlined above: sensation and perception.

1.3 The sensation–behaviour system

In the descriptions of sensation, perception, behaviour and cognition just given, information from the world is sensed, perceived, related to previous experiences, which then leads to behaviour. However, this step-by-step, linear sequence is a misleading over-simplification. For one thing, the nerve connections between receptors and brain are not one-way: we also have to take account of how sensation itself is actively driven by the brain.

For example, eyes are not passive receivers, but rather directable organs, and the very act of directing the eyes towards a particular part of the environment selects what can be perceived. Even very young babies actively select what they will look at and for how long they will look at it. Although the ears are much less directional, because sound and vision are linked in all sorts of ways, people (including babies) turn towards sounds; in other words, they attend selectively. In this sense, the operation of attention means that both sensation and perception can be regarded as the results of behaviour, or even as a form of behaviour; thus the distinctions outlined above are not at all clear-cut.

It is more appropriate to talk about these four processes making up a single dynamic system and to recognize that when psychologists are studying infant perception they are looking at the total behaviour of a complex set of interacting processes. The sorts of questions addressed by the research in this chapter are concerned with how this system develops. Although we shall examine some of the components in the perceptual systems separately, we cannot easily isolate the performance of one part from the performance of the system as a whole.

Summary of Section 1

- Infants are born with physically immature sensory and nervous systems. Psychologists are interested in understanding how this immaturity impacts on their sensing and perception of the world.
- Many developmental theorists make assumptions about how infants perceive the world. Piaget assumed that the child can only learn from their sensory experiences through acting on the world. Other theorists claim that infants are born with a basic understanding of some aspects of their environment, either physical features, or social aspects of it.
- Sensation, perception, cognition and behaviour are part of an integrated, dynamic system.

2 Vision

One question that many parents have as they gaze into the eyes of a newborn child is, 'How much and what can he or she see?' This question has led to all sorts of popular beliefs, such as 'babies are effectively blind for the first few weeks', 'they see only in black and white', and 'they have better vision than adults'. Psychologists, too, have different positions on this question: empiricists argue that perception has to be learned, while nativists suggest that perception is possible from birth.

Activity I   What can babies see?

Allow about
5 minutes

This activity will help you clarify your ideas about what you expect babies to be able to see.

Consider what you think babies can see. If possible discuss your thoughts with people who are parents to assess whether their views differ from your own.

Write down your own views on this question, and if possible discuss it with people who are parents. Do their views differ from your own?

Where do you think these views come from?

If you are a parent, what do you remember thinking about this question when your own child was born?

Did you get any information about your baby's vision from relatives, nurses or from media such as baby books?

Keep your notes and refer back to them when you have finished the chapter.

2.1 The development of the visual system

An infant's visual system develops significantly during the first few months after birth. The immature visual system of the infant is nevertheless 'good enough' for some important perceptual processes to be possible, such as discrimination and recognition.

Structures

Accommodation
The muscular adjustment of the curvature of the lens to produce a focused retinal image of objects at different distances.

At the time of birth, the infant's eye is nearly completely mature. The actual image formed on the retina by the lens has about as much clarity and colour as that in an adult's eye. However, infants have very sluggish and inefficient accommodation. This may be due to the insensitivity of the retina to fine detail, or to immaturities in other parts of the visual neural pathways. The visual nervous system can be divided into four main parts: the retina, the optic nerve, the lateral geniculate nucleus and the visual cortex (see Figures 1 to 4).

When the eyes are fixated on something in the visual environment, a focused (upside-down) image of the scene is cast on the retina, stimulating the visual receptors, the rods and cones, in the retina. Electro-chemical signals leave the retina via the optic nerve fibres. The optic nerves from each eye are joined and cross at the optic chiasm. The optic nerves then connect with the lateral geniculate bodies, which then 'project' onto the visual cortex. The visual cortex is richly interconnected with the rest of the cerebral cortex. Each of these parts of the system is anatomically immature at birth; the following summarizes the development of these parts.

The retina

Figure 1 (b) shows that the retina is a complex organ: the rods and cones do not have simple one-to-one links with the optic nerves. The signals that the rods and cones produce when light falls on them are processed by a series of neural layers before reaching the neural pathways to the cortex (Figure 2). Studies of the electrical activity in the optic nerve fibres show that a lot of this processing involves recognizing features such as high contrast edges and spots of light. In adults, the fovea, the central area of the retina, contains a high density of cones. This makes it particularly sensitive to the fine detail and colour of retinal images. The rest of the retina contains a higher proportion of rods, and hence is sensitive mainly to black and white light and not so sensitive to detail.

Although no new rods or cones are formed after birth, in the newborn's eye the fovea does not have a high density of cones, and there is a migration of cones towards the foveal area as the retina continues to develop: a migration that only completes when the child is about 11 (Abramov *et al.*, 1982). The speed of this migration is probably greatest during the 2 – 3 months after birth, since the ability to resolve fine detail (acuity) appears to undergo its greatest improvement in this period. This imposes an absolute limit on the perception of images that are being fixated by the eye, and the acuity measurements of infants' eyes suggest that one consequence of the immaturity of the fovea will be a great deal of 'blur' in this image. The other result may be that the image will be lacking in colour intensity; only 'washed-out', pastel colours will be perceived (Hainline, 1998).

Acuity
Sensitivity to fine detail.

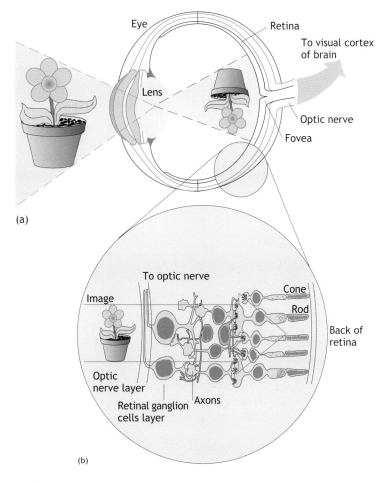

Figure 1 (a) The lens of the eye focuses a sharp image on the retina, which contains the eye's light receptors. (b) The retina's structure: light travels through the processing layers and falls on and stimulates the light receptors, the rods and cones.

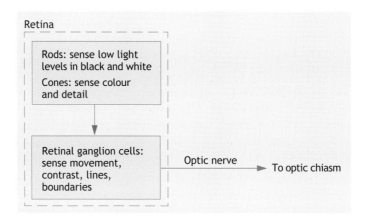

Figure 2   The processing of information in the eye before it is passed on to the brain.

The optic nerves

The optic nerves are all formed by the time of birth, but lack much of their myelin coating. Myelin sheaths on nerves both speed up and insulate nervous impulses travelling along them. Myelination of the optic nerves is virtually absent at birth, and does not reach mature status until the baby is 3 months old (Yakovlev and Lecours, 1967). Hence, in the many poorly myelinated fibres which run through the optic nerves, retinal information will travel relatively sluggishly and will be diffused by the time it reaches the end of the optic nerves. The optic nerves from the two eyes meet at the optic chiasm: from this area, most nerve fibres from the right eye go towards the left side of the brain, while most from the left eye go to the right side (Figure 3). The next 'processing stations' for information from the eyes are the lateral geniculate nuclei which lie at the base of the brain.

Myelin
A substance that forms along the length of nerve cells, and serves to insulate the electrical impulses of the nerve cell and improve the speed at which they travel.

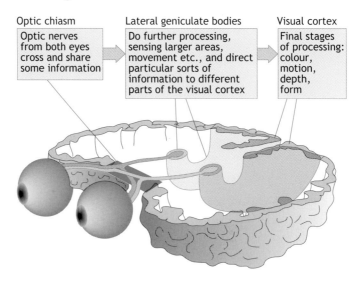

Figure 3   Continuing the flow of visual information: from the optic nerve to visual cortex.

The lateral geniculate nucleus

The optic nerves from each retina terminate in the lateral geniculate nucleus (LGN). This complex, layered structure lies at the base of the brain. It is possible to identify parts of the LGN that are fed by particular parts of the visual field, and it has been found that the retinal image is 'mapped' into the LGN in a systematic way. This mapping appears to be preserved to some extent in the LGN's connections into the cortex. A main function of the LGN is to compare inputs from nerve fibres that come from adjoining areas of the retina and to respond to differences in the amount of light falling on the centre as opposed to the periphery of these areas. This sort of processing has already been done to some extent by the retina, but the LGN enhances detail in the retinal image. It takes about 12 months for the LGN to reach its adult developmental status (Hickey, 1977); before that, the LGN cells that process information from the central area of the retina are less mature than the peripheral cells, further contributing to a lack of clarity in the centre of the visual field.

The visual cortex

Compared to the retina and the LGN, the visual cortex of the brain (Figure 4) is a highly complex structure and the way that it works is by no means fully understood. A basic function of the visual cortex is to compare inputs from the different receptive fields covered by the nerve fibres from the LGN (Hubel and Wiesel, 1962). Some of the cells in the visual cortex respond to static line stimuli, such as light and dark lines and boundaries between light and dark areas, the so-called 'simple cells'. Others, known as 'complex cells', also respond to such features, but are primarily sensitive to their movement. 'Hypercomplex' and 'concentric' cells take their inputs from larger receptive fields and are sensitive to size and colour of stimuli in these fields (Michael, 1978). There is evidence that the organization of these cells into complex structures continues for at least 6 months after birth (Horton and Hedley-Whyte, 1984).

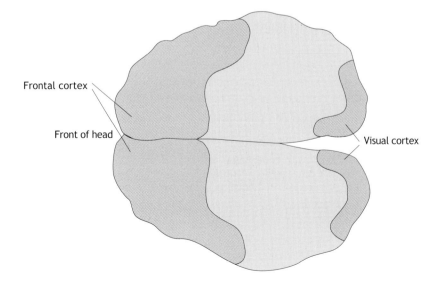

Figure 4   The brain from above, showing the visual cortex and the frontal cortex.

Neuron
A nerve cell.

Most of the neurons in the visual cortex have been formed by the time of birth, but they are relatively poorly interconnected. At this stage they have only a few short axons which are poorly myelinated (their myelination follows the same course as the optic nerve axons). The number of connections between these neurons in the visual cortex increases greatly during the first 6 months after birth.

Visual capacity

The complete visual system takes some months to develop from relative immaturity at birth to a relatively mature status, and this must constrain young infants' perception. However, the precise effects of these constraints are hard to assess on the basis of neurological and anatomical data alone. Instead, we must turn to behavioural evidence, to studies of what babies actually can and cannot do when exposed to visual experiences. By examining behaviour we are looking at the performance of a more complex system, because behaviour involves further neural pathways, from the cortex through the systems that control motor activity such as eye movements. These systems also continue to mature through the early years of life, and it should be remembered that evidence from behaviour about the nature of infant perception will be limited not only by the capacity of the input system to the brain (sensory systems), but also by the capacity of the output system (the cognitive system) that controls this key aspect of visual attention.

So far you have considered visual perception as though it operates on stationary images cast on the retina by the lens. However, vision is not this simple: fixations (stationary retinal images) certainly are a major type of visual input, but other things have to go on to allow the eye to fixate on a particular part of the visual world. When you look at a complex scene you fixate one point of detail, and then another and another and so on. There are several different types of eye movement that allow you to change the direction of looking, usually three or four a second. These successive fixations are related to the nature of the scene you are looking at, such that you fixate points of particular interest. Also, the visual world is rarely stationary, and much of the information that is important is contained in these movement patterns. You will see that while much of the early work on infant perception used static, two-dimensional, graphic images. Later research with more complex, dynamic stimuli suggests that the capacity of an infant's systems may be greater for these 'information-rich' stimuli and that babies can seem more competent in more naturalistic situations.

Scanning

During the first months after birth, infants' scanning patterns change dramatically, until at the age of 2–3 months their scanning is similar to that of older children and adults. In normal circumstances, infants', older children's and adults' eyes view the visual world in a series of fixations, in each of which the eyes are stationary, giving the retinae stable images of the object(s) of visual attention, with the central foveal regions receiving these images. Between fixations, the eyes scan in a straight line from one fixation point to the next. These eye movements, called saccades, are very brief, only a few milliseconds in duration. By reflecting a beam of infrared light from the surface of the eye and recording its motion, it is possible

Saccade
A quick eye movement that is made between fixations.

to observe which parts of the visual field are fixated. Two developmental features of scanning patterns are of note: first, young infants do not inspect nearly as many parts of the visual image as older people do, and secondly, their fixations tend to be concentrated around the edges of images rather than on features inside them.

As you have already seen, the foveal region of the young infant's retina is not yet adapted to detect fine detail. Hence, fixating on any part of the visual field does not necessarily serve the same ends for a baby as it does for older people. This is another major problem in understanding the development of visual perception, since (like adults) infants do scan, from the moment they are born, and they scan predictable features of images such as their edges. It may be that the gross features of scanning (i.e. bringing objects of interest into the centre of the visual field) are relatively mature, but 'inspection' of fine detail only emerges as the visual system as a whole matures.

BOX 1

Development of visual scanning: the 'externality effect'

Figure 5 shows the fixations and scanpaths of a 1 month old (left) and a 2 month old (right) viewing a schematic drawing of a human face. You can see that the younger infant's fixations are heavily concentrated on two particular parts of the edge of the face, while the 2 month old not only scans to several points on the edge, but also devotes the majority of fixations to the internal features of eye and mouth. This is a general developmental pattern found in most infants. Much the same pattern of concentration on one or two peripheral features, such as a corner or an edge, is found for the scanpaths for geometric shapes.

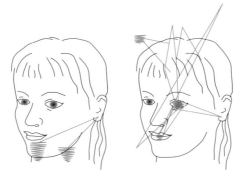

Figure 5   From Maurer and Maurer, 1998, p. 123.

Visual attention and acuity

Answering the question of 'What can babies perceive?' is important to understand what the infant's early psychological experience is like. It is only within the last 40 years that evidence on this has begun to accumulate. A major breakthrough came from the work of Fantz who, in the 1950s, pointed out that while infants may be linguistically and motorically underdeveloped, they are able to inspect their world visually. He had the simple idea of observing how often babies look towards different visual stimuli. He reasoned that if babies consistently look at some things rather than others, then they must be able to perceive differences between them.

Using the apparatus shown in Figure 6, one person presented the infant with one or two visual stimuli at a time, and an observer recorded the lengths of fixations for each stimulus by observing the infant's direction of gaze and corneal reflection (the reflection of the stimulus over the cornea of the eye).

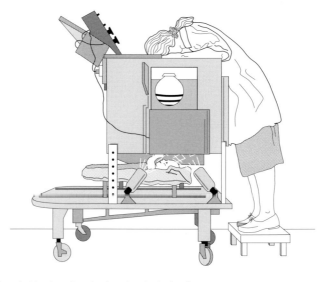

Figure 6   Fantz's 'viewing chamber' and typical stimuli.

Where two stimuli were presented at a time, the observer recorded the 'visual preference' for one stimulus over the other. This method is commonly called 'forced-choice preferential looking' (Atkinson, 2000). In a well designed experiment of this type, the observer does not know which stimuli are being presented on which side, to prevent any expectations she may have from influencing her judgement. She simply records the total amounts of time the baby spends looking to each side. Preferential looking has been used to examine how much fine detail babies can perceive (the 'acuity' of their visual system). The method is to present infants with pairs of stimuli, one containing fine detail and one which is a uniform grey. The stimuli are matched for overall brightness so that brightness preferences do not interfere with the results.

RESEARCH SUMMARY 1

How much detail can babies see?

The development of visual acuity has been tested using sets of stripes like those in Figure 7. Each pattern was paired with a grey square of equal overall brightness at a distance of 25 cms from the infant's face. Up to the age of one month, babies only show a visual preference for stripes over the grey square when shown the thickest set of stripes. Their acuity progressively improves as they get older, until by six months they are able to distinguish the finest stripes from a grey square. It is of interest to note that vision in the very young infant is not too different from that of the adult domestic cat. Like the cat, the young infant does not need the fine acuity necessary for reading or perceiving distant objects, and 'when development proceeds normally, infant vision seems perfectly adequate for the things that infants need to do.' (Hainline, 1998, p. 42).

Figure 7   Examples of stripes used in testing babies' visual acuity.

2.2 The infant's visual world

Preferred characteristics of visual stimuli

What characteristics of visual stimuli attract infants' attention? Using variations on Fantz's visual preference method, several 'natural' or unlearned preferences have been found in newborn (babies who are around 2 or 3 days old) and older infants. These characteristics include:

- *complexity* – at birth infants prefer to look at simple stimuli and prefer more complex stimuli, such as geometric shapes, as they get older;
- *symmetry* in patterns is preferred from around 4 months of age;
- *curved features* whether in face-like or geometric patterns are preferred to straight or angular ones;
- *moving stimuli* are preferred to stationary ones;
- real *three-dimensional* objects tend to be preferred to photographs of the same objects.

These preferences all make sense since they apply to the real stimuli that infants encounter in the world outside of the laboratory.

Reading

At this point you should turn to the end of this chapter and read Reading A, 'Pattern vision in newborn infants', by Fantz (1963). This is a research report of a study of 18 newborn babies, investigating their sensitivity to various patterns; a schematic face, black and white concentric circles, a piece of newsprint and coloured discs. These stimuli are shown in Figure 8. Notice that in this study Fantz was measuring the total duration of the infants' fixation on the stimulus.

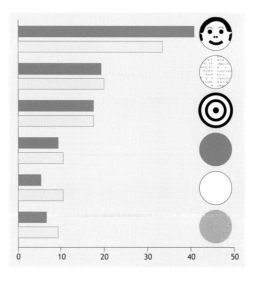

Figure 8   Pattern preferences in 2–3 month olds (dark blue bars) and infants over 3 months (light blue bars).

The stimuli used in the study are shown in Figure 8 which also shows further data on visual preferences for older infants. You can see how 'attention-grabbing' the schematic face stimulus is, and many later studies have confirmed the importance of the face as a visual stimulus for infants. An account of some of this research is given in Section 2.4.

Learning about the visually perceived world

In addition to unlearned preferences it has become apparent that at birth 'visual processing starts with a vengeance' (Karmiloff-Smith, 1999). The speed of this visual processing or learning is illustrated by two types of experimental evidence, the first from learning that occurs naturally, the second from learning in a laboratory setting.

Several studies have found that infants just 12 hours old will spend more time looking at their mother's face when she is shown paired with a stranger's face (see Figure 9). This preference is usually investigated after the baby has been separated from his or her mother for a few minutes, and can be apparent after only an hour's attention to her face, though it gets stronger with greater experience (Bushnell, 2003).

This can be considered a learned *familiarity preference*, but there is also clear evidence for *novelty preferences*, even in newborn infants. That is, the studies we have described so far have all used the visual preference method, in which pairs of stimuli are shown to the infant and observers record how much attention they pay to each of them. However, it is often the case that infants will not naturally 'prefer' one or other of the stimuli. In this instance researchers make use of *habituation*, in which one of the stimuli is shown until the infant becomes bored and no longer looks at it (i.e. the infant habituates), at which point the second stimulus is introduced and increased looking at the novel stimulus indicates that the infant has learned about the previously familiarized pattern and is able to discriminate between the two. Infants have been shown to make many discriminations between visual stimuli from a very early age, for instance between geometric shapes, different colours and faces.

Habituation
Infants pay less attention to events or objects that they have seen several times. The resulting decrease in attention towards the object is known as 'habituation'.

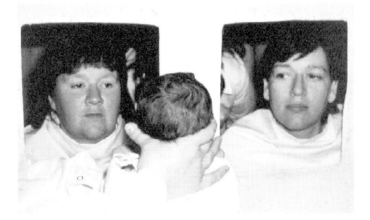

Figure 9 Only a few hours from birth infants prefer to look at their mother.

Although newborn infants' vision is much poorer than ours, their visual world is highly organized. An experiment on *size constancy* serves to illustrate this.

Slater *et al.* (1990) showed newborn infants (2 days old) a single object – either a small or a large cube, which, over trials, was shown at different distances from the eyes. Figure 10 shows a baby being tested. On subsequent test trials the babies looked more (i.e. showed a 'novelty preference') at a different-sized cube than at the same-sized one, even though the two cubes were at different distances in order to make their retinal sizes the same. This finding demonstrates that size constancy is an organizing feature of perception that is present at birth. Note that, like habituation, this procedure is dependent on the infants learning about the characteristics of the stimulus shown in the early 'familiarization' trials, and also on the infants subsequently preferring to look at novel stimuli on the later test trials.

Size constancy
Refers to the fact that we perceive an object as being the same size despite changes to its distance, and hence changes to the size of image it casts on the retina.

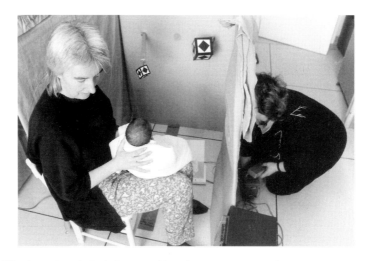

Figure 10   A newborn baby being tested in a size constancy experiment.

As we have said, at birth infants can discriminate between a variety of shapes, including people, and their visual world is structured and organized by mechanisms such as size constancy, but they have a long way to go before they fully comprehend the world of objects. As you look around you most of the objects you will see are partly covered (occluded) by objects that lie in front of them – a book occludes that part of the table it is lying on, a tree occludes part of the horizon, and so on. Babies begin to realize that partly occluded objects are whole, or complete, behind an occluder from about 2 months of age (Figure 11). By around 5–6 months infants are beginning to understand that two objects that are touching are two, not one. By 6–8 months they have learned about support and gravity – that an object hanging off the end of a table should fall, that ball-bearings will travel further when rolled down a longer rather than a shorter ramp. They learn about the relative importance or reliability of different types of information from experience, so that their experiences and actions on the world of objects help shape up their understanding of physical laws. In this respect they are becoming 'budding intuitive physicists, capable of detecting, interpreting and predicting physical outcomes' (Baillargeon, 1993, p. 311).

Are these two objects shaped ...

... like this? ...

... or like this?

Figure 11   From around 2 months of age infants begin to appreciate that an object that is occluded by another is whole or complete behind the occluder.

2.3 Depth perception and binocular vision

Stereopsis
The fusion of the retinal images from both eyes which is the basis of three-dimensional vision.

Binocular vision refers to the interaction of vision between the signals from our two eyes. Our eyes are a small distance apart, which means that when we look at a particular object each eye receives a slightly different image of it. The fusion of these images, known as stereopsis or stereo vision, provides a powerful cue to depth – the presentation of slightly different images to the two eyes is the basis of three-dimensional movies and pictures. Experimental studies suggest that coarse stereopsis first emerges between 3 and 6 months of age, followed by rapid improvements to near adult levels between 6 and 12 months of age.

Binocular vision and the development of stereopsis are not necessary for depth perception, since individuals with only one eye can perceive depth. Evidence for size constancy, and a preference for real three-dimensional objects rather than their photographs, indicate that some degree of depth perception is present at birth, but depth perception appears to improve during early infancy. In research on infants' depth perception even more of the infant's systems are brought into play, and infants' reaching and crawling behaviours are used.

Appreciation of pictorial depth cues – those monocular cues to depth that are found in static scenes such as might be found in photographs – has been found from about 5–6 months. Sen *et al.* (2001) describe such a cue to depth, which is an illusion shape that can be seen, with one eye closed, as a pair of three-dimensional rods. This illusion is shown in Figure 12. When they tested infants with one eye patched (i.e. under monocular conditions of viewing) they found that 7 month olds, but not 5 or 5½ month olds, reached for the apparently closer end of the fronto-parallel cylinder. This finding demonstrates both perception of the illusion in the older infants, and also depth perception in that they reached for what appeared to be the nearer cylinder.

Figure 12   A two-dimensional version of the three-dimensional illusion used by Sen *et al.* (2001). When the figures are made out of wooden rods, and viewed monocularly, a powerful illusion is experienced such that the bottom of the rod on the left appears much nearer than the bottom of the rod on the right.

RESEARCH SUMMARY 2

The visual cliff

Figure 13 shows the 'visual cliff' that Gibson and Walk (1960) invented to examine depth perception in infants. This consists of a central board laid across a heavy sheet of plate glass which is supported about a metre above the floor. On one side of the board, there is a checkerboard surface immediately below the glass, while on the other side the checkerboard surface is at floor level, creating a visual deep drop. Babies from

6 months to 1 year in age were placed on the central board, and their mothers were asked to encourage them to crawl across both the visually solid and the visual cliff sides. If babies of this age were able to perceive depth, then they would be expected to be less prepared to crawl over the drop, even though it was in fact quite safe to do so.

Figure 13   The visual cliff.

The results from Gibson and Walk (1960) seem clear: only three out of 27 infants crawled to their mothers over the drop, whereas all 27 crawled over the visually solid side. This was in spite of some infants reaching out and patting the glass above the drop. Campos *et al.* (1992) found that when infants first start to crawl they will happily cross the 'deep' side, suggesting that a period of locomotor experience (e.g. crawling) is necessary for a wariness of heights to develop, but experienced crawlers almost always refused to crawl over the deep side.

2.4   A preference for faces?

The human face is one of the most complex visual stimuli encountered by the infant: it moves, it is three-dimensional, it has areas of both high and low contrast; and it contains features that change (when talking, when changing expression, when looking at or away from the baby), but which are in an invariant relationship (the eyes are always above the mouth, etc.). As a rough guide Figure 14 gives an indication of how a mother's face might look to a newborn baby. While the image is degraded and unfocused to the newborn, enough information is potentially available for the infant to learn to recognize its mother's face, and for other aspects of face perception. As you have seen, several investigators have found that infants recognize, and prefer, their mother's face soon after birth. There is considerable evidence suggesting that faces are special, right from birth. Here we will describe some of the research that has investigated other aspects of face perception at or near birth, and discuss how face perception might develop during infancy.

Figure 14 A face as it might appear to a newborn baby (left) and to an adult (right).

Attractiveness and imitation

Several researchers have found that infants prefer to look at attractive faces when these are shown paired with faces judged by adults to be less attractive (Hoss and Langlois, 2003). The 'attractiveness effect' has also been found in studies with newborn infants who averaged less than 3 days from birth at the time of testing (e.g. Slater *et al.*, 1998). The typical interpretation of the 'attractiveness effect' is that it results from a facial prototype: if many faces of the same gender are computer-averaged the resulting 'average' face, or prototype, is always perceived as being attractive. According to this interpretation attractive faces are seen as more 'face-like' because they match more closely the facial representation or prototype that infants either form from their experience of seeing faces, or with which they enter the world.

Some of the clearest evidence that faces are special for infants is the finding that infants, only minutes after birth, imitate a range of facial expressions that they see an adult produce (e.g. Reissland, 1988). Apparently, this was first discovered by one of Piaget's students, Olga Maratos, who reported to him that if she stuck out her tongue to a young baby, the baby would respond by sticking its tongue out to her (according to Piaget's theory this should not appear until the second year). Apparently, when Piaget was informed of these findings he sucked contemplatively on his pipe for a few moments, and then commented 'How rude'!

Facial imitation can be taken to indicate that babies can match what they see to some inbuilt knowledge of their own face, and can then use this match to produce the same facial expression (which might be tongue protrusion, mouth opening, furrowing of the brow, or other expressions) which the infants, of course, cannot see as they produce it. This seems to be an inborn ability and raises the question of why infants imitate. One idea is that babies imitate as a form of social interaction and as a way of learning about people's identity (Meltzoff and Moore, 2000).

These findings on the 'attractiveness effect' and imitation of adults' facial expressions support the view that infants enter the world with a detailed representation of the human face that is part of a genetic preparedness for discriminating between individuals and for bonding with carers. (e.g. Quinn and Slater, 2003; Meltzoff, 2004) and are in opposition to Piaget's constructivist view described earlier.

Early experience and learning

However elaborate the newborn infant's representation of the face may be, it still has a great deal to learn. For example, an understanding of facial expressions develops through infancy and continues to develop through childhood and later. Here, we will look at two ways in which experience affects the development of face perception in infancy.

Reading

SG

At this point you should turn to the end of this chapter and read Reading B, 'Is face processing species-specific during the first year of life?' by Pascalis *et al.* (2002). This is a research report comparing 6- and 9-month-old infants' and adults' ability to discriminate between human and monkey faces. The 9 month olds and adults only discriminated between faces of their own species, while the 6 month olds showed discrimination between individuals of both species.

Their results suggest that during the first year of life the face processing system becomes attuned to a human template. You might compare this finding with the difficulty that humans of one ethnic group often have in discriminating between individuals of another ethnicity. The authors compare their findings with the perceptual narrowing found in speech perception, which will be discussed in Section 3.3.

Infants are also able to discriminate on the basis of gender. Representing faces as female versus male is an example of categorization, a mental process that underlies one's ability to respond equivalently to a set of discriminably different entities as instances of the same class. In order to demonstrate categorization, Quinn *et al.* (2002) presented 3–4-month-old infants with a number of different exemplars (colour photographs of different faces), all of which were from the same gender category, either male or female, during a series of familiarization trials. Subsequently, during a novel category preference test, infants were presented with two novel stimuli, a new face from the familiar category, and a face from the other gender. Generalization of familiarization to the novel instance from the familiar category, and a preference for the novel instance from the novel category, are taken as evidence that the infants have grouped together or categorized the instances from the familiar category (including the novel one) and recognized that the novel instance from the novel category does not belong to this grouping (or category representation).

SG

Quinn *et al.* (2002) found that the infants could discriminate between male and female faces, but while those who had been familiarized to *male* faces subsequently showed a strong preference (novelty response) for looking at a *female* face when this was shown side-by-side with a novel male face, those familiarized to *female* faces did not show a preference for a *male* face. In their second experiement it turned out that this was because the infants had a strong tendency to look at female faces in preference to male ones! Additionally, in another experimental condition, the infants showed better recognition of individual different female faces than those of males. However, a majority of infants, at least in Western societies, are reared with a female primary caregiver for at least the first few months. When Quinn *et al.* tested infants who were reared with a male primary carer they found the opposite result – these infants fared better with male faces. Thus, it seems that the representation of gender from human faces by young infants is strongly influenced by the gender of the primary carer: those reared primarily by a female prefer to look at female faces and become 'female experts' while those reared by a male primary caregiver become 'male experts'.

It seems that the newborn infant emerges into the world with a representation of the human face that helps them to recognize individual faces, such as the mother's, and a basic understanding of people as social objects. It is also the case that early learning about faces can be very rapid. Thus, the initial state of the face recognition system is increasingly added to by experience to assist the infant in becoming a 'human face expert' and helping them to make sense of the complex social world.

Summary of Section 2

- The human visual system is immature at birth: it continues to develop for several years. In particular, young infants do not have a fully developed central area of vision which picks up fine detail and colour.
- Infants show visual preferences for some images over others from the first days after birth.
- Infants are sensitive to some depth information from birth, but this ability continues to develop up to about 6 months of age.
- The human face is particularly attractive, probably in part because the infant is attuned to stimulus features that faces embody.
- In laboratory studies that provide information-rich stimuli, infants can show remarkable visual competence, for example newborns are able to distinguish their mothers' faces from those of strangers.
- Newborn infants' preferences for attractive faces, and ability to imitate facial gestures from birth, indicate that they emerge into the world with a genetic preparedness for discriminating between individuals and for bonding with caregivers.

3 Hearing

Most of this discussion of perceptual development has been devoted to vision, because vision allows humans to engage with complex information. However, hearing is also important, particularly in relation to communication between people. Speech is a highly complex signal, containing not only information that is interpreted as words and sentences and hence meanings, but also information that communicates other meanings, for example to do with emotional states and the relationship between speaker and listener.

Before moving on to the development of auditory abilities in infancy, we will briefly overview the anatomical and neural development of the auditory system.

3.1 The auditory pathway

Sounds in the environment (rapid changes in air pressure) are funnelled towards the ear drum (the tympanic membrane) in the ear, which moves in and out rapidly in response to these pressure changes (Figure 15). These movements are then transmitted by a set of small bones (malleus, incus and stapes) onto a much smaller membrane, the stapes footplate. As this second membrane is so much smaller, the movements of the tympanic membrane are effectively amplified in their transmission to the stapes footplate. The movements of this second membrane stimulate a series of rows of tiny hairs within the cochlea. It is believed that these hairs are sensitive to different frequencies in the transmitted sounds; they have neural transmitting cells at their bases, which connect with the auditory nerve. This contains a large number of nerve fibres (30,000 or so) and connects to the auditory projection areas of the cortex (Heschl's gyrus) via a series of four 'relay stations'.

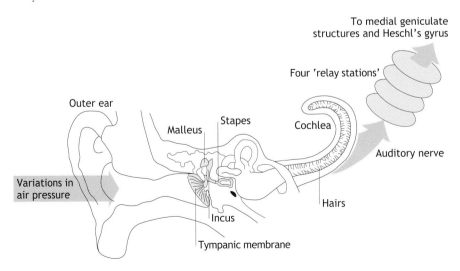

Figure 15 The hearing system.

Development of the auditory system

The onset of hearing is around the sixth month of prenatal life, and at birth the anatomical structures outlined above are remarkably mature and functional, in contrast to the structures of the visual system. The fibres throughout the auditory nerve are fully myelinated at birth, although the neurons in Heschl's gyrus show much the same pattern of development as do those in the visual cortex, not completing their interconnection until adolescence.

There is no doubt that infants can hear quite well from the time that they are born, although their auditory threshold (sensitivity to low-intensity sound) is inferior to those of adults and older children: this sensitivity gradually improves over the early years. However, the evidence suggests that infants' auditory abilities are very sophisticated even in newborns.

3.2 Auditory preferences

Just as for vision, where infants show preferences for some stimuli over others, they also show preferences for some sounds over others. A different method has to be used to assess these preferences, however, since infants do not turn their ears towards particular sounds! They do turn their heads, though, and this ability to locate sounds is demonstrated straight after birth. Head-turning towards sounds is apparent in even the youngest infants, and this behaviour is used to examine the nature of early auditory preferences.

Motherese
Also known as 'infant-directed speech', motherese refers to the way that adults change particular features of their speech when talking to very young children. Typically the voice is more high pitched, the language used is simpler, more words are stressed and intonation is exaggerated.

When adults speak to babies, they tend to do so in a way that exaggerates the pitch contour (i.e. there is more 'rise and fall' in their voices) and also raises the overall pitch. This particular kind of speech has been called infant-directed speech or 'motherese', because mothers use it so often towards their babies. In a study by Fernald (1985), 4-month-old infants were played a recording of a normal voice if they turned their heads to one side, or motherese if they turned their heads to the other side. These babies all turned their heads more frequently to hear the motherese voice. Many subsequent experiments have replicated the finding that infants prefer to listen to motherese rather than adult-directed speech. However, one characteristic of motherese is that it typically conveys positive emotion ('happy talk') and in recent research infants were found to prefer 'happy' adult talk to less happy motherese! (Singh *et al.*, 2002). This suggests that the preference for motherese might actually be attributable to a more general preference for speech that imparts positive emotion.

Psychologists have found once again that stimuli that are important to infants (e.g. mothers' voices) are well discriminated by babies. One interpretation of this is that babies are born 'attuned' to prefer the patterns of stimulation that occur most frequently in interactions with their carers. By 4 months of age, infants have had a lot of experience of human voices, and their preference might be a learned one. However, studies have been conducted with much younger infants, and two in particular are noteworthy.

DeCasper and Fifer (1980) used changes in infants' sucking rates to allow infants to control which of two stimuli they experienced. The sucking procedure they used is illustrated in Box 2. The stimuli used were audio-recordings; one of the infant's own mother's voice and one of a stranger's voice. The results were clear: infants could clearly discriminate between these two voices because they consistently sucked so as to produce the sound of their mother's voice.

BOX 2

Categorical perception of phonemes

When a 2-day-old baby sucks on a special dummy, the sound 'ba' is produced in the headphones. She learns quickly to produce the sound, and her sucking speeds up. Eventually, though, she gets used to it and her sucking decreases again (habituation). If the sound she produces is now changed to 'pa', her sucking will increase again, showing that she has perceived the difference. This is usually described as 'dishabituation'. Changing the sound's VOT to another that still signals 'ba', though, doesn't produce an increase in sucking; she still hears it as the same sound.

As these infants were newborns, it is possible that they learned something about their mothers' voices before they were born, because babies can hear sounds while still in the womb. DeCasper and Spence (1986) investigated this by asking pregnant mothers to read aloud a piece of prose repeatedly to their unborn babies. After they were born, these babies then showed a preference for this familiar prose over another matched piece that they had never heard before. These results suggest that infants' aural preferences may be due at least in part to their experiences of sounds before they are born.

3.3 Speech perception

Babies' precocious interest in human speech is matched by some very sophisticated sensitivities to those features that are used to differentiate particular speech sounds. There has been a lot of research into the way that infants perceive phonemes, the individual sounds that make up words. One set of phonemes that has been particularly intensively studied is the plosives, such as [b] and [p]. We can distinguish the two words *bat* and *pat* solely on the basis of the difference in the two phonemes at the start of each word. These two sounds are virtually identical, but a key difference between [b] and [p] is that in [b] there is little or no delay between the 'plosive' opening of your lips and the 'voicing' of the sound by your vocal chords. In [p], there is a slight delay between these two parts of the sound. Voicing onset time (VOT), as this distinction is known, is an important contrast in most languages.

Phoneme
The smallest isolatable sound unit of a given language.

Adult speakers are able to discriminate differences in VOT around the point that marks the difference *between* phonemes in their language, such as the distinctions between [b] and [p]. However, adults are unable to detect similar variation in VOT in two different examples of [p] being spoken. This so-called 'categorical perception' of speech sounds is present in a very mature, adult-like form in newborns.

Other studies have found that young infants can discriminate among all of the distinctions that are found in languages around the world, even those that they do not hear in the language used around them. However, as they grow up in a particular language community, exposed to just a small sample of these distinctions, they seem to lose this ability, and when older can recognize only those distinctions which are actually used in their first language: in Werker's (1989) term they become 'native listeners'. For example, both the [k] sound in 'key' and the [k] sound in 'ski' are members of the same phoneme in English. This means that the two [k] sounds are perceived as the same sound by English speakers despite the fact that the [k] sound in 'key' is aspirated (it concludes with a short puff of breath) and the [k] sound in 'ski' is unaspirated (it does not conclude with a short puff of breath). In contrast, the two [k] sounds are members of different phonemes in Chinese. As a result, speakers of Chinese can readily discriminate the two sounds. While young infants living in an English-speaking community can easily discriminate these sounds, older infants lose this ability: thus, speakers of English and speakers of Chinese differ in terms of their ability to discriminate the two sounds. Another example of this is given in Box 3.

BOX 3

Phonemic discrimination

Sandra Trehub designed a study to learn whether one- to four-month-olds can distinguish as well as their English-speaking parents a certain pair of sounds used in Czech. To obtain these sounds, she ordered a tape-recording of two phonemes from a linguistics laboratory. The tape arrived. Trehub played it and could hear no difference between the phonemes. She played it again, and yet again, but no matter how often she listened to it, she could not hear a difference. Eventually she telephoned the lab in a huff to complain that someone had recorded the same phoneme twice. 'No', she was told, 'Two phonemes are there'. She was firmly convinced that she was wasting her time, but she went ahead with the study anyway. Sure enough, the English-speaking parents, when forced to say which sound was which, were right only slightly better than chance. But their babies had no difficulty in telling them apart at all.

(Source: Maurer and Maurer, 1988, pp. 149–50).

Other research has demonstrated that infants develop a very sophisticated understanding of their native language before they speak. For example, by 4–5 months they can discriminate their own native language from all others, they respond to their own name by 4½ months, they start to distinguish individual words from fluent speech around 7½ months, and from around 8 months they begin to attach meanings to words. In summary, 'infants acquire considerable information about the nature and organization of their native language well before they actually begin to produce recognizable words' (Jusczyk, 2002, p. 147).

It seems that there are differences between the development of visual perception and the development of hearing. Babies appear to come into the world with an ability to discriminate sounds, particularly speech sounds, that is in some ways even more acute than that of adults. The developmental course of speech perception appears to go in two directions: infants actually become somewhat less competent in discriminating some non-native sounds as they get older, but become much more sophisticated in understanding the speech characteristics of their native language.

Summary of Section 3

- The human auditory system is more mature in its neuroanatomical structures at birth than the visual system.
- Infants show auditory preferences just as they show visual preferences.
- Infants discriminate different voices from very soon after birth, if not *in utero*. They recognize their own mother's voice and are sensitive to intonation.
- Infants are sensitive to a range of important phonemic distinctions in speech, some of which do not occur in their language community.
- Infants learn a great deal about the speech characteristics of their native language before they speak their first word.

4 Cross-modal perception

Adult perception of the world is usually not through a single sensory channel; we integrate information from different senses. For example, when people are conversing, they integrate the sound of voices with the movements of bodies, faces and mouths. Also, adults are used to co-ordinating sound with visual locations for objects that produce sound; if you hear a sound to one side of you, you may turn in order to visually find the sound source.

Can infants integrate the different sensory modalities in this way, or does this ability only develop as a result of experience? There is some evidence that newborns do have a rudimentary ability to do this sort of integration. For example, Wertheimer (1961) found that his daughter, tested immediately after birth, tended to turn her eyes to the left or the right, depending on which side a click was made. In a more recent study by Morrongiello *et al.* (1998) newborn infants were shown a toy that was accompanied by a sound, and the question of whether the babies could learn the sight–sound pairings, and if so under what conditions, was asked. They had the toy-sound coming either from the *same* place (known as spatial co-location) or from *different* places (dislocation), one to the left, the other to the right. The infants learned that the sound was an attribute of a specific object only in the spatial co-location condition.

Similarly, Slater *et al.* (1999) familiarized 2-day-old infants to two different, simple visual stimuli (a red vertical line and a green diagonal line) where each was accompanied by its 'own' sound. There were two different experimental conditions – in one the sound was presented for the whole time that the visual stimulus was shown, irrespective of whether the baby looked at the visual stimulus or not, and in the other the sound was presented only when the baby looked (it turned off automatically when the baby looked away). In this latter instance the presentation of each sound–sight pair was synchronized in that the baby either had both together or none at all. The results were clear – the babies only learned the sight–sound combinations when their on/off presentation was synchronized.

These two experiments tell us that newborn infants can learn about auditory–visual events, but that this learning is guided by the same rules that apply throughout life – people only associate stimuli from different senses if there is information that specifies that they genuinely belong together. We can see how these 'rules' work naturally in the real world – we would only associate a voice with a person if we see their lips move, we would only associate a sound with a particular animal if it comes from the same place. In technical terms the information that specifies that information from one modality is linked with that from another is called *intersensory redundancy*; that is, the information from the two (or more) modalities provide similar, or linking information. In the examples given above, the auditory–visual connections are arbitrary, in the sense that there is no necessary connection between the sound and the visual object. An important example of an arbitrary auditory–visual relation is between a person's face and their voice: there is no way of knowing in advance that a particular voice goes with a particular face. There is evidence that infants can learn this relationship at least as early as 3 months, and that learning is helped by the presence of intersensory redundancy in the sense that when a person speaks their voice is perfectly synchronized with their mouth movements.

As development proceeds infants become more and more sophisticated in their learning of cross-modal relations. For example, by 11 weeks of age, but not earlier, infants expect a single object to make a single sound, and a compound object (several small objects) to make a complex sound, when they strike a surface (Bahrick, 2001). Bahrick and Lickliter (2002) suggest that redundant information is also extremely important in infants and children learning the names for objects – the synchronous presentation of the word and the object it names assists the child in learning the arbitrary word–object associations.

Intersensory redundancy
Evidence that indicates that information from one sensory modality (e.g. an image) is also linked to information from a different sensory modality (e.g. a sound).

SG

Summary of Section 4

- Newborn infants show a rudimentary ability to co-ordinate information from different senses.
- They are sensitive to synchrony and asynchrony, and spatial co-location in learning arbitrary auditory–visual associations.
- Intersensory redundancy is an important cue in indicating that information from two senses goes together.

5   Perceiving the world: a multisensory experience

The studies in this chapter suggest that infants function at their best in experiments when they are presented with stimuli that are similar to the sorts of things that they experience in their everyday world outside the psychology laboratory. The world provides rich, complex stimulation with movement, sounds, smells and tactile sensations, such that information about objects and events is carried simultaneously through more than one sense. It seems that infants are not only able to deal with this richness, but also have perceptual systems that, though immature, function well in this context. Studies that use impoverished stimuli may not give a full picture of what babies can make of much more complicated stimulation; they do not evoke the levels of perception that are possible in more 'ecologically valid' situations.

Early studies of infant perception predominantly used static stimuli, in an attempt to isolate basic factors in visual perception. However, these sorts of stimulation are unlike the usual world of the infant. Recent research strongly suggests a preparedness at birth for dealing with dynamic perceptual experiences. This is well illustrated by considering the role of action in perceptual development.

Activity 2

Allow about 5 minutes

Testing your senses

This activity will demonstrate the role of action in perception.

People tend to think that we have only five senses – touch, taste, smell, hearing and vision – but a couple of simple demonstrations convince us otherwise. Try these actions:

(1) stand on one leg and close your eyes;

(2) with your eyes closed touch the tip of your nose with your right hand.

Comment

Note that touch, smell, taste, hearing and seeing contributed little to these tasks, but in the first instance you should not have fallen over, and in the second you should have touched your nose effortlessly! Your ability to do these sorts of tasks relies upon two senses – the sense of bodily posture and balance, which is controlled by the semi-circular canals in the inner ear (this is known as the *vestibular system*), and feedback from the nerves throughout our bodies telling us where our body parts are (known as *kinaesthetic feedback*).

The vestibular system and kinaesthetic feedback begin their development in the womb – even the foetus has been known to move its hand so that it can suck its thumb – and they constantly develop throughout infancy and later life.

You will almost certainly have had an experience like this. You are sitting in a train in a station and there is another train on the next track. This train then starts moving, but for a moment or two you are convinced that it is your train that is moving. This impression can be so strong that some individuals who are standing will lurch forwards or backwards to compensate for the movement – that is, they make inappropriate postural controls. Infants do this too. Butterworth (1981) tested toddlers for posture control in a 'moving room'. This was a small room placed in a larger room which consisted simply of three walls – front and two sides – and these were on castors so that they could move independently of the floor (which didn't move). Older infants (15–34 month olds) stood up facing the front wall and then the room moved, either towards or away from the infants. The results were clear – when the room moved towards the infant, the baby fell over backwards, and if the room moved away the baby fell forwards (the floor was soft!). Younger babies, from 2 months old, were tested in the moving room sitting in an infant chair, and their head movements were measured. For all infants there were appropriate head movements when the room moved (i.e. head movements backwards when the room moved toward the infant, and forwards when it moved back).

Such data suggests that the posture and bodily position senses help to guide the infant's behaviour from birth. What is clear is that with each new motor development – for instance, from sitting to crawling – infants need to readjust their posture and body senses to make the next 'step forward'. An example of the way in which the development of the action systems have a profound impact on the infant's perception of the world can be seen at the onset of independent locomotion (in most infants, the onset of crawling; Campos *et al.*, 2000). You have seen that when they begin crawling infants avoid the visual cliff; only after experience of crawling do they learn a wariness of heights. It is not too difficult to understand why this should be the case. For the precrawling infant the major changes to his or her visual world are through the actions of others – being held, pushed in a pram, driven in a car – and height will typically be experienced by being held aloft by a carer. In these circumstances a wariness of heights or of unexpected movement would be maladaptive, and so it has to be learned later, during independent locomotion. The onset of locomotion, with its new found autonomy, opens up a new world to be explored and brings with it a new form of social signalling, which is referred to as 'social referencing': the infant will look to his or her parents for guidance as to what is safe and what is risky.

Summary of Section 5

- Experimental work that uses ecologically valid situations and stimuli to assess infants' perceptual abilities may demonstrate higher abilities than more 'unnatural' experimental work is able to.
- Postural control and kinaesthetic feedback begin to develop in the womb, and continue to develop throughout later life in response to new experiences.

6   Conclusion

This chapter began with an account of different theories of development. Empiricism was compared with a version of *nativism* that claims that newborn infants enter the world with pre-existing representations, of objects and people. The development of the visual system and of visual perception was explored in detail and was followed by an account of auditory development with a focus on speech perception. Following this you read an account of the origins and development of cross-modal perception which pointed to the important links between perception and action.

   Although researchers will often investigate a single sensory modality it is important to appreciate that development throughout life involves the integration of information from many systems operating in parallel, and that the development of any one system or sensory modality is intimately linked with the development of others.

Further reading

Bremner, G. and Slater, A. (2004) *Theories of Infant Development*, Oxford, Blackwell.

Slater, A. and Lewis, M. (2002) *Introduction to Infant Development*, Oxford, Oxford University Press.

References

Abramov, I., Gordon, J., Hendrickson, A., Hainline, L., Dobson, V. and Labossiere, E. (1982) 'The retina of the newborn infant', *Science*, vol. 217, pp. 265–7.

Atkinson, J. (2000) *The Developing Visual Brain*, Oxford, Oxford University Press.

Bahrick, L. E. (2001) 'Increasing specificity in perceptual development: infants' detection of nested levels of multimodal stimulation', *Journal of Experimental Child Psychology*, vol. 79, pp. 253–70.

Bahrick, L. E. and Lickliter, R. (2002) 'Intersensory redundancy guides early perceptual and cognitive development', in Kail, R. and Reese, H. (eds) *Advances in Child Development and Behavior*, vol. 30, pp. 153–87, Oxford, Academic Press.

Baillargeon, R. (1993) 'The object concept revisited: new directions in the investigation of infants' physical knowledge' in Granrud, C. (ed.) *Visual Perception and Cognition in Infancy*, Hillsdale, NJ, Erlbaum.

Bushnell, I. W. R. (2003) 'Newborn face recognition' in Pascalis, O. and Slater, A. (eds) *The Development of Face Processing in Infancy and Early Childhood: current perspectives*, New York, NOVA Science.

Butterworth, G. (1981) 'Structure of the mind in human infancy', *Advances in Infancy Research*, vol. 2, pp. 1–29.

Campos, J. J., Anderson, D. I., Barbu-Roth, M. A., Hubbard, E. M., Hertenstein, M. J. and Witherington, D. (2000) 'Travel broadens the mind', *Infancy*, vol. 1, pp. 149–219.

Campos, J., Bertenhal, B. and Kermoian, R. (1992) 'Early experience and emotional development: the emergence of wariness of heights', *Psychological Science*, vol. 23, pp. 61–4.

DeCasper, A. J. and Fifer, W. (1980) 'Of human bonding: newborns prefer their mothers' voices', *Science*, vol. 208, pp. 1174–6.

DeCasper, A. J. and Spence, M. J. (1986) 'Prenatal maternal speech influences newborns' perception of speech sounds', *Infant Behaviour and Development*, vol. 9, pp. 133–50.

Fantz, R. L. (1963) 'Pattern vision in newborn infants', *Science*, vol. 140, pp. 296–7.

Fernald, A. (1985) 'Four-month-old infants prefer to listen to motherese', *Infant Behaviour and Development*, vol. 8, pp. 181–95.

Gibson, E. J. and Walk, R. D. (1960) 'The visual cliff', *Scientific American*, vol. 202, pp. 64–71.

Hainline, L. (1998) 'The development of basic visual abilities', in Slater, A. (ed.) *Perceptual Development: visual, auditory and speech perception in infants*, Hove Psychology Press.

Hickey, T. L. (1977) 'Postnatal development of the human lateral geniculate nucleus: relationship to a critical period for the visual system', *Science*, vol. 198, pp. 836–8.

Horton, J. C. and Hedley-Whyte, E. T. (1984) 'Mapping of cytochrome oxidase patches and ocular dominance columns in human visual cortex', *Philosophical Transactions of the Royal Society of London*, Series B, vol. 304, pp. 255–72.

Hoss, R. A. and Langlois, J. H. (2003) 'Infants prefer attractive faces', in Pascalis, O. and Slater, A. (eds) *The Development of Face Processing in Infancy and Early Childhood: current perspectives*, New York, NOVA Science.

Hubel, D. H. (1963) 'Integrative processes in central visual pathways of the cat', *Journal of the Optical Society of America*, vol. 53, pp. 58–66.

Hubel, D. H. and Wiesel, T. N. (1962) 'Receptive fields, binocular interaction and functional architecture in the cat's visual cortex', *Journal of Physiology*, vol. 160, pp. 106–54.

Jusczyk, P. W. (2002) 'Language development: from speech perception to first words', in Slater, A. and Lewis, M. (eds) *Introduction to Infant Development*, Oxford, Oxford University Press.

Karmiloff-Smith, A. (1999) 'The connectionist infant: would Piaget turn in his grave?', in Slater, A. and Muir, D. (eds) *The Blackwell Reader in Developmental Psychology*, Oxford, Blackwell.

Maurer, D. and Maurer, C. (1988) *The World of the Newborn*, New York, Basic Books.

Meltzoff, A. N. (2004) 'The case for developmental cognitive science: theories of people and things', in Bremner, G. and Slater, A. (eds) *Theories of Infant Development*, Oxford, Blackwell.

Meltzoff, A. N. and Moore, M. K. (2000) 'Resolving the debate about early imitation', in Muir, D. and Slater, A. (eds) *Infant Development: the essential readings*, Oxford, Blackwell.

Michael, C. R. (1978) 'Colour vision mechanisms in monkey striate cortex: dual opponent cells with concentric receptive fields', *Journal of Neurophysiology*, vol. 41, pp. 572–88.

Morrongiello, B. A., Fenwick, K. D. and Chance, G. (1998) 'Cross-modal learning in newborn infants: inferences about properties of auditory-visual events', *Infant Behavior and Development*, vol. 21, pp. 543–53.

Pascalis, O., de Haan, M. and Nelson, C. (2002) 'Is face processing species-specific during the first year of life?', Science, vol. 296, pp. 1321–3.

Piaget, J. and Inhelder, B. (1966) *The Psychology of the Child*, trans. by H. Weaver, published 1969, London, Routledge and Kegan Paul.

Quinn, P. C., Yahr, J., Kuhn, A., Slater, A. and Pascalis, O. (2002) 'Representation of the gender of human faces by infants: a preference for female', *Perception*, vol. 31, pp. 1109–21.

Quinn, P. C. and Slater, A. (2003) 'Face perception at birth and beyond', in Pascalis, O. and Slater, A. (eds) *The Development of Face Processing in Infancy and Early Childhood: current perspectives*, New York, NOVA Science.

Reissland, N. (1988) 'Neonatal imitation in the first hour of life: observations in rural Nepal', *Developmental Psychology*, vol. 24, pp. 464–9.

Sen, M. G., Yonas, A. and Knill, D. (2001) 'Development of infants' sensitivity to surface contour information for spatial layout', *Perception*, vol. 30, pp. 167–76.

Singh, L., Morgan, J. L. and Best, C. (2002) 'Infants' listening preferences: baby talk or happy talk?', *Infancy*, vol. 3, 365–94.

Slater, A., Mattock, A. and Brown, E. (1990) 'Size constancy at birth: newborn infants' responses to retinal and real size', *Journal of Experimental Child Psychology*, vol. 49, pp. 314–22.

Slater, A., Quinn, P. C., Brown, E. and Hayes, R. (1999) 'Intermodal perception at birth: Intersensory redundancy guides newborn infants' learning of arbitrary auditory-visual patterns', *Developmental Science*, vol. 2, pp. 333–8.

Slater, A., Von Der Schulenberg, C., Brown, E. *et al.* (1998) 'Newborn infants prefer attractive faces', *Infant Behavior and Development*, vol. 21, pp. 345–54.

Spelke, E. (1998) 'Nativism, empiricism, and the origins of knowledge', *Infant Behavior and Development*, vol. 21, pp. 181–200.

Werker, J. F. (1989) 'Becoming a native listener', *American Scientist*, vol. 77, pp. 54–9.

Wertheimer, M. (1961) 'Psychomotor co-ordination of auditory and visual space at birth', *Science*, vol. 134, p. 1692.

Yakovlev, P. I. and Lecours, A. (1967) 'The myelogenetic cycles of regional maturation in the brain', in Minkowski, A. (ed.) (1967) *Regional Development of the Brain in Early Life*, Philadelphia, F. A. Davis Company.

Readings

Reading A: Pattern vision in newborn infants

Robert L. Fantz

Abstract. *Human infants under 5 days of age consistently looked more at black-and-white patterns than at plain colored surfaces, which indicates the innate ability to perceive form.*

It is usually stated or implied that the infant has little or no pattern vision during the early weeks or even months, because of the need for visual learning or because of the immature state of the eye and brain, or for both reasons[1]. This viewpoint has been challenged by the direct evidence of differential attention given to visual stimuli varying in form or pattern[2]. This evidence has shown that during the early months of life, infants: (i) have fairly acute pattern vision (resolving 1/8-inch stripes at a 10-inch distance); (ii) show greater visual interest in patterns than in plain colors; (iii) differentiate among patterns of similar complexity; and (iv) show visual interest in a pattern similar to that of a human face.

The purpose of the present study was to determine whether it was possible to obtain similar data on newborn infants and thus further exclude visual learning or postnatal maturation as requirements of pattern vision. It is a repetition of a study of older infants which compared the visual responsiveness to patterned and to plainly colored surfaces[3]. The results of the earlier study were essentially duplicated, giving further support for the above conclusions.

The subjects were 18 infants ranging from 10 hours to 5 days old. They were selected from a much larger number on the basis of their eyes remaining open long enough to be exposed to a series of six targets at least twice. The length of gaze at each target was observed through a tiny hole in the ceiling of the chamber [...] and recorded on a timer. The fixation time started as soon as one or both eyes of the infant were directed towards the target, using as criterion the super-position over the pupil of a tiny corneal reflection of the target; it ended when the eyes turned away or closed[4]. The six targets were presented in random order for each infant, with the sequence repeated up to eight times when possible. Only completed sequences were included in calculating the percentage of total fixation time for each target.

The targets were circular, 6 inches in diameter, and had nonglossy surfaces. Three contained black-and-white patterns – a schematic face, concentric circles, and a section of newspaper containing print 1/16 to 1/4 inch high.

The other three were unpatterned – white, fluorescent yellow, and dark red. The relative luminous reflectance was, in decreasing order: yellow, white, newsprint, face and circles, red. Squares containing the pattern of colors were placed in a flat holder which slid horizontally into a slightly recessed portion of the chamber ceiling to expose the pattern of color to the infant through a circular hole in the holder.

The chamber and underside of the holder were lined with blue felt to provide a contrasting background for the stimuli, and to diffuse the illumination (between

10 and 15ft-ca) from lights on either side of the infant's head. The subject was in a small hammock crib with head facing up directly under the targets, 1 foot away.

Table A **Relative duration of initial gaze of infants at six stimulus objects in successive and repeated presentations.**

Mean percentage of fixation time								
Age group	N	Face	Circles	News	White	Yellow	Red	p*
Under 48 hrs	8	29.5	23.5	13.1	12.3	11.5	10.1	.005
2 to 5 days	10	29.5	24.3	17.5	9.9	12.1	6.7	.001
2 to 6 mths**	25	34.3	18.4	19.9	8.9	8.2	10.1	.001

* Significance level based on Friedman analysis of variance by ranks
** From an earlier study (2).

The results in Table A show about twice as much visual attention to patterns as to plainly colored surfaces. Differences in response to the six stimuli objects are significant for the infants both under and over 2 days of age; results from these groups do not differ reliably from each other, and are similar to earlier results from much older infants. The selectivity of the visual responses is brought out still more strikingly by tabulating the longest-fixated target for each newborn infant: 11 for face, 5 for concentric circles, 2 for newsprint, and 0 for white, yellow, and red. For comparison, the first choices of infants 2 to 6 months were distributed as follows: 16, 4, 5, 0, 0, 0.

Three infants under 24 hours could be tested sufficiently to indicate the individual consistency of response. Two of these showed a significant (.005 and .05) difference among the targets in successive sets of exposures, one looking longest at the face pattern in 7 of 8 exposures, the other looking longest at the 'bull's-eye' in 3 of 6 exposures. The third infant 10 hours after birth looked longest at the face in 3 of 8 exposures.

It is clear that the selective visual responses were related to pattern rather than hue or reflectance, although the latter two variables are often thought to be primary visual stimuli. Specification of the prepotent configurational variables is unwarranted at this time. The results do not imply 'instinctive recognition' of a face or other significance of this pattern; it is likely there are other patterns which would elicit equal or greater attention[5]. Longer fixation of the face suggests only that a pattern with certain similarities to social objects also has stimulus characteristics with considerable intrinsic interest or stimulating value; whatever the mechanism underlying this interest, it should facilitate the development of social responsiveness, since what is responded to must first be attended to.

Substantiation for the visual selection of patterned over unpatterned objects is given in an independent study of newborn infants in which more visual attention was given to a colored card with a simple figure, when held close to the infant, than to a plain card of either color[6].

The results of Table A demonstrate that pattern vision can be tested in newborn infants by recording differential visual attention; these and other results call for a revision of traditional views that the visual world of the infant is initially formless or chaotic and that we must learn to see configurations[7].

References and notes for Reading A

1   See for example, Evelyn Dewey, *Behaviour Development in Infants*, (Columbia University Press, New York, 1935); K. C. Pratt, in *Manual of Child Psychology*, L. Carmichael (ed.) (Wiley, New York, 1954); B. Spock, *Baby and Child Care* (Pocket Books, New York, 1957).

2   R. L. Fantz, J. M. Ordy, M. S. Udelf, *J. Comp. Physiol. Psychol.* 55, 907 (1962); R. L. Fantz, *Psychol. Rec.* 8, 43 (1958).

3   R. L. Fantz, *Sci. Am.* 204, No. 5, 66 (1961).

4   High reliability of a similar technique, using the same criterion of fixation, was shown with older infants (1). Since eye movements are less coordinated and fixations less clear-cut in newborn infants, a further check of the response measurement is desirable; I plan to do this by photographic recordings.

5   I chose the targets for their expected attention value for the older infants of the earlier study; this may be different for newborn subjects: response to the newsprint may be decreased by less acute vision (although some patterning would be visible without resolution of individual letters); 'bulls-eye' elicited strong differential attention only over 2 months of age in another study (3); and is preferred to red and yellow by newborns. The face pattern might for these reasons have a relative advantage for newborns.

6   F. Stirnimann, *Ann. Paediat*, 163, 1 (1944).

7   Supported by research grant M-5284 from the National Institute of Mental Health. I am indebted to Booth Memorial Hospital for making the subjects available; to Major Purser, Caroline Holcombe, R.N., Dr. R.C. Lohrey, and other staff members for their co-operation; and to Isabel Fredericson for invaluable assistance.

Source: Fantz, R. L. (1963) 'Pattern vision in newborn infants', *Science*, vol. 140, pp. 296–7.

Reading B: Is face processing species-specific during the first year of life?

Olivier Pascalis – Department of Psychology, The University of Sheffield, Sheffield S10 2TP, UK. Michelle de Haan – Institute of Child Health, Developmental Cognitive Neuroscience Unit, University College London, London WC1N 2AP UK. Charles A. Nelson – Institute of Child Development, Department of Pediatrics, and Center for Neurobehavioral Development, University of Minnesota, Minneapolis, MN 55455, USA.

Between 6 and 10 months of age, the infant's ability to discriminate among native speech sounds improves, whereas the same ability to discriminate among foreign speech sounds decreases. Our study aimed to determine whether this perceptual narrowing is unique to language or might also apply to face processing. We tested discrimination of human and monkey faces by 6-month-olds, 9-month-olds, and adults, using the visual paired-comparison procedure. Only the youngest group showed discrimination between individuals of both species; older infants and adults only showed evidence of discrimination of their own species. These results suggest that the "perceptual narrowing" phenomenon may represent a more general change in neural networks involved in early cognition.

At first glance the development of the ability to recognize faces appears to follow a typical trajectory: rapid change during infancy, followed by more gradual improvement into adolescence (*1*). This pattern contrasts with some aspects of language development. For example, speech perception is characterized by a loss of ability with age, such that 4- to 6-month-olds can discriminate phonetic differences that distinguish syllables in both their native and unfamiliar languages, whereas 10- to 12-month-olds can only discriminate the phonetic variations used in their native language (*2, 3*). Here we describe a similar phenomenon for face recognition: Specifically, we demonstrate that 6-month-old infants are equally good at recognizing facial identity in both human and nonhuman primates, whereas 9-month-old infants and adults show a marked advantage for recognizing only human faces.

Nelson (*4*) has proposed that the ability to perceive faces narrows with development, due in large measure to the cortical specialization that occurs with experience viewing faces. In this view, the sensitivity of the face recognition system to differences in identity among the faces of one's own species will increase with age and with experience in processing those faces. By adulthood the extensive experience with human faces can be mentally represented as a prototype that is "tuned" to the face inputs most frequently observed (human faces), with individual faces encoded in terms of how they deviate from the prototype (*5*). Because infants begin to show evidence of forming face prototypes by 3 months of age (*6*), their face recognition should become more "human face specific" some time after this. This leads to the prediction that younger infants, who possess less experience with faces than older infants and adults, should be better than older infants or adults at discriminating between individual faces of other species.

This hypothesis is indirectly supported by several lines of research. For example, human adults are far more accurate in recognizing individual human than monkey faces; the opposite is true for monkeys (*7*). Such species-specificity may be due to the differential expertise in the two groups: monkeys are more familiar with monkey than human faces, whereas humans are more familiar with human than monkey faces. Human infants, of course, likely have no experience with monkey faces and relatively little experience with human faces. This may confer upon them a more broadly tuned face recognition system and, in turn, an advantage in recognizing facial identity in general (i.e., regardless of species). This prediction is supported by a preliminary study (8) in which it was demonstrated using event-related potentials (ERPs) that young infants, but not adults, could discriminate monkey face identity across changes in facial orientation. A second ERP study examined the influence of stimulus inversion, a manipulation that in behavioral studies impairs adults' recognition of identity of human faces more than objects (9). In adults, inversion affected only the processing of human faces and not monkey faces, whereas in 6-month-olds, inversion affected the ERPs similarly for human and monkey faces (10). This suggests that infants were processing facial identity in the two species comparably. It is noteworthy that this was not because they failed to detect the difference between the two species, as the early-latency sensory components of the ERP differed for human and monkey faces for both ages. None of these studies directly tested the discrimination abilities of older and younger infants and adults in the same experimental procedure. We compared the ability of 6- and 9-month-old infants and adults to process human and monkey faces with the same visual paired-comparison procedure. We hypothesized that if face recognition follows the same developmental pattern as language, the ability to process other species' faces will be present only in the youngest age group studied. A similar development (tuning period) for face recognition and for language may indicate a more general sensitive or tuning period for various cognitive functions. A visual paired-comparison procedure (VPC) was used to assess recognition in both infants and adults. VPC indexes the relative interest in the members of a pair of visual stimuli made of one novel item and one item already seen in a prior familiarization period. Recognition is inferred from the participant's tendency to fixate the novel stimulus significantly longer. The stimuli were colored pictures (Fig. 1) of human Caucasian (male and female faces from our collection) and monkey faces (*Macaca fascicularis*) [details of materials and methods (11)].

Eleven adult participants with no special expertise in monkey face recognition were tested (11). For human face stimuli, the average looking time toward the novel stimulus during the 5-s recognition tests was significantly longer (2.79 s) than that toward the familiar stimulus (1.63 s) (paired two-tailed t test, $t = 3.93$, df = 10; $P < 0.01$). By contrast, for monkey face stimuli, participants looked as long at the novel stimulus (2.42 s) as at the familiar stimulus (2.31 s) (paired two-tailed t test, $t = 0.30$, df = 10; $P > 0.05$).

Infant participants were 30 healthy, full-term 6-month-old infants and 30 healthy, full term 9-month-old infants. No differences were found in the amount of time required to reach the familiarization time between age groups nor between species of face (11). In 6-month-olds, for human face stimuli, the average looking time toward the novel stimulus during the 10-s recognition test for human face stimuli was significantly longer (4.55 s) than that toward the familiar face (3.57 s) (paired two-tailed t test, $t = 2.67$, df = 14; $P < 0.05$). During the parallel test for monkey face stimuli, 6-month-olds looked at the novel face significantly longer (4.04 s) than at the familiar face (2.31 s) (paired two-tailed t test, $t = 3.78$, df = 14; $P < 0.05$). During the 10-s test for human face stimuli, 9-month-old infants looked significantly longer toward the novel stimulus (4.50 s) than toward the familiar stimulus (3.63 s) (paired two-tailed t test, $t = 3.44$, df = 14; $P < 0.05$). In contrast, for monkey face stimuli,

9-month-olds looked as long at the novel stimulus (3.86 s) as at the familiar stimulus (3.74 s) (paired two-tailed t test, $t = 0.35$, df = 14; $P > 0.05$).

Our results with adults support our prediction and are consistent with prior findings (7). It is important to note that this failure to recognize monkey face identity is not due to the lack of explicit instruction to do so. Our previous work shows that even in a classic forced-choice task, human adults are worse at recognizing monkey faces (55%) than human faces (73%) (12).

The infants' results support our predictions: 9-month-olds showed a pattern similar to that of adults, whereas 6-month-olds showed a preference for the novel facial identity both when tested with human faces and with monkey faces. The results of 6-month-olds and adults are also consistent with previous electrophysiological studies showing a difference in the specificity of face processing between these ages (8, 10). Our experiments support the hypothesis that the perceptual window narrows with age and that during the first year of life the face processing system is tuned to a human template (4). This early adjustment does not rule out the possibility that later in life individuals can learn how to discriminate a new class of stimuli on a perceptual basis (13). As is the case for speech perception, our evidence with face processing indicates the existence of an early tuning period that is likely dependent on experience. Although it is difficult to compare directly the tuning of speech perception with the tuning of face perception, there may be overlap between these systems. By 3 months of age infants are already relating these two types of information, as they are able to associate faces with voices (14). Systems for processing faces and for processing speech may thus develop in parallel, with a similar timing and a mutual influence. One possibility is that there is a general perceptuo-cognitive tuning apparatus that is not specific to a single modality and that can be described as an experience-expectant system [for discussion see (15)]. Alternatively, the concordance in age may simply be a developmental coincidence, thus reflecting a modality-specific, experience-dependent process. Distinguishing between these views will be facilitated by further developmental and comparative studies.

Figure 1 Examples of stimuli used (11).

References and Notes for Reading B

1   M. de Haan in *Handbook of Developmental Cognitive Neuroscience*, M. Luciana, C. A. Nelson, Eds. (MIT Press, Cambridge, MA, 2001) pp. 381–398.

2   M. Cheour *et al. Nature Neurosci.* 1, 351 (1998).

3   P. K. Kuhl, K. A. Williams, F. Lacerda, K. N. Stevens, *Science* **255**, 606 (1992).

4   C. A. Nelson, *Infant Child Dev.* **10**, 3 (2001).

5   T. Valentine, *Q. J. Exp. Psychol. A Hum. Exp. Psychol.* **43**, 161 (1991).

6   M. de Haan, M. H. Johnson, D. Maurer, D. I. Perrett *Cogn. Dev.* **16**, 659 (2001).

7   O. Pascalis, J. Bachevalier, *Behav. Process.* **43**, 87 (1998).

8   C. A. Nelson, in *Developmental Neurocognition: Speech and Face Processing in the First Year of Life*, B. de Boysson-Bardies, S. de Schonen, P. Jusczyk, P. MacNeilage, J. Morton, Eds. (Kluwer Academic Publishers, Dordrecht, Netherlands, 1993), pp. 165–178.

9   R. K. Yin, *J. Exp. Psychol.* **81**, 141 (1969).

10 M. de Haan, O. Pascalis, M. H. Johnson, *J. Cogn. Neurosci.* **14**, 199 (2002).

11 Materials and methods are available as supporting material on *Science* Online (see below).

12 O. Pascalis, M. Coleman, R. Campbell, (2000) *Cognitive Neuroscience Abstract Book*, Seventh Annual Meeting of the Cognitive Neuroscience Society, San Francisco, CA, 10 April 2000 (Cognitive Neuroscience Society, MIT Press, Cambridge, MA, 2000), p. 76.

13 I. Gauthier, M. J. Tarr, A. W. Anderson, P. Skudlarski, J. C. Gore, *Neurosci.* **2**, 568 (1999).

14 H. Brookes *et al, Infant Child Dev.* **10**, 75 (2001).

15 W. T. Greenough, J. E. Black, in *Developmental Behavioural Neuroscience: The Minesota Symposia on Child Psychology,* M. R. Gunnar, C. A. Nelson, Eds. (Lawrence Erlbaum, Hillsdale, NJ, 1992) pp. 155–200.

Supporting Online Material

www.sciencemag.org/cgi/content/full/296/5571/1321/DC1

Source: Pascalis, O., de Haan, M. and Nelson, C. (2002) 'Is face processing species-specific during the first year of life?', Science, vol. 296, pp. 1321–3.

Chapter 4
Early cognitive development

Dennis Bancroft and Emma Flynn

Contents

Learning outcomes

After you have studied this chapter you should be able to:

1   describe the development of object permanence;
2   provide an account of research into the development of children's ability to imitate;
3   use your knowledge of (1) and (2) to illustrate the differences between the interactionist and nativist positions;
4   explain the importance of representation for human life and activity;
5   understand how children's use of models develops;
6   use the investigations presented in the chapter to illustrate some of the techniques used by psychologists to investigate the origins of thought in infants.

1   Introduction

This chapter considers the origins and development of children's early thinking, examining the relationships between perception (discussed in Chapter 3), cognition and behaviour. To do this, we will focus on three aspects of early development. The first is infants' understanding of objects, which Piaget regarded as the essential basis of a child's cognitive system. As an adult, you know that the book you are now reading will continue to exist even when you cannot see it because it is covered by other papers on your desk or it is in your bag or you move into the kitchen to make a cup of tea. You can plan your activities with respect to the book safe in the knowledge of its continuing existence. But there was a time when, as an infant, you did not see the objects around you as having that permanent status. If objects disappeared from view you behaved as though they no longer existed. It has been argued that developing an awareness of the permanence and individual identity of objects is one of the major achievements of the early part of a child's life and for this reason is worthy of study (Butterworth, 1981). When a child understands that objects continue to exist even when not visible or when partially visible, then that child has a basis for mental activities such as planning and prediction. Also since *people* comprise a particular set of 'objects' one might suppose that understanding of this kind would be an important basis for social relationships. This relates to the second topic which explores one aspect of the ability of infants to respond in a special way to people, as distinct from other physical objects in their environment – in this instance the development of the ability to imitate. Chapter 3 touched upon the question of whether infants are born able to imitate or whether this is something that develops in the early months of life. This chapter will consider this discussion in more detail in terms of social development.

By discovering how imitation develops and how children represent objects we begin to comprehend the development of children's ability to hold representations of the world in mind and how they understand changing stimuli in the environment. This research addresses questions such as 'How long do representations stay in a child's mind?', 'Do they fade quickly or can the representations be recalled after a few hours, or even a full day?'.

The final section describes a later development in the infant's use of representation: the ability to use models as representations of the real world. Although this ability develops late in infancy it relies heavily on earlier developments. For example, you may hold in mind a picture of a book that is lying underneath a pile of papers: a simple representation-to-object link. However, other representation-to-object connections are more complex. A photograph of an apple is an external, tangible representation of an object. Nevertheless, you understand that you are dealing with a representation of an object and not the real thing; you know, for example, that you cannot eat the apple in the photograph. We are dealing, then, with two representations: one of the object of interest (i.e. the apple), and one of the external form of representation, (i.e. the photograph).

In exploring these important aspects of early cognitive development psychologists face some of the same methodological problems that were highlighted in the previous chapter. For example, cognitive processes cannot be observed directly, but must be *inferred* by observing what infants do in their normal relations with the world and by using this as evidence of their understanding. In practice, this natural observation is supplemented by research that presents children of differing ages with scenarios carefully designed to answer questions about the form and limits of their understanding. This is not always an easy task and you will notice in much of what follows how imaginative investigators can be and how rarely unambiguous evidence is obtained.

A number of the activities included in this chapter encourage you to reflect on the significance of the outcomes of the research studies described when it comes to making sense of the behaviour and understanding of infants. Some of the activities will also ask you to evaluate the techniques used to investigate this understanding. You may find it helpful to keep notes in a way that will ultimately allow you to compare the ages at which certain forms of understanding become apparent and under what conditions. You may also identify ways of refining and improving the procedures described.

During the course of the chapter you will become increasingly aware of the contrasting interpretations from the interactionist and nativist positions. Note these as they arise and assimilate them into the picture that develops through the book.

2   Understanding objects

If a 4-year-old child drops a ball that then rolls out of sight they usually try to retrieve it and may even move objects in the process. This behaviour demonstrates knowledge that objects continue to exist even when they cannot be seen. Infants under 6 months old behave quite differently. They do not undertake any search and appear to forget about the ball; behaviour which suggests that they do not understand that the ball continues to exist when it is out of sight. If this is true, then there are some important questions for psychologists to investigate:

(a) What do infants know about objects?

(b) When do children come to know what we as adults know about objects?

(c) If infants do not have adult understanding, how does this understanding develop?

2.1 Piaget: a starting point

As with many areas of developmental psychology it is the work of Jean Piaget that provides our starting point (see Chapter 2). On the basis of his investigations (e.g. Piaget and Inhelder, 1969), Piaget asserted that in the early months of life infants behaved as if they thought that an object that they could no longer see had ceased to exist. In addition he reported that infants gradually developed the knowledge that objects continue to exist while out of sight as a result of their various chance explorations, so that by about 8 or 9 months they would look for objects which had 'disappeared'.

In order to understand Piaget's claims it is important to know how he obtained his evidence. This section focuses on his studies of the first 2 years of a child's life, the period that coincides with the *sensori-motor stage* (see Chapter 2, Section 4.3).

Figure I   Responses of babies to a hidden object.

In these investigations Piaget examined how children responded when an object which was initially visible was then hidden from sight. He showed the child an attractive toy in the manner shown in Figure 1, and once he had gained the child's attention, placed the toy on a flat surface within easy reach and covered it with a soft cloth. Sometimes the toy was completely covered by the cloth and sometimes it was only partially covered, so that some of it was still visible. Piaget then recorded the child's actions. This procedure was repeated regularly over the first year of the child's life in order to observe any changes in behaviour when the toy was covered up.

Piaget noted that, even though the infants by 6–7 months of age were capable of the actions necessary to retrieve the toy, had their attention focused on it and had seen it being hidden, they made no attempt to retrieve it. As the months passed there came a point at which the child would retrieve the toy if part of it was still visible but not if the toy was completely hidden. Finally, at about

9 months of age, children would move the cloth and retrieve the toy even if it had been completely hidden. The explanation that Piaget offered was that for the younger infants the object had, in effect, *ceased to exist* once it was covered over. The understanding that an object continues to exist even when out of sight is called 'object permanence'. His observations suggested that an understanding that objects continue to exist even when not visible develops in stages.

Piaget's findings were based on detailed observations of a few children and in this way he was able to produce data that were rich in quality and allowed comparisons to be made between the behaviours of the same children at different ages. The small size of his sample has raised questions about whether these results are true of children in general. However, the many researchers who have since adopted Piaget's experimental procedures have produced similar results in terms of the ages and stages at which object permanence develops. In Piaget's description of infants' cognitive development this understanding of the nature of objects has a very important place. Indeed it is sometimes considered to be *the* major accomplishment of the first year of life, since understanding that objects have an independent, permanent existence is clearly essential for many aspects of life.

2.2   Expectation as a clue to understanding

The evidence so far offers strong support for Piaget's notion of stages in the development of children's understanding of objects. Another possible explanation of what he observed is that the younger children were just unable to co-ordinate their actions. Although infants under 9 months of age can both reach and grasp, it may be impossible for them to produce these actions together. This would mean that although the younger infants in Piaget's experiments understood that the toy existed, they could not retrieve it because they could not co-ordinate the actions required to remove the cloth.

Inspired by Piaget's work, several investigators have sought to identify what infants know about the existence of objects. For example, Bower *et al.* (1971) devised a number of tasks to investigate object permanence without making demands on infants' physical co-ordination. They reasoned that while infants might have some difficulty in co-ordinating their reaching and grasping behaviour, they had good control over their visual system so an experiment was devised that made use of that fact.

Children of about 2 months of age were positioned in such a way that they could see a toy train moving from one end of a length of track to the other, passing behind a screen placed half way along the route (Figure 2). Part of the procedure involved stopping the train behind the screen and when that happened the direction of the child's gaze was recorded. If the child had no understanding that the train continued to exist when it was behind the screen then there should be no specific direction for his or her gaze. However, if the infants did understand that the train continued to exist while behind the screen it was predicted that their gaze should follow along the direction of the track, as they would expect the train to emerge from the screen. With respect to Piaget's findings, the results were surprising. Once the train had disappeared behind the screen, the children looked at the part of the track that it would have reached had it not stopped. Children of only 2 months would follow the progress of the train, and appear to anticipate its reappearance from behind the screen. In a variation of this procedure, children were shown one object disappearing behind the screen and a different object appearing from the other side. In this case their pattern of gaze did not follow the path of motion smoothly, but was apparently disrupted by the appearance of the new object.

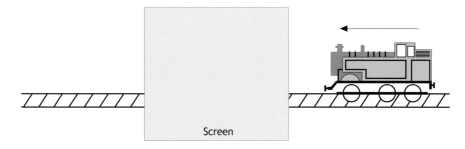

Screen

Figure 2   A toy train moving along a track towards a screen.

Activity 1   *The disappearing train*

Allow about
10 minutes

This activity invites you to consider the implications of Bower et al.*'s findings for Piaget's account of the emergence of object permanence.*

How do Bower's *et al.*'s findings prompt a rethinking of Piaget's conclusions? Just as Bower investigated an alternative explanation for Piaget's findings, can you suggest any explanations for the way that the children behaved in Bower's study that are different from his own?

Comment

Bower concluded that in order to anticipate the reappearance of the train from behind the screen, the child must know that the train continues to exist even when it is out of sight.

To be disconcerted by the appearance of a different object implies that the children were able to recognize the change. In other words they had retained a *memory* of the initial object even after it had disappeared and could tell that the new object did not conform to that memory.

However, there is at least one possible alternative explanation for these findings. Perhaps, once the children had begun to follow or 'track' the object they continued this motion, not because they expected the object to reappear but because they have a predisposition to track the path of moving objects. This would give the appearance of anticipation, but would not indicate understanding of the object's continued existence.

In order to test out this alternative explanation Bower introduced a refinement into the procedure, a refinement which proved to be instructive (Bower and Paterson, 1973). In the new procedure the train was stopped just *before* it disappeared from view. If the children were actually tracking the train's movement then their gaze should remain on the stationary, visible train. What happened, though, was that the children's gaze continued to move along the track, just as it had done in the earlier experiment. This indicated that in the earlier experiment the pattern of the child's gaze was not an indication of anticipation of the train's movement and therefore did not show an understanding of the train's continuing existence when concealed. Rather, it was a predisposition to continue to look along the path of a moving object even when that object had stopped.

2.3   The violation of expectations

One of the research tools introduced in the previous chapter was the ingenious yet simple habituation technique, which relies on the fact that children, like adults, lose interest if they look at the same object or event over and over again. When children are exposed to repetitions of the same event they begin to pay less and less attention to it. This loss of interest suggests that the children have committed the object or event to memory, since in order to know that something is familiar you have to have a memory that you have seen it before.

Another procedure used by researchers investigating early cognitive development is known as the 'violation of expectations' technique. This is similar to the habituation technique but relies on the principle that people spend longer looking at events that they believe to be impossible. This is true even when they have seen the event before and it is no longer novel. For example, if children understand that when objects are dropped they fall to the ground rather than float in mid-air, then they spend longer looking at 'floating' events even if these events have been seen previously. In research with infants, they are familiarized with a certain event and once habituated to it they are shown two variants of it. One of the variants involves a possible event that is different from the original event, and the other variant is an impossible event, which is the same as the original event but made 'impossible' by some new feature.

These two techniques were used by Baillargeon and her colleagues. They showed 5-month-old infants a sheet of card lying flat on a table (Baillargeon *et al.*, 1985). As the infants watched, the sheet moved upwards and away from them, rotating along one edge in an action resembling the raising of a drawbridge (Figure 3a). Once it had become vertical the drawbridge continued to rotate until it lay flat on the table once more, having travelled through 180 degrees. This procedure was repeated until the infant had become habituated. Baillargeon then placed a wooden block on the table, clearly visible to the infant, in a position where the drawbridge would make contact with it having travelled about two-thirds of its path (see Figure 3b). There were two conditions in the experiment. In one the drawbridge stopped after travelling 120 degrees just as would be expected as the block impeded its progress (the 'possible event' shown in Figure 3biii). In the other, the experimenter discreetly removed the block once the drawbridge was vertical and screening it from the infant's gaze (Figure 3cii) and then it made the full 180 degree rotation (Figure 3ciii). This condition was referred to as the 'impossible event' as, in one interpretation of events, the existence of the block should have impeded the progress of the drawbridge beyond 120 degrees. The investigators measured the amount of time the infants spent looking at these two contrasting events.

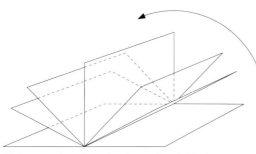

(a) Preparations (introduction to drawbridge)

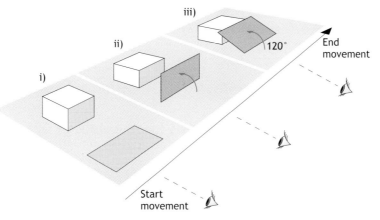

(b) Possible event
   i)   Starting point — the block is visible on the table and the drawbridge is flat.
   ii) Mid-point — the drawbridge is vertical, obscuring the block from view.
   iii) Final point — the drawbridge has rotated 120°, resting on the block.

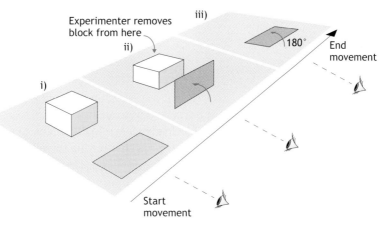

Figure 3
(a) Preparation
(habituation to
the drawbridge);
(b) possible test
event and
(c) impossible
test event.

(c) Impossible event
   i)   Starting point — the block is visible on the table and the drawbridge is flat.
   ii) Mid-point — the drawbridge is vertical, the block is removed out of view of the child.
   iii) Final point — the drawbridge is flat on the table having rotated 180°.

Activity 2   Predicting outcomes

Allow about
5 minutes

This activity will help you to test your understanding by predicting infant responses in an experiment.

From what you have read so far, how do you think the infant would react in Baillargeon's experiment outlined above and why?

Comment

It is already established that infants prefer to look at novel happenings. The relative amount of time spent looking at each of these two presentations indicates whether they found one more interesting than the other. If the infants are familiar with the 180 degree rotation (as they were) they should find the drawbridge which stopped after 120 degrees of rotation more 'interesting' and therefore spend more time looking at it. Yet, as you have learned in this chapter it is also known that children like to look at events that they believe to be impossible even when they have seen that event occur before.

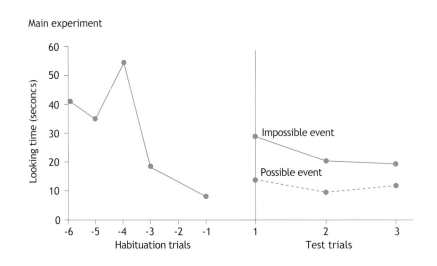

Figure 4   Looking times of participants (from Baillargeon *et al.*, 1985).

Figure 4 shows, on the left, the decline in interest during the habituation phase of the experiment and, on the right, the difference in attention paid subsequently to the 'possible' and 'impossible' events. The infants spent more time watching the 180-degree rotation, even though they were familiar with it.

One interpretation of this result might be that the infants were interested in the fact that the drawbridge could apparently pass through a solid object. In other words, perhaps these 5-month-old infants were like adults in that they understood that the block remains an obstacle to the progress of the drawbridge even though they are unable to see it because as the drawbridge rises it obscures the object. Therefore these infants apparently acknowledged the continuing existence of an object that they could not see.

Could it be, though, that the infants spent more time watching the 180-degree rotation because it took longer for the drawbridge to travel the full distance? The investigators thought of this possibility and for some trials placed the block to one side of the drawbridge so that it was still there but did not impede the rotation. Now the infants looked at the quicker, 120-degree rotation and the longer, 180-degree rotation for equal amounts of time, thus showing no preference. This demonstrated that the difference in looking time for the possible and impossible events was not due to the length of the procedure (see Figure 5).

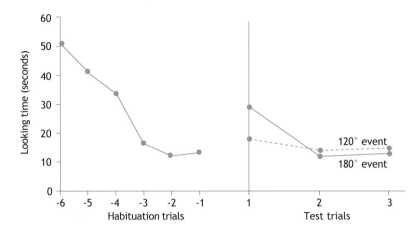

Figure 5 Habituation trials and looking times for displaced block (from Baillargeon *et al.*, 1985).

Once again, looking times declined during the habituation trials from an average of 50 seconds to an average of 12 seconds. However, the amount of time then spent looking at the alternative test presentations was very similar.

The infants in this study behaved in a way consistent with two important ideas: (i) that they 'believed' the block continued to exist even though it was completely obscured by the drawbridge and (ii) even more surprising, the infants' behaviour suggested that they 'understood' that the presence of an object that they could not see constituted an obstacle to the progress of the screen.

Baillargeon (1986) conducted a further investigation of this notable phenomenon. Infants aged from 6 to 8 months were shown a toy car, a slope, a length of flat track and a screen coming down on the track. As illustrated in Figure 6a, the infants saw the car roll down the slope, run along the flat track, disappear behind the screen and then appear on the other side. They were shown this event several times until, after a while, they became habituated to it and so less interested in it.

At this point the apparatus was altered in full view of the infants. First the screen was removed so that the whole extent of the track was visible. Next, a box was placed either on the track (Figure 6b) or by the side of the track (Figure 6c). The screen was then replaced, so that the box was no longer visible to the child. Each infant was shown the toy car rolling down the slope again. In each case the vehicle moved behind the screen and out the other side, even for event (a), as the box had been secretly removed from the track. Adults, who know about objects and obstructions, would be surprised to see the car move freely in condition (a) when there is an obstruction in its way. Yet adults would not be surprised when the car reappears in condition (b), as the box is not on the track. But how did the infants behave?

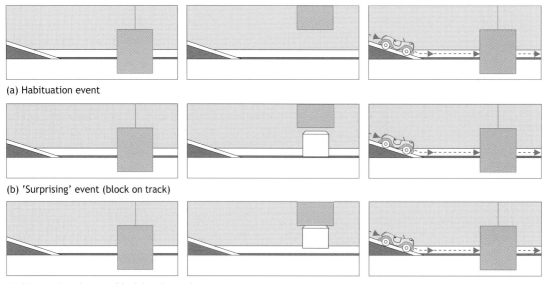

(a) Habituation event

(b) 'Surprising' event (block on track)

(c) 'Unsurprising' event (block beside track)

Figure 6   Habituation and test events (from Baillargeon, 1986).

Baillargeon showed that 6–8-month-old infants behaved in a similar way to adults. The infants paid more attention to the event when they had been shown the block on the track and less attention when they had been shown the block beside the track. Baillargeon concluded the infants showed a preference for the impossible event rather than the possible event. This work has been replicated with even younger children. Baillargeon and DeVos (1991) demonstrated that infants as young as 3½ months were surprised to see the car reappear when they knew that a hidden object was blocking its path. Such results imply that the infants understood that:

(a) the box continued to exist, in its same location, after it was hidden (occluded) by the screen;

(b) the car continued to exist, and pursued its trajectory, after it disappeared behind the screen; and

(c) the car could not roll through the space occupied by the box.

More recent work by Aguiar and Baillargeon (2002) has shown a number of steady changes in the understanding of objects in the first few months of life. For example, 2½ month olds expect any object to be hidden when behind any occluder, irrespective of the relative size and shape of the two objects. However, by 3 months infants are more sophisticated in their thinking and realize that objects become temporarily visible when passing behind an occluder with an opening in its lower edge. But it is only by 3½ months that infants can integrate factors, such as the height of the occluder and the size of the object. Before

3½ months children expect both tall and short objects to be hidden by a short occluder, but by 3½ months children realize that only tall occluders will fully hide a tall object. So, whereas Piaget regarded the realization that objects continue to exist even when hidden from view as the main developmental task for young infants, Aguiar and Baillargeon claim that, from the start, infants recognize that objects continue to exist when occluded.

2.4 Searching behaviour in the dark

One feature of the experiments described so far is that the procedures used to explore children's understanding of objects have become more complex. By contrast, Hood and Willatts (1986) carried out a study to examine similar issues, but using a simple procedure involving a Christmas tree decoration, surrounded with tinsel and mounted on the end of a short wooden rod.

The participants were thirteen infants, aged 5 months. Each child sat in a chair with the experimenter crouching in front of it. Initially the eye-catching object was presented directly in front of the child to arouse interest. It was then removed and the mother, who was seated behind the child, restrained the child's hands by holding them. Three trials were then carried out. For one of these the object was presented to the left, for another it was presented to the right and one of the trials involved the object not being presented. The order of presentation of the three trials was randomized across the children. On the object-present trials the object was presented to one side of the infant within the infant's reach and when the infant was attending to the object the room lights were switched off and the object was removed. After a brief delay the mother released the infant's hands. For 25 seconds the experimenter and mother remained silent, while the child's behaviour was recorded using a camera with infra-red recording ability. After the 25 seconds the lights were switched on again. On the no-object-present trials, the experimenter showed the child the object in front of them, the experimenter then removed the object, while the room lights were still on. The mother restrained the child's hands for a period of 10 seconds until the room lights were switched off and the child's behaviour was again recorded.

When the researchers analysed the video tapes using strict criteria for what constituted reaching towards the object they found that the infants not only regularly reached out, they also did so more often in the direction where the object had been seen than in any other direction.

Table 1 presents some of the data from the thirteen infants. The second column shows the average number of times each infant reached to the object's new position after the lights had been switched off. The third column gives the average number of reaches made by each infant when the object had been removed from the midpoint before the lights went out.

Table 1   **Mean number of reaches by individual infants when object present and not present**

Participant	Moves (object present)	Moves (no object present)
1	0.50	1.00
2	2.00	0.00
3	2.75	3.25
4	6.25	2.50
5	0.75	1.00
6	2.50	2.00
7	0.50	0.00
8	3.00	2.50
9	1.25	0.50
10	1.00	1.00
11	0.50	0.75
12	2.50	2.25
13	1.00	0.00
Mean	1.88	1.33

Source: adapted from Hood and Willatts, 1986, p. 60.

When inspecting the data and drawing conclusions it is important to understand the significance of the third column which provides an indication of the infants' behaviour under 'normal' conditions where there is no manipulation (so called 'base-line' data). This is important as some infants may make more reaches in a certain direction and not another, irrespective of whether the toy is present or not. It is only by comparing behaviour under the experimental condition, (i.e. when the toy is present) with their base-line behaviour, (i.e. when the toy is not present) that any meaningful comparison can be made. This provides what is referred to as the 'within-participant' comparison. A 'between-participant' comparison can also be made by comparing performance across children (within a single column).

Activity 3   *Analysing the data*

Allow about 10 minutes

This activity will provide you with experience of analysing and interpreting data.

Taking account of the comments above, look at the data in Table 1 and make notes on your interpretation of it. What do you conclude from comparisons of data in columns two and three? What about the between-participant comparisons in each of those columns?

Comment

There is a great deal of variability within both the second and third columns. For example, when the object is present (column two) participant 4 reaches, on average, over six times towards the object, whereas four participants (1, 5, 7 and 11) reach less than once over a number of trials. Nevertheless, beyond this variability, a comparison of the means at the foot of columns two and three shows a difference that is statistically significant and allows Hood and Willatts to observe that 'Five-month-old infants reached more to the place where they had seen an object than to a ... place where no object had been shown, even though the room was in darkness and nothing at all was visible.' (Hood and Willatts, 1986, p. 61).

The conclusion which seems to follow is that *some* infants of 5 months of age have an understanding of the continuing existence of objects which have become lost to sight.

▲

However, Shinskey and Munakata (2003) argued that although infants appear to search for objects hidden by darkness at an earlier age than they search for hidden objects in light, this may be due to the methodological differences of the two search tasks. The two sorts of experiments differ on a number of points including whether the hidden object made a sound and the number of familiarization trials with visible objects and these may account for the difference in performance. However, when they conducted a controlled comparison of 6½-month-old infants' search behaviour for a toy hidden in the dark or under a cloth in the light, their results supported those of Hood and Willatts (1986).

2.5   Memory and object permanence

Although Piaget found that children aged 8–9 months were able to retrieve a toy that had been concealed in front of them, he also noticed that after that age they still had difficulty retrieving the toy under certain circumstances. In a variant of the well-established procedure, Piaget placed *two* cloths side by side in front of children; this time aged 9–12 months. As before, their attention was attracted to a small toy which was then hidden under one of the cloths (location A). Infants older than 9 months typically found the toy. After a number of such trials the toy was hidden under the other cloth (location B) in full view of the child. Typically the children would watch the toy being hidden in the new location (B) and then turn back to cloth A and look for the toy under it. Sometimes the children would investigate cloth B, but unless the toy was immediately obtained they would turn and search under cloth A. This error is known as the 'A-not-B error' and is a *perseveration error.*

Perseveration error
When a person repeats an action which they have previously performed even when that action then becomes inappropriate in the current context.

This finding was taken as further evidence of Piaget's view of infants as egocentric. Piaget used this term in a particular way to mean that infants do not make a clear distinction between objects in the world and their own actions on them. Objects are not understood to exist independently. In this case Piaget suggests that the infant connects the rediscovery of the object under the first cloth (A) with his or her own actions in lifting the cloth. The infant is said to reason thus: 'if I wish to find it again I must do what I did before'.

This evidence is incompatible with earlier findings which suggested that 5-month-old children understand that objects continue to exist even when not visible. Why is it that children aged 8–9 months, who understand that objects still exist when hidden and see an object being hidden in a particular location, nevertheless search for the object in the wrong location?

This conundrum was investigated by Harris (1973) who repeated Piaget's experiment but with a significant modification. As before, the children were shown an object hidden under cloth A and allowed to retrieve it. This happened several times. They were then shown the object being hidden under cloth B. On some occasions the infants were allowed to try to retrieve the object straight away, while on other occasions there was a delay of 5 seconds. Those infants who were able to begin their search straight away had no difficulty in retrieving the hidden object from under cloth B. However, those infants who were made to wait for 5 seconds before they were allowed to begin their search often went to cloth A for the toy. Harris's interpretation of these different outcomes (Harris, 1989) starts with the assertion that the infants see and understand that the object is hidden under cloth B. Those who are allowed to search for it immediately have no difficulty remembering where it is and looking in the correct location. However, the memory for the new hiding place is so fragile that if there is only a short delay before they are allowed to search and they then catch sight of cloth A, the new information is disrupted and replaced by the more established information based on the earlier trials.

This is a neat explanation since it is compatible with the findings that have been described so far. It explains a puzzle without returning to the Piagetian position, that children cannot detach objects from their own actions upon those objects.

Harris's explanation in terms of the fragility of infant memory may appear compelling, but it was soon called into question by an ingenious experiment that followed the same procedure except that the covers at points A and B were transparent (Butterworth, 1977). This meant that there were no demands on memory as the toy was always visible. Butterworth found that the infants were still likely to make the mistake of searching for the toy under the transparent cover A even though it was visible throughout under cover B.

Butterworth's explanation identified a possible competition between two different ways of coding or memorizing the position of objects, which comes about when an object is moved from one place to another. The first option is to memorize the position with respect to oneself, an 'egocentric' code. The alternative is to memorize the position of one object with respect to some other object, termed an 'allocentric' code. The argument runs like this: the children who make the A-not-B error do so because they have memorized the position of the toy in one of these ways, but they have memorized the position of its cover in the other way. The toy is moved to another position leaving the cover in place. Because only one of the objects has been moved, only one of the codes will be updated. If infant behaviour is governed by the unchanged code, then the infant may reach for the wrong place.

There is one final set of evidence related to object permanence. Diamond (1985) returned to the original task devised by Piaget and charted the development of 25 infants from the age of 7–12 months. Following Harris's earlier observation that children made the mistake of searching for a toy under the wrong cloth if there was a short delay between hiding it and being allowed to search for it, she varied the length of the delay at each age until the child began to make that error.

Activity 4   *Interpreting data*

Allow about
10 minutes

This activity provides more experience of analysing and interpreting data from research.

Figure 7 summarizes Diamond's results at each of the ages that the infants were tested. The thick blue line joins the average delay required at each age before they began to make the A-not-B error. The vertical lines indicate the extent of the variation between the infants of the same age.

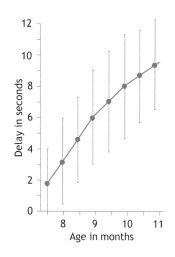

Figure 7   Delay at which the A-not-B error occurs by age (Diamond, 1985).

Study the data in Figure 7 and write a brief account of Diamond's findings.

Comment

Diamond found that the younger infants began to make errors if their search was delayed by as little as 3 seconds. As the children grew older so they became more able to cope with a longer delay. At 12 months of age the infants could manage a delay of 10 seconds between the object being hidden and carrying out a successful search.

Diamond proposed that when an object which has often been hidden under cloth A is now hidden under cloth B, the infants are faced with a choice. The information about the new hiding place is possessed by the children since they have just seen the object being hidden. This information is held in a part of the memory system that is used for holding temporary bits of information (short-term memory). It is known that people vary considerably in the efficiency with which they use this system and that children improve with age. It would not be surprising if infants in the first year of life were in the process of developing this ability. Diamond argues that 7-month-old children can hold information in this temporary store for only a brief period. As well as this temporary memory system, infants have developed the habit of finding the object under cloth A. The proposal is that when the information in the temporary memory system begins to fade, the established habit takes over and the infant looks for the object where it was previously found.

Diamond believes that A-not-B errors are caused by two factors: an inability to hold in memory the location of the desired object after a time delay, and the inability to inhibit an incorrect action which has become a habit. She claims that infants are capable of these two skills when they are required separately, but are unable to co-ordinate the two when a task requires that they are used together. She proposes that the ability to hold two representations in mind, and inhibit undesired actions, is the primary function of the frontal cortex, which is located at the very front of the brain. The frontal cortex does not fully develop until late childhood, and therefore young children have difficulty with tasks which require these skills. The evidence, summarized in Figure 7, shows that increasing memory demands for young children do increase the errors that they make. However, her account does not fully explain why children make errors when the memory demands are all but removed, for example, when transparent covers are used.

Summary of Section 2

- The findings that Piaget originally produced have proved remarkably robust although the interpretations he placed upon them have been strongly challenged by subsequent researchers.
- Some studies have shown that infants of 5 months of age behave in ways that are consistent with an understanding that things continue to exist even when they are no longer visible.
- The findings of investigations with younger infants are ambiguous but suggest that children as young as 2 months have some appreciation of the properties of objects.
- While infants may have some idea of the permanence of objects, keeping track of objects which move from place to place is a more difficult problem since it makes demands on various parts of their still developing cognitive system.
- Children's apparent lack of 'object permanence' can also be explained in terms of the development of short-term memory abilities.

3 People: the social object

Piaget was interested in the origins and development of children's understanding of their world. His starting position was that infants are born with a small repertoire of behaviours (reflexes) over which they have little or no control. Piaget considered that a child's ability to think and reason developed from this. One issue of particular interest to him was the development of children's ability to store experiences in memory. When a child can create such a store, it becomes possible to use memory of the past to influence or guide actions in the present; in other words to *think* and to reason.

Piaget believed that the ability to imitate showed the beginnings of the development of this memory. In other words, when infants see something and later on repeat the event for themselves, Piaget felt that one could be sure that they have 'coded' and 'stored' the earlier experience, and had access to it as a guide to their own behaviour.

Table 2 Piaget's stages of imitation in infancy

Levels of imitative development	Stages of imitative development	Approximate age (months)	Selected developments in imitation
Level 1	1	0–1	Imitation of crying
	2	1–4	Imitation of hand gestures (hand opening/closing)
	3	4–8	Imitation of actions-on-objects (hitting or banging an object)
Level 2	4	8–12	Facial imitation (mouth opening, tongue protrusion)
	5	12–18	Imitation of certain new behaviours never before performed by the infant
Level 3	6	18–24	Deferred imitation

Source: Butterworth, 1981, p. 88.

3.1 Imitating Piaget

A number of Piaget's ideas grew out of his day-to-day experiences of his own children, Jacqueline, Lucienne and Laurent. Like Darwin (Chapter 1) he kept careful records of his children's behaviour. The following example concerning tongue-poking reveals something of the technique that Piaget used, as well as his daughter's behaviour.

> OBS. 17 at 0;5 (2) [i.e. observation seventeen at five months and two days of age] J. put out her tongue several times in succession. I put mine out in front of her, keeping time with her gesture, and she seemed to repeat the action all the better. But it was only a temporary association. A quarter of an hour later, no suggestion on my part could induce her to begin again. There was the same negative reaction the next few days.
>
> At 0;6 (1) I waved goodbye, then put out my tongue, then opened my mouth and put my thumb into it. There was no reaction, since the first movement did not correspond to a known schema [see explanation below], and the others involved parts of her face which she could not see.

(Piaget, 1951, pp. 27–8)

This extract exemplifies two points that Piaget thought were very important. The first is that in the early stages of the development of imitation, children can only imitate actions that they are already able to perform and not new actions. The second point of difficulty for infants at this age is that they are unable to imitate actions that require them to use parts of their bodies which they cannot see, for example, most especially their own face.

Note that Piaget is using the term 'schema' here to refer to a pattern of actions or behaviours. So an older child with a schema for picking up flat rectangular objects (like 'Marmite soldiers') would 'know' the pattern of looking, reaching and grasping.

> OBS. 18. L at 0;6 (19), when she put out her tongue I imitated her, and mutual imitation followed, lasting at least five minutes. L. carefully watched my tongue and seemed to find a connection between her gesture and mine. But shortly afterwards, and on the following days, she failed to react to the stimulus.
>
> (Piaget, 1951, p. 28)

The point to notice here is that at 6 months 19 days Lucienne was able to play a part in this episode of mutual imitation. Piaget took the view that to be certain that a child can retain a memory and reproduce some behaviour, there should be a time lag. It is for this reason that he repeats the exercise on the following days and notes the lack of success. Some writers have thought that this insistence on a long delay between seeing some behaviour and reproducing it was rather too great and prevented a full recognition of infants' true abilities.

> OBS. 20. At 0;8 (9) I put out my tongue in front of J. ... At first J. watched me without reacting, but at about the eighth attempt she began to bite her lips as [she had done] before, and at the ninth and tenth she grew bolder, and thereafter reacted each time in the same way.
>
> The same evening her reaction was immediate: as soon as I put out my tongue she bit her lips.
>
> ... At 0;8 (13) she put out her tongue, biting as she did so. When I imitated her she seemed to imitate me in return, watching my tongue very carefully. But from the next day onwards and until 0;9 (1) she began to bite only her lips when I put out my tongue at her without her having done so. Biting the lips thus seemed to her the adequate response to every movement of someone else's mouth ...
>
> At 0;9 (2), however, J. put out her tongue and said *ba ... ba* at the same time. I quickly imitated her, and she began again, laughing. After only three or four repetitions, I put out my tongue without making any sound. J. looked at it attentively, moved her lips and bit them for a moment, then put out her tongue several times in succession without making any sound. After a quarter of an hour I began again, and then about half an hour later. Each time she again began to bite her lips, but a moment later distinctly put out her tongue.
>
> (Piaget, 1951, p. 31)

In this extract Piaget describes the appearance of behaviour that he would confidently describe as 'direct imitation'. This expression means the absence of delay between the demonstration presented to the child and the child's reproduction of the event. Infants are finally able to see some behaviour, store it and reproduce a version of it after an interval. This occurs at some point in the second year of life. In the following sections you will be able to compare the criteria for imitation adopted by Piaget with that used by other investigators.

3.2   A closer look at imitation

Piaget's observations were important evidence in the attempt to understand the mental abilities of infants. Recognition of this importance by developmental psychologists led to a number of attempts to replicate Piaget's findings. As is often the case in science, we can be more confident about a piece of evidence if several different investigators can reproduce it in separate enquiries.

As has already been noted, Piaget's study of the development of imitation was based on the development of his own three children. While there is no reason to suppose that these children were different from others, there is also no reason to suppose that their development was 'typical'. One study carried out in the USA sought to replicate Piaget's findings on imitation using a somewhat larger sample (see Research summary 1).

RESEARCH SUMMARY 1

A study of imitation

The earliest observations confirmed Piaget's report that in early imitation, infants would only produce actions that were already in their repertoire. They were unable to imitate an action that they had not already produced for themselves. Uzgiris and Hunt (1975) studied the development of twelve children from 1 month until they were 2 years old. In the middle of the first year children were seen to attempt to imitate quite complex behaviours, even though they did not always complete the action.

The next development, which was noticed between 9 and 12 months, involved the infants imitating behaviours which they were unable to see themselves doing. For example, if a baby imitates a wave, the baby can see both the original wave and the movement of their own arm. You might imagine that if babies are able to see their own attempts in this way then they are able to observe how close they have come to producing a good copy of the behaviour. In the case of tongue-poking, the baby is able to see the original behaviour but not their own attempt. It was Piaget's proposition that this form of 'unseen imitation' is a more sophisticated development.

Last, from 12 to 18 months infants are able to imitate novel actions. That is, they have reached a level of development such that they are able to match new visual experiences with new movements of their own.

This sequence of development is similar to that described by Piaget. This means that groups of children from America and Europe appear to produce similar sorts of behaviours as they develop. One important point to note is that the ability to imitate facial gestures seems to appear between 9 and 12 months.

No sooner had one group of investigators concluded that infants only become able to produce a particular behaviour by the end of the first year, than another group began to look for the same behaviour patterns occurring earlier.

 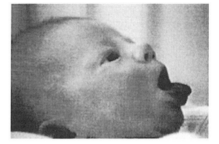

Figure 8   Infant imitation.

Meltzoff and Moore conducted a series of investigations into infant imitation beginning in 1977. Their findings excited a considerable amount of interest and comment, and are considered contentious by some psychologists due to their nativist stance. For this reason, their investigation is worth describing in some detail since it then becomes possible to see how the various criticisms apply

Meltzoff and Moore demonstrated four behaviours – tongue poking, lip protrusion, mouth opening and finger movement – to six infants who were between 12 and 21 days old at the start of the study. Each child was shown one of four gestures four times during a 15-second period, after which there was a space of 20 seconds when the investigator's face was immobile. During this time the infant was video-taped. The video tapes were played to six judges who were told that the infant had been shown one of four behaviours but were not told which one. (This arrangement leads to them being labelled 'blind' judges, because they were unaware of the details or aims of the experiment). Once they had watched the tape the judges were asked to say which of the four possible gestures had been demonstrated. One limitation with this procedure is that there was no item on the judges' list to indicate the possibility of no imitation. Without this possibility, the number of 'correct' guesses that occur by chance is increased. Such 'false positives' risk biasing the findings. On the basis of these ratings, Meltzoff and Moore concluded that the infants were able selectively to imitate the adult's behaviours shown to them (see Figure 9).

(a) Lip protrusion shown to infant

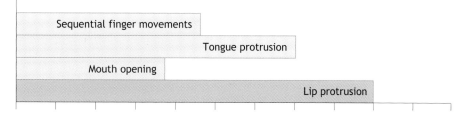

(b) Mouth opening shown to infant

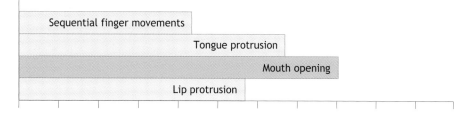

(c) Tongue protrusion shown to infant

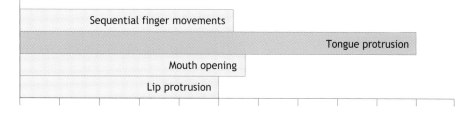

(d) Sequential finger movements shown to infant

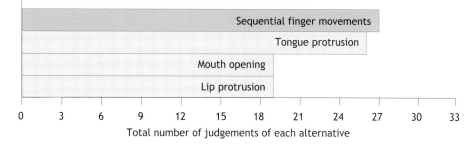

0   3   6   9   12   15   18   21   24   27   30   33
Total number of judgements of each alternative

Figure 9   Selective imitation by six infants (from Meltzoff and Moore, 1977).

These investigators reported another study which involved twelve 2-week-old infants. First they were shown an impassive adult face, followed by a 15-second demonstration of either tongue protrusion or mouth opening; they were then filmed for 2½ minutes, during which time the investigator's face was once again immobile. The procedure was then repeated so that the infants could be shown a behaviour which they had not yet been shown. Thus, for example, children saw either a demonstration session of tongue protrusion followed by a session of mouth opening, or of mouth opening followed by tongue protrusion. This allowed Meltzoff and Moore to discover whether the infants really were imitating the different actions or whether they were simply performing idiosyncratic actions to all demonstrations, for example, opening their mouth to all demonstrations. The video tapes were watched by an independent person whose task it was to count the number of infant tongue protrusions and mouth openings during each of the 2½ minute segments of film. As before, the judges did not know which of the two behaviours had been demonstrated by the adult, but they identified significantly more infant tongue protrusions in the film made following the adult demonstration of this behaviour, and more mouth openings in the film made following the adult demonstration of that behaviour. Once again, Meltzoff and Moore felt able to claim that their evidence was consistent with the idea that 2-week-old infants are capable of selective imitation.

Activity 5   *Questioning the evidence*

Allow about
10 minutes

This activity provides further experience of analysing and interpreting research data.

Figure 9 shows a summary of data from Meltzoff and Moore (1977). For each of the four behaviours that were shown to the infants there is a record of the number of judgements made as to which had been demonstrated, based on observations of the video tape of the infants. For ease of interpretation, the bar that corresponds to the behaviour actually demonstrated is shaded more heavily.

Look at the data in Figure 9 and, for each behaviour shown to the infants, compare how many judgements were correct with how many were incorrect. Look also at the extent to which the judgements increased when a particular behaviour was shown compared with the (incorrect) judgements of that behaviour in the other conditions.

For each shown behaviour consider whether the evidence supports the hypothesis that these infants were actually imitating the shown behaviours.

Other investigators have scrutinized the evidence produced by Meltzoff and Moore very carefully. If it can be accepted, we would have to agree that imitation is present from the earliest days of an infant's life. In examining a similar set of data based on twelve infants, Kaye (1982) has pointed out that between them the infants poked out their tongues on a total of 39 occasions after they had been shown an adult poking out a tongue. The infants also poked out their tongues on fifteen occasions after having seen an adult demonstrating mouth opening, and on another fifteen occasions after the presentation of an immobile face. Only a few of the infants produced any 'imitations' at all and some produced nothing. Therefore, although the differences are statistically significant, by looking at the total number of responses produced by the group of infants as a whole, one loses sight of, first, the low response rate and, second, the fact that several of the infants produced nothing at all.

   One issue to consider is the wisdom or otherwise of investigating children in groups and hoping to generalize, from the evidence thus obtained, about all children. Psychologists can sometimes appear to assume that children are similar, that they all develop in the same sort of way. However, there can be considerable individual variation in psychological development. If this is so, we should not be surprised to find children who do not do as we (and our theories) suppose.

Activity 6   Different research approaches

Allow about
10 minutes

This activity helps to clarify how differences in methodology can affect the generation of data and its interpretation.

Write a short account of the differences between the experimental approach adopted by Piaget, as described earlier in the chapter, and the approach adopted by Meltzoff and Moore (1977). Think about issues such as the number of participants, the experimental controls and the positive and the negative aspects of each approach.

Comment

A comparison between these two experimental approaches is very revealing. First, Piaget observed the behaviour of only a few children. This raises the question of whether his results were true of children in general. In contrast, Meltzoff and Moore recruited groups of children and placed them into different conditions, to try to establish the developmental changes that occur in children's imitative ability. Second, Piaget followed the development of the same children, repeating the experiments over months and years. This allowed the small changes that occurred in individual children's behaviour to be recorded, and removed the problem of the variability which occurs when making comparisons across groups of children, as children behave in a variety of ways even when in the same condition. This variability within conditions can make it difficult for psychologists to develop straightforward theories. Focusing on the development of only a few children as Piaget did allows a clearer theory to be developed, which can then be examined using larger groups of children. In contrast, Meltzoff and Moore compared larger groups of children of different ages to establish the changes in ability with age. Using groups is more representative than concentrating on a small number of children but often the data are reduced to average scores across groups and the variability of individual children's behaviour, which is often very revealing, is overlooked. One final benefit of considering groups of children is that by comparing children within different conditions, or at different ages, it is possible to see how children behave in different settings. Manipulating the conditions allows different theories to be investigated. For example, can young children only imitate behaviours for body parts that they can see, or can they successfully imitate behaviour using body parts which they cannot see?

Jacobson (1979) also produced evidence that contributes to the investigation of early imitation. Twenty-four infants were observed at the ages of 6, 10 and 14 weeks. They were shown a variety of objects and behaviours and their responses were video-taped. In addition to the tongue protrusion and finger movements used by Meltzoff and Moore, Jacobson presented the infants with a white ball and a felt-tipped pen, each of which were moved slowly towards the infant's mouth, and a ring which was moved up and down.

The stimulus of tongue protrusion was found by Jacobson to be the most effective means of getting the infants to poke out their tongues. However, her data showed that some of the other stimuli were almost as effective. She argued that if it is possible to have infants of this age respond to a pen or a ball moving towards them just as they did to a poking tongue, then one could not claim that the infants of this age selectively imitate.

Meltzoff and Moore (1983) produced more evidence in an attempt to address the criticisms that their earlier work attracted and to move the focus of their investigation down to even younger infants. Their motive was, in part, to discover the extent to which infants are born already possessing mental and physical abilities. The main problem that confronts those interested in this line of enquiry is that infants seem to be able to learn from very early on in life. An investigation of what infants can do at the age of some weeks is unable to answer the question of how much ability they were born with since it is possible that what they can demonstrate has been learned since birth. Accordingly, psychologists make considerable efforts to study very young infants which allow them to claim that what these infants can do must have been present from birth because they have not had time to learn.

In this subsequent investigation, Meltzoff and Moore once again attempted to investigate infants' ability to imitate facial gestures, but this time the 40 infants involved were less than 72 hours old. As before, the procedure was recorded on video tape which was seen by judges who were told the range of behaviours that they might see but not what they might see on any given occasion. A proportion of the judges' scores was checked by other judges and received a high degree of confirmation. The evidence from this study suggested that of these 40 newborn infants, 30 produced more mouth opening during the mouth opening phase of the experiment than during the tongue poking phase. Also, 25 infants did more tongue poking during the tongue poking phase than they did during the rest of the study. The investigators also note that twelve of the 40 infants did in fact produce more tongue poking when they were being shown mouth opening by the investigators.

Thus, in apparent contradiction to Piaget's assertion that infants are unable to imitate until they reach 9–12 months of age, several investigators have produced evidence that suggests infants begin postnatal life with this ability consistent with a nativist position.

Although doubts have been raised about some of the evidence, if we accept it, then the challenge is to develop an interpretation that is consistent with all of the facts.

Activity 7   Forming a view?

Allow about
30 minutes

This activity will help you draw conclusions from reviewing the evidence.

Do you think that the competing strands of evidence concerning imitation in this chapter are incompatible or is it possible to produce an account of the developmental history of imitation which includes all the evidence presented? Review the material describing the studies and then outline the interpretations of the findings in search of a shared understanding.

Comment

If you accept all the evidence then you might take the view that there are some early infant behaviours which look much like imitation. There are also many reports that describe the appearance of imitation as happening between 9 and 12 months. These studies also describe the apparent difficulty of demonstrating imitation before this time. Piaget did not use the investigative techniques that produced the evidence that Meltzoff and Moore describe. It is possible that had he done so he might have made observations consistent with theirs.

3.3   A final note on imitation

Perhaps the difference between the theory of imitation development described by Piaget on the one hand and Meltzoff and Moore on the other is that they are looking at different aspects of imitation. For example, Piaget only considered behaviour to be a 'true' indicator of imitative ability if it involved a time delay between the demonstration of the 'to-be-imitated' action and the infant's production of the act. A time delay between these actions suggests that infants are able to hold a representation of a behaviour in mind over a period of time. Piaget suggested that it was only in the second year that children became capable of deferred imitation. However, more recent work by Meltzoff and Moore suggests that the ability may develop much earlier. This section ends with an account of their study of 40 6-week-old infants (Meltzoff and Moore, 2002).

In this study each infant was placed in one of four conditions, where they saw either: (a) a passive face, (b) a mouth opening movement, (c) a tongue protrusion to the mid-point or (d) a tongue protrusion to the side. Each infant saw the same imitative behaviour on 3 consecutive days. For example, the infants in the mouth opening group saw the experimenter demonstrate only mouth opening and never saw the tongue-poking demonstration. Across the 3 days there were five 90-second test periods, three of which were immediate imitation trials as the infant was able to respond straight after the experimenter had finished the demonstration. However, the other two 90-second test periods were delayed trials as they were carried out 24 hours after the last demonstration. Therefore on the first day of testing the children witnessed a demonstration of the 'to-be-imitated' action. Following this, the children were video-taped for 90 seconds to see if they imitated the action. The second and third days of testing had the same sequence of testing, however, at the beginning of the testing session the children came face-to-face with the experimenter who maintained a neutral, passive face. The infants were video-taped for 90 seconds to see if they then produced the action that they had seen demonstrated 24 hours earlier. This was followed by the demonstration session and then the 90-second video-taped response period. Meltzoff and Moore found that 6-week-old infants were able to imitate from memory after a 24-hour delay. This suggests that these infants can generate actions on the basis of a stored representation.

Consider for a moment what an accomplishment this is. To imitate a tongue protrusion, infants need to receive some input from the visual sense. They also need to be able to store this input so that it can be called upon later, and they need to be able to translate the visual input into a pattern of physical behaviour of their own. It is clear that a complex level of mental activity is involved: reception, store, translation and action. To say that newborns can imitate is to claim that they possess considerable cognitive sophistication. It is even more surprising to find that they can store and translate an action up to 24 hours after they have learned it.

Meltzoff and Moore were also interested in whether infants could adapt their behaviour to make their actions more similar to the experimenter's behaviour. To do this they examined the behaviour of the children in the 'tongue protrusion to the side' condition. Such an action is novel to the infants and therefore not easily produced. Yet Meltzoff and Moore discovered that over the period of testing, the infants became more accurate in their production of this action. This suggested that infants have some control and understanding over their actions and are able to relate their behaviour to what they have observed others do, even when they cannot see the part of their own body making the action.

Meltzoff and Moore do not believe that 'there is no development in imitation' (Meltzoff and Moore, 2002, p. 54). For example, in previous work they found that 2–3-month-old children had better imitative ability than 6-week-old children. Similarly 9-month-old children begin to imitate body movements using people as a source of knowledge about how to act on objects, but it is only by 18 months that children infer the actions that someone is intending to undertake when they are not successful. Therefore Meltzoff and Moore see their findings not as a definitive marker of when children have developed the ability to imitate, but as an indication of the building blocks needed for later cognitive development.

In Chapter 2 you read about Piaget's position that development happens as a process of interaction between an infant equipped with a small range of reflexes and an environment that constantly poses challenges. These challenges require the infant either to incorporate the new with the old (assimilation) or to modify behaviour to cope with the demands of this particular challenge (accommodation). Thus it is argued that a complex skill such as using a pen has developed in small stages which began with the grasping reflex with which the child was born.

In Piaget's view, the ability to represent the world symbolically is an outcome of the complex interaction between child and environment and it takes time to achieve. The development of imitation described by Piaget is consistent with this philosophical perspective. Piaget's account begins with the absence of imitation and describes progressive sophistication until 'true' imitation begins. However, as shown in subsequent studies, the evidence that infants are able to imitate from the earliest days (even hours) of life undermines Piaget's philosophical position. Piaget's detailed observations provide a sound base of evidence, but his interpretation of them is questionable.

Meltzoff and Moore take a radically different view concerning the nature of the newborn infant's cognitive system. For them, infants do not need to embark on the developmental process suggested by Piaget since they are born with an ability to symbolize (or represent) their world. The basis for this belief is evidence that suggests that infants can imitate in the first hours of life.

Summary of Section 3

- Research sheds light on imitation, experimental techniques and theories of the nature of childhood.
- Piaget took the view that knowledge of the world is constructed as a result of the interaction between infants and their environments.
- Other theorists are inclined to the view that infants are born with much more comprehension than Piaget allowed.
- Piaget's original studies suggested that the development of imitation is a lengthy process which is not complete until 9–12 months.
- Subsequent investigations reported by Meltzoff and Moore presented counter-evidence that infants in the first days of life have the capacity to imitate behaviours demonstrated by an adult. Evidence also showed that infants of 6 weeks can store a 'to-be-imitated' action and perform it 24 hours later.

4 The development of understanding representations

The ability to represent objects, whether they are toy trains or people, provides researchers with information about the development of reasoning. One of the critical skills needed to reason about our environment is the ability to hold in mind a representation of the world. Mental representations exist in the sense that we are able to *symbolize* items in the world. When we reason we are manipulating an abstracted representation of our environment.

Activity 8   *Using representations*

Allow about
5 minutes

This activity explores the significance of mental representations in everyday life.

Make a list of activities you could still undertake if you could *not* hold representations in your mind.

Comment

Automatic reactions, such as shutting our eyes when we sneeze or being startled when we hear an unexpected loud noise, are made without holding a representation in mind. However, it is impossible to undertake any conscious action without representing the world. For example, the simple act of getting out of bed requires representations. You must represent where the bed is in relation to the walls of the room. You need to represent your feet and where you must put them on the floor in order to stand up successfully. Think for a moment of what it's like getting out of an unfamiliar bed, in a hotel for instance. An action such as this may seem simple, but yet when it is broken down into its components it becomes much more complex. Imagine how many representations one needs to use in order to undertake more complex actions such as baking a cake or driving to work.

▲

People do not only represent concrete objects but also abstract 'objects', such as emotions, thoughts and concepts. Humans are flexible in their use of this symbol system and flexibility contributes to our ability to make new thoughts from old and to deal with new demands from the environment. One of the great challenges that face psychologists is to understand how representations are symbolized and stored.

It is important to be aware that the term 'representation' is used in different ways by different authors and this can make unravelling the idea rather tricky. Mandler (1983) made the helpful distinction between two kinds of representation: *procedural* and *declarative*. Procedural representations are 'know how' kinds of knowledge – all those things that one knows how to do, but that are difficult to explain. An adult example would be something like riding a bicycle. Early infant knowledge of behaviours like reaching or grasping is said to be of this kind. Declarative knowledge is the description given to the kind of knowledge that you have represented and that is available to your conscious thinking (e.g. 2 + 2 = 4). As it is available to you in this way, it is possible for you to tell others of your knowledge and to pass it on. Because of its flexibility and power, developmental psychologists have been very interested in the origins and development of declarative knowledge.

There are many different representational systems that we use every day. The procedural/declarative distinction is one way in which representations can be categorized. Other representational systems include words, photographs, maps, drawings, gestures, sign language and models. One of the many uses of language is to refer to objects and events in the world. Another is to express feelings in a way that is clear to other humans. These functions may be achieved by words or gestures or, indeed, any conventional form. It follows that when people use gestures or sounds in this way they are revealing something of their present understanding of the world. Similarly for children, the use of words or conventional gestures to refer to other things or events indicates some kind of symbolic mental activity.

We have explored a range of evidence concerning children's representations of objects (Section 2) and children's representations of people (Section 3). More recent evidence suggests that, contrary to Piaget's theory, children are able to hold some representations in mind from very early in life. As children's understanding of representations improves then this has significant implications for the development of other skills. For example, it is not surprising that along with the ability to hold in mind the permanent existence of objects and the development of sophisticated imitative ability, we also see changes in children's language acquisition and their ability to use an object to represent other objects in pretend play. However, evidence also shows that children are not able to understand some representations until later in infancy. To conclude this chapter we will explore one of these later developments; the understanding of models.

4.1 Understanding models

When do children begin to understand the relationship between symbols and the actual objects that they represent? This question has been explored by DeLoache in terms of models and the spaces that they represent (DeLoache, 1987, 1989).

In one of her early experiments two groups of children, one with a mean age of 2 years and 7 months and the other with a mean age of 3 years and 2 months, were invited to examine both a room and a smaller model of the same room (see Figure 10). The model contained smaller versions of all the furniture to be seen in the larger room. In this experiment two dolls were used; a small doll in the model room and a larger one in the full-scale room. The small doll was hidden at a series of different locations in the model room and a child was asked to find the larger doll in the corresponding full-scale room. Before the children began their search the experimenter explained the relationship between the smaller doll and the larger doll, and the children were told that the larger one was hidden in the 'same place' as the smaller one. Children of 3 years or more were able to deduce the location of the large doll from the position of the small doll in the model room. Children who were 2 years and 6 months or younger were unable to use the representational correspondence between the model and the full-size room, and instead searched incorrectly. Later questioning showed that younger children were able to recall the exact location of the small doll, suggesting that their problem was not one of memory but rather an inability to understand the representational relationship between the two rooms.

The most common error made by the young children was to search at the location where the toy was hidden in the previous test trial. Therefore the young children are making similar errors to children in the A-not-B search task described in Section 2.5. This suggests that the error may be due to problems of inhibiting an action which is now incorrect but was previously successful. To explore this Sharon and DeLoache (2003) examined the searching behaviour of 129 children aged between 2 years and 4 months and 2 years and 8 months using the model-room task. They suggested that if young children's incorrect searches were due to problems of inhibiting their previously correct action then they should be more likely to be correct on their first trial as this is not preceded by any action. They found that 77 per cent of the children failed to find the doll on their first trial even though the inhibitory control demands were minimal.

Sharon and DeLoache (2003) followed this up using the same procedure, but specifically reduced the inhibitory control demands within the task by altering the model to show the child that the location in which the doll had previously been hidden was now empty. For example, if the doll was previously hidden in a basket, then before the next trial the basket was turned on its side so that it was now clear to the child that it was empty. This time the children did not make the perseveration errors for it was clear to them that the previously successful location was now empty. However, it did not improve their performance. Rather than go to the correct location, illustrated by the location of the doll in the model room, children now searched around the previously successful location, for example near the basket. These results show that problems with inhibitory control contribute very little to the difficulty with the task that children aged 2 years and 6 months experience. Instead, the results confirm that young children's great difficulty is appreciating the relationship between models and the spaces they represent.

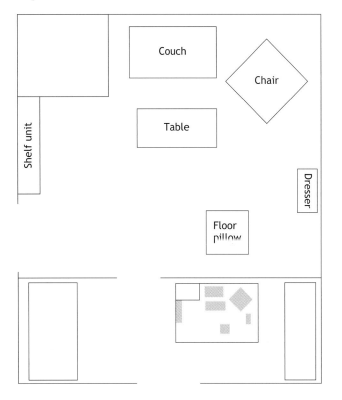

Figure 10   Layout of the experimental space. Shaded areas in the scale model correspond to labelled items of furniture in the room. Room dimensions: 4.80 m × 3.98 m × 2.54 m. Model dimensions: 71.1 cm × 64.8 cm × 33.0 cm (from DeLoache, 1989).

This work, therefore, shows that significant changes in children's understanding of representations and objects continue to occur later in infancy. Towards the end of the third year of life children show significant advances in their understanding of external representations. These changes have been illustrated by children's successful use of external representations (i.e. models) to find objects in the world. This sophisticated level of cognition entailed in the ability to understand the relationship between an external representation and the real world relies heavily on, and extends (i) the earlier developments of understanding the continuing existence of objects that are out of sight, and (ii) holding in mind representations of a changing environment and one's behaviour in relation to that environment which is needed for successful imitation.

Summary of Section 4

- The ability to hold in mind and understand representations is essential to be able to carry out planned actions. These representations can take many forms including words, numbers, gestures and expressions.
- A great deal of development in the understanding of representations occurs in the first year of life, including the understanding of the existence of objects which are out of sight and the ability to hold in mind and replicate actions performed by other people.
- There are also significant developments which occur later in life including the understanding of models as representations of the real world.

5   Conclusion

The early part of this chapter focused on two key issues: the development of the understanding that objects continue to exist even when they are not accessible to the senses, and the development of the ability to imitate. Selected studies were used to trace the history of psychological investigation in these areas. Underlying the concern with the conduct of the various investigations and the surface meaning of the evidence was the idea that a review of this kind might shed some light on the more profound debate concerning the nature of human infants. Representations are critical to cognitive development and significant changes occur very early in a child's life, perhaps with some skills being present from birth (nativism). However, other skills involving the understanding of representations develop later (Piaget's constructivism), such as the understanding of models.

Understanding how much children know about the world is difficult for two reasons. First, it is not possible simply to ask young children about their reasoning skills. Second, often children's difficulties in experiments may be due not to the limitations of their cognitive ability, for example, their ability to understand the relationship between a model and the space it represents. Instead, the difficulties may be due to problems in co-ordinating their knowledge with their behaviour (i.e. overcoming perseverative errors in the A-not-B task). The current level of our understanding has only been possible through the ingenuity of psychologists, who have developed techniques which have allowed us to infer the content of a child's knowledge through his or her actions.

References

Aguiar, A. and Baillargeon, R. (2002) 'Developments in young infants' reasoning about occluded objects', *Cognitive Psychology*, vol. 45, pp. 267–336.

Baillargeon, R. (1986) 'Representing the existence and the location of hidden objects: object permanence in 6 and 8 month old infants', *Cognition*, vol. 23, pp. 21–41.

Baillargeon, R. and DeVos, J. (1991) 'Object permanence in young infants: further evidence', *Child Development*, vol. 62, pp. 1227–46.

Baillargeon, R., Spelke, E. S. and Wasserman, S. (1985) 'Object permanence in 5 month old infants', *Cognition*, vol. 20, pp. 191–208.

Bower, T. G. R. and Patterson, J. G. (1973) 'The separation of place, movement and object in the world of the infant', *Journal of Experimental Child Psychology*, vol. 15, pp. 161–8.

Bower, T. G. R., Broughton, J. M. and Moore, M. K. (1971) 'Development of the object concept as manifested in the tracking behaviour of infants between 7 and 20 weeks of age', *Journal of Experimental Psychology*, vol. 11, pp. 182–93.

Butterworth, G. E. (1977) 'Object disappearance and error in Piaget's stage IV task', *Journal of Experimental Child Psychology*, vol. 23, pp. 391–401.

Butterworth, G. E. (1981) *Infancy and Epistemology*, Brighton, Harvester Press.

DeLoache, J. (1987) 'Rapid change in the symbolic functioning of very young children', *Science*, vol. 238, pp. 1556–7.

DeLoache, J. (1989) 'Young children's understanding of the correspondence between a scale model and a larger space', *Cognitive Development*, vol. 4, pp. 121–39.

Diamond, A. (1985) 'Development of the ability to use recall to guide action, as indicated by infant's performance on $A\overline{B}$', *Child Development*, vol. 56, pp. 868–83.

Harris, P. L. (1973) 'Perseveration errors in search by young infants', *Child Development*, vol. 44, pp. 28–33.

Harris, P. L. (1989) 'Object permanence in infancy', in Slater, A. and Bremner, J. G. (eds), *Infant Development: recent advances*, Hove, Lawrence Erlbaum.

Hood, B. and Willatts, P. (1986) 'Reaching in the dark to an object's remembered position: evidence of object permanence in 5 month old infants', *British Journal of Developmental Psychology*, vol. 4, pp. 57–65.

Jacobson, S. W. (1979) 'Matching behaviour in the young infant', *Child Development*, vol. 50, pp. 425–30.

Kaye, K. (1982) *The Mental and Social Life of Babies*, Chicago, University of Chicago Press.

Mandler, J. (1983) 'Representation', in Mussen, P. H. (series ed.) Flavell, J. H. and Markman, E. M. (vol. eds), *Handbook of Child Psychology vol. 3, Cognitive Development*, New York, Wiley.

Meltzoff, A. N. and Moore, M. K. (1977) 'Imitation of facial and manual gestures by human neonates', *Science*, vol. 198, pp. 75–8.

Meltzoff, A. N. and Moore, M. K. (1983) 'Newborn infants imitate adult facial gestures', *Child Development*, vol. 54, pp. 702–9.

Meltzoff, A. N. and Moore, M. K. (2002) 'Imitation, memory, and the representation of persons', *Infant Behaviour and Development*, vol. 25, pp. 39–61.

Piaget, J. (1951) *Play, Dreams and Imitation in Childhood*, London, Routledge and Kegan Paul.

Piaget, J. and Inhelder, B. (1969) *The Psychology of the Child*, London, Routledge and Kegan Paul.

Sharon, T. and DeLoache, J. (2003) 'The role of perseveration in children's symbolic understanding and skill', *Developmental Science*, vol. 6, pp. 289–96.

Shinskey, J. L. and Munakata, Y. (2003) 'Are infants in the dark about hidden objects?', *Developmental Science*, vol. 6, pp. 273–82.

Uzgiris, I. and Hunt, J. McV. (1975) *Assessment in Infancy: ordinal scales of psychological development*, Urbana, IL, University of Illinois Press.

Willatts, P. (1985) 'Adjustments of means-ends coordination and the representation of spatial relations in the production of search errors by infants', *British Journal of Developmental Psychology*, vol. 3, pp. 259–72.

Chapter 5
Temperament and development

John Oates and Jim Stevenson

Contents

Learning outcomes

After you have studied this chapter you should be able to:

1 describe the concept of individual differences in development and how studying them complements research into developmental processes;

2 describe the various factors that may be involved in the development of psychological differences between children;

3 describe the concept of temperament and its relationship to infant individuality;

4 compare alternative frameworks that have been put forward to describe temperamental differences;

5 evaluate alternative methods for measuring temperamental differences;

6 describe and illustrate what is meant by a transactional model of how temperament and development are related.

1   Introduction

Differences between individuals can become apparent as early as the days after their birth; some are placid and easy-going, others seem less at ease with the world. Some are more active than others, some seem more easily able to focus their attention. The concept of temperament has been developed by psychologists to sum up these sorts of differences. This chapter looks at the ways in which temperament has been explored and the extent to which it affects development after infancy.

1.1 Two approaches in developmental psychology

Developmental psychology takes two broad approaches to the study of development. One seeks to identify and explain the changes shown by most children as they become adults as part of a typical pattern of psychological development, asking the question 'What makes people develop in similar ways?'. At a descriptive level, this approach aims to define developmental milestones that children reach and to describe approximate average ages by which they are typically reached. At a more explanatory level, this approach also seeks to identify underlying processes which can explain how and why children develop in these common ways.

Figure 1 What makes people develop in similar ways?   **Figure 2** What makes people different from each other?

The second approach is interested in the variations around these general patterns and the influences that help to create these 'individual differences' between people, asking 'What makes people different from each other?'. This way of studying psychological development also sets out to reveal underlying processes, but is more focused on the individuality of people.

In practice, although the questions that each approach is tackling are clearly different, they often share some similarities of method. So, for example, a study of what factors lead to most infants uttering their first word by 1 year of age might try to find out what environmental factors are associated with infants who achieve this especially early. This would be making use of individual differences as a way of identifying common processes in development. Similarly, a study that is looking for reasons why some children understand how to count earlier than others, thus focusing on individual differences, might nevertheless be seeking to describe a common process that leads to these.

This chapter examines differences between young children's temperaments and the extent to which these can explain differences in development, that lead to differences in adults, such as personality differences.

1.2 Adult personality

One of the most significant ways in which adults differ is in their personality. A crucial aspect of personality is that it represents a relatively stable set of qualities of a person. So, for example, if someone's personality is seen as outgoing, then one would expect them to be more outgoing than others most of the time and in most situations. If this person was very withdrawn and quiet on a particular day, we might say 'that's not like them at all', recognizing that personality, who a person 'is', is something that is relatively enduring.

At the same time we would recognize that some variations in people's behaviour are to be expected. Thus we might note that our outgoing friend is a little quieter than usual one day, and simply say 'they seem to have something on their mind' without thinking that this is atypical behaviour. Personality, therefore, represents a tendency to behave in particular ways and is not a rigid, fixed characteristic.

1.3 Character type or trait?

A common way of making sense of differences between things is to categorize them; to say 'that's an X, and that's a Y'. So, saying that someone is 'an outgoing person' is implicitly categorizing them as a member of the group of 'outgoing persons'. This is an appealing approach because it is rather black and white, someone either is, or is not, 'an outgoing person'. The idea that people can be assigned to one or another of a limited set of character types has a long history, going back to the ancient Greek philosophers. Theophrastus (371–286 BC) described six 'Characters':

- the garrulous – outgoing, talkative, vivacious;
- the mean – selfish, miserly;
- the tactless – insensitive, clumsy;
- the flatterer – using compliments to achieve own ends;
- the dissembler – deceitful, evasive;
- the avaricious – grasping, covetous.

Hippocrates (460–377 BC) first used a term similar in meaning to temperament ('humour') to define four basic types of people, and he named these as:

- Choleric – easily aroused, easily angered;
- Phlegmatic – cool, detached;
- Sanguine – impulsive, excitable, optimistic;
- Melancholic – depressive, pessimistic.

He believed that each of these was caused by an excess of one of the four 'humours' or bodily fluids; blood (sanguine), phlegm (phlegmatic), black bile (melancholic) or yellow bile (choleric).

The Hippocratic set of types was widely promoted by the Roman philosopher and physician Galen (129–210 AD) in his medical textbook *Pericraison, De Temperamentis* and was the dominant model of personality until the sixteenth century AD. Indeed, to the extent that you recognize the Hippocratic categories, it still offers a plausible grouping, even though the underlying theory of the humours has no scientific validity.

The notion of distinct types of people is still held by some psychologists, for example the Myers-Briggs Type Inventory (Briggs Myers and Myers, 1995) is a widely-used 'personality test' that seeks to categorize people as either 'Thinkers', 'Feelers', 'Sensers' or 'Intuiters', based on the profiles of their answers to a series of questions. However, even as long ago as Hippocrates, Plato (427–347 BC) realized that there is a alternative way of thinking about the differences between people and he argued that these could be more easily explained if people were seen as varying on two dimensions (or 'traits'):

- anxiety versus calmness;
- impulsivity versus reflectivity.

Plato's scheme languished somewhat until Wundt (1832–1920 AD), one of the founders of the science of psychology, came to the same conclusion as Plato. Wundt proposed that Galen's four types could be fitted into a simple scheme that recognized two dimensions (or traits) much like Plato's, named changeability and excitability:

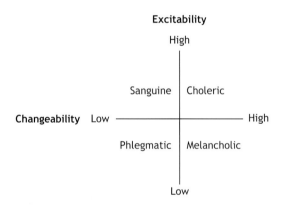

Figure 3   Wundt's dimensions and Galen's types.

The modern study of adult personality still bears the marks of these two contrasting approaches, type versus trait.

Twentieth century psychologists started their quest for a definitive set of traits by assembling all the different words that are used to describe people and grouping them into a discrete number of traits. This is achieved by using statistical techniques such as factor and cluster analysis to find out which tend to go together and have similar or identical meanings. This research then went on to collect data by rating many people using these traits and using further techniques to find out how valid these traits are.

Trait
A dimension along which people vary, for example, extraversion versus introversion.

Type
A category into which certain people can be classified, for example, moody.

1.4 The three main trait theories

Although there are still numerous competing models, there are three main contrasting trait theories. In order of increasing complexity, first, Eysenck's theory (Eysenck, 1981, 1991) proposes two primary traits, introversion–extraversion and neuroticism–stability, and two secondary traits of intelligence and psychoticism. His view is that a person's temperament is largely definable in terms of their positions on these two main traits and that this is biologically based on the characteristics of their nervous systems, for example, how easily they are aroused or bored. Like most 'personality tests', a person's position on each of Eysenck's traits is scored from a series of questions, several on each dimension, in the Eysenck Personality Inventory (EPI).

Another dominant model is the 'Big-5' personality theory, which, in some slightly differing variants (e.g. Costa and McCrae, 1997), puts forward five primary traits:

- Neuroticism–Stability;
- Extraversion–Introversion;
- Agreeableness–Disagreeableness;
- Openness to experience–Resistance to change;
- Conscientiousness–Laxity.

Another model that, like the 'Big-5', proposes a small number of 'super factors' is offered by Tellegen's Multidimensional Personality Questionnaire (MPQ), which groups eleven primary factors into the three traits of Positive Affectivity, Negative Affectivity and Constraint, reflecting 'pleasure', 'anger' and 'fear' respectively (Tellegen, 1982).

Finally, the third dominant model asserts a much larger number of factors and one of the most widely used is the Cattell 16-PF (Personality Factor) model (Cattell and Kline, 1977), which proposes the following sixteen factors:

Warmth–coldness	Liveliness	Vigilance	Openness to change
Reasoning	Rule consciousness	Abstractedness	Self-reliance
Emotional stability	Social boldness	Privateness	Perfectionism
Dominance	Sensitivity	Apprehension	Tension

There is some overlap between these three models. Each has an extensive body of research supporting it, so 'Which of these is the right one?' is not really the right question to ask. It is more that at one extreme there is a simple, broad-brush analysis of personality structure and at the other a more fine-grained analysis. The existence of these three main approaches, and there are many other variants as well, means that in the field of personality research it is often difficult to compare a study that has used one measure with another that has used different measures.

What all three approaches share is a view that there is a limited set of stable personality characteristics, which can be viewed as dimensions along which people vary. These traits will be evidenced in behaviour across contexts and across time. Where they differ, though, is in the underlying assumptions about the origins of the individual differences between people that are revealed by their positions on these dimensions.

The three approaches lie along a continuum, from the strongly nativist view of Eysenck that these differences are biologically based and hence originate to some degree in genetic variation, to the view that the relatively fixed adult character arises from an amalgam of experiences and choices as well as genetic predispositions.

1.5 Stability of adult personality

It is now well-established that adult personality, at least as measured by these multi-trait questionnaires, shows a high degree of stability during adulthood (Jones and Meredith, 1996; Costa and McCrae, 1997). In other words, people's personalities do not seem to change a great deal, at least in these global respects, once they are adults. However, this is looking at stability statistically across large groups of people. It does not imply that everyone's personality is genetically fixed at birth and completely stable, nor does it rule out the possibility of major changes in adulthood.

There might well be much more instability in the earlier portion of life. Looking at the traits of adult personality, it can be seen that some of these cannot be evident in infants and young children, because they involve behaviours that have not yet developed, so any links with early life need to be explored using different measures. This is especially the case for very young children, since all of the 'tests' outlined above rely on self-completed written questionnaires, so different approaches have to be used to study infants.

1.6 Infant 'personality'

It is often said that it is not until the birth of their second child that parents properly consider the effects of biological influences on behaviour. This can be illustrated by the following quotation from the influential American psychologist, Maslow:

> Our first baby changed me as a psychologist. It made the behaviourism I had been so enthusiastic about look so foolish that I could not stomach it any more. It was impossible. Having a second baby, and learning how profoundly different people are even before birth, made it impossible for me to think in terms of the kind of learning psychology in which one can teach anybody anything.

> (Maslow, 1973, p. 176)

Children of the same parents and living in the same family are often strikingly different from each other from a very early age. One may be active, sociable and anxious while the other is passive, solitary but relaxed. For example, in describing her 4 year old, a Nottingham mother said:

> Well, I think it's a sort of mixed relationship. He's full of fun, he's a lively little boy, and he's also a very self-willed one. I enjoy the fact that he is lively, and that I can play with him and do things with him. The older boy is more a dreamer and a thinker, and you could hold much more of an intelligent conversation with him at 4 than you can with Neil; but I can romp with Neil far more than Martin wanted to romp.

> (Newson and Newson, 1970, pp. 66–7)

Putting aside for the moment the fact that a second child will inevitably have a different experience to a first child (in terms of sharing parental attention and other factors), what most parents experience is a strong feeling that there is something that can be summed up in the word 'constitution' that has a profound effect on way that children behave right from the moment of birth. In other words, this is part of their 'make-up' and the implicit belief is likely to be that this is 'in their genes'.

Although this belief will be challenged from various perspectives as the chapter progresses, this notion of some fixed, biological basis to infants' characters is summed up in the term commonly used in developmental psychology, 'temperament':

> Temperament ... consists of biologically rooted individual differences in behaviour tendencies that are present early in life and are relatively stable across various kinds of situation and over the course of time.

> (Bates, 1989a, p. 4)

1.7 Temperament

Differences in temperament lead to differences between children in their habitual styles of responding to people and events, that is, their individuality. As Rutter (1987) suggests, temperament is an abstract notion of a trait or disposition to act or behave, not evidenced in just one behavioural act but rather in consistent qualities of behaviour over extended periods of time. According to this meaning of the term, temperament differences do not preclude anyone from showing any particular behaviour. Instead they are general features of behavioural style which can be seen as influencing the child's behaviour in a wide variety of settings and which are stable over months and possibly years.

Activity I

Allow about
10 minutes

What is temperament?

This activity will help you to think about temperamental differences between children of different ages and how these might be categorized.

Note down a list of the ways in which you might describe the behavioural style of a child aged I year, and a child aged 5 years. Also think of particular behaviours that would be good indicators of the type of temperament of the child, for example, friendly: at age I year – smiles at familiar people; at age 5 years – asks to play with other children. If you have little experience of children at these ages ask a parent with appropriately aged children.

Comment

Have you used the same indicators for both ages? How do these contrast with indicators that differ between ages? Your responses are likely to suggest that underlying temperamental differences, even if they are stable during development, may nevertheless be expressed in different ways at different ages.

Temperament is generally seen as separate from more cognitive aspects of development. Aspects of behavioural style and social interaction influenced by temperamental differences are distinct from differences in either cognitive ability or cognitive style, for example, approaches to problem solving. Empirically this distinction is supported by studies that have failed to show any association between temperament profiles and measures of ability such as intelligence test scores. Differences in temperament are thus likely to be seen in children of all ability levels. In the following section, the ways in which child temperament has been conceptualized and measured are examined in more detail.

Summary of Section 1

- Developmental psychology is concerned with both the pattern of normal development and with individual differences in development.
- In the history of the study of adult personality, two contrasting approaches favoured either type or trait definitions.
- Generally, modern adult personality theories favour the use of a number of traits as measures.
- Temperament has been defined as 'biologically rooted individual differences in behaviour tendencies that are present early in life and are relatively stable across various kinds of situations and over the course of time' (Bates, 1989a, p. 4).
- Temperamental differences are shown in children's behavioural styles.
- Temperament is independent of individual differences in cognitive ability.

2   Individual differences

2.1 Identifying character traits

Just as in the study of adult personality, the study of infant and child temperament has tended to focus on defining a limited number of traits and then gathering data from large numbers of children to examine variation among them. But this research has also attempted to incorporate the notion of types as well, recognising that a personality type may reflect a specific profile on a set of traits.

Three key questions thus arise: what are these traits, how many of them are there, and what influences the variation in their occurrence? One criterion for identifying traits is that they should be independent of each other. For example, for activity and impulsiveness to be recognized as independent traits, knowing a child's activity level should not strongly predict the child's level of impulsiveness. At the same time it may be that the most impulsive children are those who show the highest activity levels, although across the majority of other children activity level and impulsiveness are unrelated. In other words, children may show a wide range of activity levels at all degrees of impulsiveness. However, the most extreme activity levels may only be shown by the most impulsive children.

Therefore, it may be possible to identify a number of different types or profiles from these traits, that is, patterns of high and low scores on traits that are often found to occur together in sub-groups.

The basic approach of temperament research is therefore:

- to identify underlying dimensions which are reflected in children's behaviour;
- to identify the causes of such variation; and
- to establish whether these temperamental differences have any consequences for the child's current experiences and subsequent development.

This approach to temperamental differences emphasizes the *quantitative* differences between children on a limited number of underlying dimensions of behaviour. That is, it sets out to measure these differences in systematic ways, not just to describe them.

2.2 Dimensions of temperament

How complex is the pattern of traits that define the differences between children? Can they be reduced to a small set of dimensions or do we need to think of many independent dimensions that can be measured? As for the study of adult personality, there is disagreement about the range of behaviours in which temperament differences are thought to be shown and the exact number of dimensions that should be included. However, there does appear to be an emergent picture of three broad categories of behaviour that are involved with infants and pre-school children. Bates (1989a) identifies these as:

1   *Emotional responses*: the child's general quality of mood (sunny, out-going and positive or the opposite), reaction to unfamiliar people or settings and the child's tolerance of and response to internal states such as hunger and boredom.

2   *Attentional orientation patterns*: such as how readily the child can be comforted when distressed or how easily they are distracted from an activity.

3   *Motor activity*: the vigour and frequency of activity, including the ability to modify activities appropriately.

Activity 2   *Dimensions of temperament*

Allow about
5 minutes

This activity encourages you to consider the similarities and differences between your own views of temperamental differences and Bates's categories.

Look back at your answers to Activity I and compare them with the three categories offered by Bates. How many of your descriptions are covered by these categories?

Comment

You probably found that most of the items in your list could be allocated to one or other of Bates's categories. If not, you are conceptualising temperament in a somewhat different way.

▲

2.3 Stability versus continuity in development

It is important to make clear the distinction between regularities in individual differences in a characteristic and regularities in the development of the characteristic itself. Regularity in individual differences – *stability* – suggests that those persons who show a relatively high (or low) level of some characteristic at a given point in time will also tend to be the same people that will show a relatively high (or low) level of that same characteristic some years later. Note here that it is the degree to which a characteristic is present compared to other people that is important. It may be that all children show a decrease in their level of activity as they get older. Stability is shown when those children with high activity levels compared to other children of the same age are also the ones with the highest relative activity levels 1 or 2 years later.

Stability refers to regularity of individual differences across a long period of time, that is, years rather than months. It has to be recognized that children's behaviour may vary from day to day, reflecting the influence of who the child is with, the setting they are in and factors such as the child's health, hunger or tiredness. Accurate and reliable temperament measurement is achieved when the same or closely similar 'score' on a measure is obtained for repeated measurements over weeks rather than days.

Regularity in the development of the characteristic itself – *continuity* – is tested by whether the child shows, for example, a similar range of behaviours indicating fearfulness at age 18 months and 3 years. At both these ages crying may be an indicator of fearfulness (thus showing continuity) whereas verbalization may play a very different role in fearfulness at the two ages. An 18 month old may verbalize to explain the fear and verbalizing may itself be part of the fear response. This use of the term continuity is largely dependent on individual differences in behaviour showing similar correlations with other behaviours at different ages. In this sense it refers to similarity in the structure of behavioural differences across age.

2.4 The emergence of temperament

The first 5 years of a child's life are a time of many changes and especially the emergence of many new behaviours, as outlined in Table 1.

Table 1   Temperament development in early childhood

Developmental period	Temperament component
Newborn	Distress and soothability; activity; orienting and alertness (attention); approach/withdrawal to novel situations/people.
Early infancy	All of the above and smiling and laughter; vocalization; stimulus seeking and avoidance; frustration.
Late infancy	All of the above and inhibition of approach; effortful control; fear.
Pre-school years and beyond	All of the above with continuing development of effortful control.

Source: adapted from Rothbart (1989).

Figure 4 Temperament is expressed in different ways at different ages.

By the end of the first year of life, a significant stage is reached where infants are able to resist their tendency to approach the unfamiliar. It is this behaviour that Kagan (1988) calls *behavioural inhibition*. There is variation in the extent to which children seek out and explore new situations and are happy to meet unfamiliar people. Behavioural inhibition is shown when children are shy and withdraw from contact with the unfamiliar. This is recognized to be a very stable temperamental feature. Rothbart also identifies *effortful control* as emerging at about this time. The importance of the emergence of effortful control is that it allows the child to undertake active planning for future action and to react flexibly to the environment. Rothbart defines this as 'the ability to inhibit responses to stimuli in the immediate environment while pursuing a cognitively represented goal' (Rothbart, 1989). Note that what Rothbart is pointing to here is the emergence of differences between children in this aspect of temperament, as, for example, in individual differences in the extent to which a child will assemble the toys and materials needed for a particular game. Some children will be better able to sustain this play whereas others will be more easily diverted into other activities.

Having begun to explore some of the features of temperament and its development, in the following section we turn to clarifying its definition.

Summary of Section 2

- Aspects of temperament in children are examples of what psychologists call 'traits', that is, common psychological dimensions along which people vary.
- The notion that there may be 'types' of children may be based on specific profiles of traits.
- There are three broad characteristics that have been proposed as descriptors of temperament: emotional responses, attentional orientation and motor activity.
- Stability and continuity are two distinct aspects of individual differences. Stability refers to the extent to which individual differences remain constant over time. Continuity refers to the way in which a particular characteristic may be consistently linked to another characteristic at a later age or ages.
- There is a developmental progression in the components of temperament that becomes apparent as the child gets older.

3 | Problems in defining temperament

It is difficult to come up with a definition of temperament that receives general acceptance. McCall made the following observation in the course of one of the debates on defining temperament:

> Temperament researchers have been troubled by their apparent inability to consent to a common definition of temperament. I do not believe they are far away from a reasonably uniform definition and, even if they were, I would not be disturbed by this situation. We have no very good definition of intelligence either, but that has not stopped us from studying it ... To me, definitions are not valid or invalid, confirmable or refutable. Instead, they are more or less useful.
>
> (McCall, in Goldsmith *et al.*, 1987, p. 524)

Psychologists, like other scientists, rarely talk about theories being 'true'; theories are helpful (or not) in generating useful research questions. However, as McCall suggests, there is something like a consensus definition emerging. As we saw in the last section, Bates's three categories of temperament (emotional responses, attentional orientation patterns and motor activity) point to the main areas that a 'helpful' theory of temperament needs to explain.

3.1 Abstract tendencies versus visible behaviours

It has often been asserted that temperament is not shown by what a person is doing at a particular time and place. Rather temperament refers to a *general tendency* to behave in particular ways or to show a particular *style* of behaviour; or as Bates puts it 'a property of the organism that organizes interactions with the environment over a wide range of situations' (Bates, 1989a, p. 5). So temperament is not a visible feature of behaviour as it is in the everyday use of the term when, for example, we say that someone who is behaving in a petulant or quarrelsome way is being 'temperamental'. Rather, these behaviours are a reflection of underlying temperamental differences. In developmental psychology temperament refers to a general characteristic of the behaviour of an individual. In that sense it is an abstraction which is inferred from an individual's behaviour at different times and contexts.

3.2 Biological (genetic) basis

As noted earlier, temperament has generally been seen as based in biological differences between people. The 'biological rootedness' of temperament has caused some conceptual confusion. Hinde (1989) noted that theorists such as Buss and Plomin (1984) have used a criterion of 'genetically based' to differentiate temperament dimensions from other aspects of individual differences. Hinde argues that all behaviour has a genetic basis. The question should really be whether some aspects of individual differences in behaviour could be more influenced by genetic differences between people than others. Some characteristics may be strongly influenced by genetic differences between people;

others may be more closely related to differences in the environments experienced by children. It has been argued that the impact of genetic differences on individual differences in a characteristic can be indexed by the *heritability* statistic. Heritability has been defined as the proportion of the variation in a characteristic in a population that is attributable to genetic differences between individuals.

Buss and Plomin suggested that a high heritability might distinguish temperament from other individual differences in behaviour which may show lower heritabilities. Yet this only raises a further objection from Hinde that this would lead to arbitrary distinctions. There is no obvious cut-off point for heritability below which we could consider a behavioural dimension to not be a component of temperament. Furthermore, Hinde points out that heritability estimates for the same behaviour can change with age and with the range of environments experienced.

Data on the heritability of temperament consistently suggest that all of the three dimensions identified by Buss and Plomin, that is, Emotionality, Activity and Sociability, may have a significant genetic component. Emotionality covers individual differences in aspects of fear and of anger. Activity comprises differences in the tempo, vigour and endurance of behaviour. Sociability has components of affiliation (i.e. seeking out other people) and responsivity when with others. Buss and Plomin (1984), summarizing data from four studies on twins of about 4 years of age, found that the average correlation between monozygotic (identical) twins is 0.63 for Emotionality, 0.62 for Activity and 0.53 for Sociability. These figures show that identical twins do tend to be quite similar on these three measures. The correlations for dizygotic twins are not significantly different from zero, in other words, there is no similarity at all in their scores. These results are consistent with individual differences in temperament on all three dimensions being strongly influenced by individual differences in genetic constitution at this pre-school age.

Although not disputing these findings on heritability, Hinde goes on to argue that it is not its 'biological rootedness' that is distinctive about temperament. He suggests that the usefulness of temperament in developmental psychology lies in its ability to explain or predict the *coherence* of the child's behaviour across situations or time. In his terms, temperament therefore provides the means of identifying regularities within the changing repertoire of the child's behaviour and in a flux of shifting relationships. As far as the biological basis of temperament is concerned, twin studies can only indicate the extent to which variation between children in an aspect of temperament is attributable to variation in genetic make-up or to the variety of experiences in children's lives. Once twin studies have indicated the relative size of the effects attributable to these sources it is necessary to move on to studies that actually look at the way the child's biology influences their behaviour and the way this process interacts with the quality and variety of the child's experiences. To achieve this, studies such as those described in Box 1 need to investigate variation in central nervous system structure and function, how this relates to temperamental differences and how experience impinges on this relationship between physiology and behaviour.

BOX 1

The reward pathway

Two important parts of the brain, the mesocortical and mesolimbic systems, form what is often called the 'reward pathway'. They connect parts of the brain that are associated with emotions, such as the amygdala, to other parts, such as the prefrontal cortex, that control planning, problem solving and attention regulation.

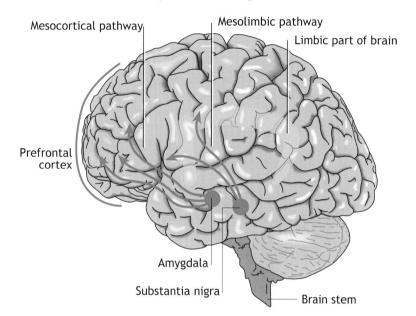

Figure 5 Mesocortical and mesolimbic pathways in the brain.

One function of these systems is to maintain attention and involvement with rewarding situations. A key neurotransmitter chemical in this pathway is dopamine and the structure of the dopamine receptors in the pathway is determined by a specific, known gene on chromosome 11, a gene which has a number of different variants (polymorphisms). One of these polymorphisms (7r) codes for dopamine receptors that are less efficient than more common forms. Although results are still mixed and controversial, there is evidence that this variant is associated with temperamental differences in infants, including reduced sustained attention, fewer signs of pleasure and greater activity levels (Auerbach *et al.*, 2001). In older children there is evidence for an association of the 7r variant with increased risk for problems with attention and risk-taking behaviour (Schmidt *et al.* 2001; Faraone *et al.*, 2001), and aggression (Schmidt *et al.*, 2002).

3.3 Stability of individual differences

The distinction between stability of individual differences and continuity in development has been discussed above. It has been assumed that a temperament feature should show high medium-term stability, that is, over a year or two. This necessarily entails that temperament will also show short-term stability over months. It is the enduring quality of temperament that is one source of its potential power to influence the child's development. But there are other processes in play that make the picture much more complex. Attitudes towards the child set by early behaviour may then influence parents' responses towards the child over an extended period of time. When considering the long-term influences of temperament on children's development we have to recognize both the more direct impact of consistent features of temperament and the possible enduring influence of early behaviour indirectly via its impact on parental attitudes, expectations and behaviour.

RESEARCH SUMMARY I

Genetic and environmental influences on development

Longitudinal
Following the progress of a single sample of children.

The Colorado Adoption Project is a longitudinal study of adopted children being undertaken by Plomin *et al.* (1988). By studying adopted children, their biological and adoptive parents and their siblings, it is providing a unique insight into the effects of genetic and environmental differences on development and the correlations and interactions between these biological and experiential influences. As the study is longitudinal they can investigate age to age correlations (stability) in children's scores. If correlations are high (0.6 or greater), this means that children's scores at one age are quite good predictors of their scores at a later age. In relation to temperament this study found that Emotionality and Sociability had age 1 year to age 2 year correlations of about 0.60 with Activity showing a slightly lower stability. From age 2 years to age 3 years all three stabilities were a bit higher at just under 0.65. One year later these high stabilities were maintained but activity dropped below 0.60 once again.

The stabilities established in Plomin *et al.*'s study were obtained using parental ratings of temperament and it is known that such ratings are subject to bias (Neale and Stevenson, 1989). This might mean that parents are rating their children more as they remember rating them the previous time than as they are actually behaving now. However, data on temperament obtained from video-recordings of children's behaviour show lower but still significant stabilities in temperament which tend to increase during the second year of life (range of stabilities 0.30–0.60). This suggests that although the parental source of bias may exist, it is not the sole reason for the stabilities that are identified.

Figure 6 Do early temperament differences continue throughout life?

This pattern of stability in temperament indicates that short-term to medium-term stability increases from infancy and into early childhood. But how far does a person's temperament, as expressed in infancy and early childhood, continue as an influence on their adult characteristics, that is, their personality? Typically, personality is thought of as resulting largely from the experiences that people encounter during childhood, but perhaps temperament also has ongoing effects. To address this issue it is necessary to carry out longitudinal studies, which, although costly and time-consuming to conduct, nevertheless can provide uniquely valuable data.

RESEARCH SUMMARY 2

Assessing long-term stability

One important longitudinal study has been following a cohort of about 1,000 children, all born between April 1972 and March 1973 in Dunedin, New Zealand and representing more than 90 per cent of births there during that period (Caspi et al., 2003). When the children were 3 years old, they took part in detailed assessments of temperament, based on which the researchers grouped them into five main 'types' as follows:

- Well-adjusted (n = 405; 48 per cent male);
- Under-controlled (n = 106; 62 per cent male);
- Confident (n = 281; 52 per cent male);
- Inhibited (n = 80; 40 per cent male);
- Reserved (n = 151; 48 per cent male).

Twenty-three years later, the participants took part in a series of assessments of their adult personalities, using the MPQ, and close friends also assessed them on a 'Big-5' questionnaire (Benet-Martinez and John, 1998).

Each of the five groups identified at age 3 years were found to have a specific profile on the Big-5 personality factors as rated by friends at the age of 26 years.

- Confident children were rated as the most Extraverted adults, and the Inhibited children as the least Extraverted.
- Under-controlled children were rated as the least Agreeable and Conscientious adults and highly Neurotic.
- Well-adjusted and Confident children were rated as more Open to Experience than the other groups.

There were also significant differences between the groups on the three MPQ 'super-factors':

- Under-controlled children grew up to be rated highest on Negative Emotionality.
- Confident children grew up to be least inhibited (low Constraint).
- Inhibited children became most inhibited (Constraint) and showed lowest levels of Positive Emotionality.
- Reserved children also showed low levels of Positive Emotionality.

However, it must be realized that despite these statistical links, they describe group differences and not how individual children change or stay the same as they become adults. These general patterns also conceal a great deal of variation.

What then are the implications of studies on the stability of individual differences in temperament? During the first year of life it appears that temperamental differences between children are influenced by a wide range of factors and the net effect is that temperament shown during this period does not strongly relate to the child's later behaviour. However, beyond the first year, stability of individual difference is well established and temperament becomes a significant enduring influence on the child's behaviour. Although there is a fair amount of individual variation, it is still possible to detect links between infant temperament and later adult personality.

3.4 Situation specificity

By definition, temperamental differences influence behaviour over a wide range of settings and contexts. Temperament theorists would not deny the part played by situations, especially the social context, on the child's behaviour. However, the idea of temperament is that it should be demonstrated by a behavioural style that will tend to hold across both time (stability) and settings (not be situationally specific).

   If temperament is something that stems from biological factors within the individual child (a trait) then we should expect to see it exhibited in a consistent fashion in a variety of settings.

RESEARCH SUMMARY 3

Measures of coherence of temperament

Hinde and Tobin (1986) studied 4 year olds both at home with their mothers and with a combination of adults and similar aged children in pre-school playgroups. They found what they called 'coherence of temperament', referring to regularity in children's behaviour across settings but not necessarily in the simple sense of the child's behaviour being the same in all contexts. In different contexts they found that the children did not necessarily show the same individual differences on the same behaviours but rather that certain temperamental features identified in one context were systematically related to behaviour shown in another. Commenting on these findings, Hinde (1989) suggests that different aspects of temperament show different patterns of home/pre-school consistency and do so differently for boys and for girls:

> *Intense* children showed generally similar behaviour in the two situations: they tended to show both more friendly behaviour and more hostile behaviour to the mother at home, and at school interacted more with peers, though the proportions of hostile and friendly interactions were not proportionately changed. The characteristic *Active* was related to similar but different behaviour: at home Active children had fewer friendly interactions with their mothers than non-Active children, but at school they showed more hostility to teachers and peers. In the case of *Shy* children, Shy girls tended to have better relationships with their mothers than non-Shy girls, but Shy boys tended to have worse ones ... Shy boys tended (non-significantly) to be more hostile to peers in school than non-Shy boys, whereas Shy girls were significantly less hostile. Finally, *Moody* seemed to be 'expressed' directly in school whereas its correlates at home concerned items indicating the mother's response to its expression.

> (Hinde, 1989, p. 32)

Hinde suggests that the value of temperament to the developmental psychologist is that it provides a way of describing *coherence* in children's behaviour. Note that he does not mean that children behave in the same way in different situations and with different people. Rather, they behave in predictable ways across many contexts and within the medium term. The prediction as to how children will behave depended on their sex and age. Under Hinde's formulation, temperament is not a fixed style of behaving but rather a set of regularities or associations between individual differences in behaviour in different contexts and, for Hinde, the most salient feature of these contexts is the quality of the child's relationships with other people.

3.5 Early emergence of individual differences

It has often been assumed that if temperament has a biological basis then its pervasive effects will mean that individual differences will be apparent from an early age. This need not be the case; there are many characteristics that are under biological control which do not manifest themselves until later in development. For example, language, as shown by word combinations, does not emerge until the second year of life although it may have origins in very early interactions between caregiver and child. Many forms of mental illness, such as schizophrenia or manic depression, are not shown until adolescence or later.

Figure 7 Some temperament characteristics may be more affected by genetic factors during adolescence.

As far as individual differences are concerned it has been demonstrated that many characteristics, for example intelligence, show *higher* heritabilities in young adulthood than in early childhood (Wilson, 1983). So, although early emergence is not a *necessary* characteristic of a biologically rooted behaviour, it has generally been accepted that the temperament construct should be applied to features of individual differences that are present early on in life. In the following section, we turn to measures of temperament.

Summary of Section 3

- Temperament is a general quality of a child's behaviour inferred from measurements of behaviour in different situations and at different times.
- Temperamental differences have been shown to be influenced by genetic differences between children.
- Temperamental differences can be detected during the first year of life but these are not highly related to temperamental differences at age 3 or 4 years.
- Temperament shows increasing stability as children get older.
- Child temperament types have been found to lead on to specific adult personality types.

4   Measuring temperament

A major concern in the study of temperament, as for any key concept in psychology, is how it can be measured most appropriately. The earliest systematic approaches to measuring temperament were reliant on parents as observers or recorders of their children's behaviour. For example, parents made 24-hour diary records of their children's behaviour in the New York Longitudinal Study (NYLS) of Thomas and Chess (1977). It was argued that parents were the only people with sufficient access to their child's behaviour over a wide range of settings and over a long period of time to be able to report on temperament. Such an extensive exposure to the child is essential to allow for fluctuations in the child's behaviour resulting, for example, from illness or stress. However, there are marked drawbacks in relying on parents as reporters on their children. In particular there are dangers of parents biasing their descriptions in terms of either social desirability or in terms of their expectations about behaviour rather than the child's actual behaviour. These are most likely to occur when the parents are using questionnaires or checklists, although diaries are also subject to such bias. In identifying these potential difficulties, it should not be assumed that parents are responsible for difficulties in obtaining reliable and valid measures of temperament.

Interviews give an opportunity to ask parents more direct questions about their children. They can also be asked to complete records based on their direct observation of the child's behaviour. Although potentially more accurate than rating scales, the reliability and validity of such temperament assessment measures have also been found wanting. Nevertheless, Hagekull *et al.* (1984) have shown that the validity of parental reports on temperament agreed adequately well with direct observation. The validity was indicated by the agreement between the parent report and the direct observation score. These results range from 28 per cent (Sensory sensitivity) to 69 per cent (Attentiveness) agreement. A high percentage indicates a good agreement between the two sets of measures.

Activity 3

The emotionality, activity and sociality (EAS) temperament scale

Allow about 30 minutes

This activity will give you the opportunity to try out one of the measures of temperament that is used in research and to assess its effectiveness.

Below is an example of ten items taken from a temperament questionnaire: the Buss and Plomin (1984) EAS scale. Fill in the ratings for a child you know under the age of 5 years. Make a note of those items that you find difficult to rate and summarize the implications of these difficulties for the accurate assessment of temperamental differences.

Table 2 The EAS temperament survey for children: parental ratings

Please circle the rating on each of the items for your child	Not typical			Very typical	
1 Child tends to be shy	1	2	3	4	5
2 Child cries easily	1	2	3	4	5
3 Child likes to be with people	1	2	3	4	5
4 Child is always on the go	1	2	3	4	5
5 Child prefers playing with others rather than alone	1	2	3	4	5
6 Child tends to be somewhat emotional	1	2	3	4	5
7 When child moves about, he usually moves slowly	1	2	3	4	5
8 Child makes friends easily	1	2	3	4	5
9 Child is off and running as soon as he wakes up in the morning	1	2	3	4	5
10 Child finds people more stimulating than anything else	1	2	3	4	5

Source: Buss and Plomin (1984).

Comment

You may have felt that the 1–5 scale used in the EAS is not sufficiently well defined. You might also have felt that for some of the behaviours the child behaves differently in different situations. The use of words like 'tends to' and 'usually' in the descriptors might have also made you feel that the measures are imprecise.

Summary of Section 4

- Measuring temperament has most often been done by asking mothers to observe/record their children's behaviour.
- There are issues regarding the reliability of parental reports.
- Nevertheless, there is some evidence that mothers' reports agree reasonably well with results of direct observation of children.

5   Four temperament theories

As yet, developmental psychologists have not found a single, agreed framework to define and measure temperament. So, in this section, we are going to look at four competing theories about the structure and organization of temperament and attempt to evaluate their strengths and weaknesses.

5.1 Thomas and Chess: nine-dimensional framework

One of the major influences on temperament research has been the New York Longitudinal Study (NYLS) initiated during the 1950s (Thomas and Chess, 1977). Thomas and Chess were the first researchers to develop a systematic theory of temperament. The researchers used a nine-dimensional framework for describing children's temperament across a wide age range from infancy to adolescence:

1   Activity Level: how much and how vigorously the child moves about.
2   Quality of Mood: whether the child is predominantly happy or whiny and miserable.
3   Approach/Withdrawal: whether the child willingly meets new people and situations or whether they tend to be reluctant.
4   Rythmicity: whether the child's biological functions (i.e. eating, sleeping, going to the toilet) are very regular and predictable or the opposite.
5   Adaptability: how readily the child accepts changes in routine.
6   Threshold of Responsiveness: how much stimulation the child needs to trigger a response – this can be both pleasurable and aversive.
7   Intensity of Reaction: when the child does react, is this a mild or a vigorous response?
8   Distractibility: how easily the child can be distracted from their present activity.
9   Attention Span/Persistence: in the absence of distracters, how long the child will persevere with an activity.

One of the major difficulties with this framework is that it has not been possible to confirm these nine dimensions as independent aspects of temperament. When developing theories and measurements in psychology such independence is used as one of the validating criteria because, if two dimensions are highly correlated,

Parsimony
Preferring the
simplest solution
or the one that
makes fewest
assumptions.

this implies that a single dimension could be used instead of two. In the present case it may be that there are fewer than nine independent influences on children's behaviour. Principles such as parsimony then lead to the rejection of the over-complex theory. For example Distractibility and Attention Span are correlated with one another (at least at the extremes), that is, a child who is very distractible is also very likely to have a short attention span. It may be more helpful to describe these as reflecting related facets of a more general dimension of 'maintaining attention' along which children can vary.

It has been difficult to replicate the NYLS nine-dimensional framework on separate samples of children (Hubert *et al.*, 1982). It can be concluded that the nine dimensions postulated by Thomas and Chess are not all independent from each other and that a smaller number of factors underlies temperamental variations.

One of the particular features of the Thomas and Chess approach is their suggestion that as well as there being nine independent dimensions of temperament, distinct temperament types could be identified. On the basis of the NYLS sample they suggest that three temperament types can be identified early in infancy: these are the 'easy' child, the 'slow to warm up' child and the 'difficult' child. These labels are given to reflect the general properties of the behavioural style shown by the children. Thomas *et al.* (1968) presented findings that indicated that children who were rated high on Intensity and Reaction and on Negative Mood and low on Adaptability, on Rhythmicity and on Approach (the 'difficult' temperament style) were at increased risk of later behaviour disorders. The presence of this link was supported by findings from longitudinal studies of early temperament and later behaviour problems (Earls and Jung, 1987; Maziade *et al.*, 1989).

The difficult temperament construct has been the subject of much controversy. It was initially argued that the concept was primarily a product of the parents' *perceptions* of their children rather than a reflection of differences in the child's *actual* behaviour. This concern reached its height when it was found that mothers' ratings of temperament could be reliably identified *before* the child was born. Vaughn *et al.* (1987) measured aspects of mothers' personalities and attitudes towards child-rearing during their pregnancies and found them to be related to their later ratings of the child's temperament. Since their attitudes were measured before the mothers had the opportunity to experience their child's behaviour (except via activity in utero), it was argued that the temperament measure was being strongly influenced by characteristics of the mother rather than the child.

It has also been found that parental perceptions of infant emotionality at 4 and 8 months infant age predict independent measures of infant emotionality at 8 and 12 months respectively (Pauli-Pott *et al.*, 2003), suggesting that infant temperament may be partly shaped by parental perceptions, rather than the other way round.

Figure 8   Do mothers' perceptions of infant temperament affect subsequent development?

Such associations could in part reflect genetic factors which would tend to produce correlations between maternal attitudes and child personality. The most likely explanation is that maternal ratings based on questionnaires and checklists are inevitably influenced by aspects of the mother's personality that will produce bias whatever is being rated. This does not completely invalidate mothers' ratings of temperament. Like any measure based upon ratings of behaviour the question of the value or validity of the measure rests on the extent to which the ratings reflect the real temperament features of the child's behaviour. As long as the correlation between the ratings and a true measure of temperament is high then the rating may still provide a useful indicator of temperamental differences.

Bates has been an active critic of the supposed link between difficult temperament and child behaviour problems. However, in his own research he found that once differences in the mother's personality and the quality of the mother–infant relationship had been taken into account there was still a link between temperamental differences reported by the mother during the first 2 years of life and behaviour problems at 3–6 years of age (Bates and Bales, 1988).

In a recent review of this aspect of the relevance of the difficult temperament Bates states that:

> mother perceptions of infant and toddler characteristics of difficultness, unadaptability to novelty and resistance to control of activity predict later perceptions of the child's behavioural adjustment. There are some interesting differentiations in how the different infancy measures predict to different kinds of outcome adjustment dimensions, e.g. early unadaptability predicting better to later anxiety problems than acting-out problems.

> (Bates, 1989b, p. 351)

In conclusion, any distortions in mothers' perceptions of their child's temperament will bear some relationship to their behaviour towards the child and hence influence the mother–child relationship and the child's subsequent development.

5.2 Buss and Plomin: EAS framework

Partly in response to these criticisms of the over-complexity of the Thomas and Chess framework, Buss and Plomin (1984) developed their simpler, alternative system for classifying temperamental differences. They were more strongly influenced by theories of adult personality than were Thomas and Chess. Buss and Plomin suggested that both experimental laboratory studies and analyses of questionnaire data indicated that there were just three independent temperament dimensions – Emotionality, Activity and Sociability. They also discussed Impulsivity and Shyness as further possible dimensions.

In developing the EAS system, Buss and Plomin sought to identify traits that showed early emergence and strong genetic influence since they considered that these characteristics identify the traits as the basis for adult personality. The personality theory that has had most influence in this field is Eysenck's (1981). He suggests that there are two major dimensions along which personality characteristics vary, that is, extraversion and neuroticism. These terms are not readily applicable to the characteristics of infants but extraversion does conceptually relate to Sociability and Impulsivity, and Neuroticism to Emotionality. Of the four approaches being contrasted in this section, that adopted by Buss and Plomin is the one most closely allied to classical psychometric test construction. This is an approach to attitude and personality measurement that relies on a detailed analysis of the interrelationships (correlations) between responses to standard items on questionnaires. Statistical procedures are used which are designed to uncover the most important common dimensions that can account for the correlations obtained between responses to items. With such an approach Buss and Plomin suggest that just the three dimensions that they identified can account for most variations in temperament and that these dimensions relate quite directly to Eysenck's theory of adult personality.

5.3 Kagan: inhibition to the unfamiliar

Rutter (1982) has argued that the traditional dimensional approach of Thomas and Chess might not be the most appropriate method of arriving at a good definition of temperament. He suggests that the procedures developed to identify temperament 'profiles' or 'clusters' are a more useful approach from the perspective of a clinician. Kagan's studies of behavioural inhibition represent a preference for a categorical theory of temperament types rather than a dimensional-based analysis. Both the Buss and Plomin, and Thomas and Chess approaches see temperamental differences as varying along a continuum. In contrast Kagan and his colleagues very much emphasize *qualitative* distinctions between temperament types. They have been studying children whom they see as belonging to distinct categories as determined by their response to unfamiliar events and people, in other words, temperament types. On the basis of a systematic series of observations of their behaviour in the laboratory, they suggest that 15 per cent or so of children aged 2–3 years of age are very shy and timid when faced with the unfamiliar. A roughly equal percentage are uninhibited and socially responsive when confronting unfamiliar people. These two groups show a high degree of stability into middle childhood with the children becoming quiet and cautious, and talkative and sociable respectively. In each case about 75 per cent of the children in these two groups show such a stability of individual differences (Kagan, 1988). This means, for example, that for the substantial majority of children who show extreme shyness in middle childhood, this is not simply a consequence of recent stresses and upsets but rather a reflection of enduring qualities of their behaviour.

In considering the origins and the degree of stability of these temperamental categories Kagan postulates very specific sites in the brain, which regulate emotional behaviour and long-term memory, as responsible for differences in behavioural style. He has shown some physiological differences between these groups of children on measures of psychophysiological reactivity (i.e. such features as heart rate, heart rate variability, pupil dilation and cortisol secretion rates). These are all features which indicate the degree of the child's emotional reactions to experiences. However, even here, there is evidence that children should not be seen as simply victims of their biology. This is acknowledged by Kagan (1988) who quotes the case of a very inhibited boy who made a successful conscious effort to overcome his social inhibition.

5.4 Dunn and Kendrick: embedding temperament in social relationships

Dunn and Kendrick (1982a) have offered an alternative model for the nature of temperamental differences. They found that most children showed some behavioural reaction to the arrival of a new baby in the family, such as disturbed sleep, increased demands for attention and more tearfulness. They also found that certain features of such responses were related to temperamental characteristics of the older children, as measured before the new sibling was born. They found that temperamental differences were also related to differences in the quality of the interaction between the mother and the older child:

> temperamental differences were not important in accounting for the dramatically wide differences in the quality of interactions between the siblings. Here, the important variables were the quality of interaction between the mother and firstborn, the way in which the mother had discussed the baby as a person with wants and feelings, and the sex constellation of the sibling pair. Such a contrast between the significance of temperamental differences in the first children's behaviour with their mothers and the unimportance of these differences in relation to behaviour directed towards the sibling reinforces the point that temperamental differences must be viewed as closely bound up with differences in children's relationships with their mothers.

(Dunn and Kendrick, 1982b, p. 98)

The point that Dunn and Kendrick are emphasizing is that children's behaviour is not independent of the situations in which they find themselves. In particular, behaviour is influenced by the social context, that is, by the other people who are present with the child. They suggest that the behavioural style that a child will show in a particular setting will be consistent. This consistency is a property of the relationship between the child and the other person. To the extent that this relationship is stable so then will the temperamental differences be stable. Using this explanation it can be seen that the continuing action of genetic effects on behaviour is not the only mechanism that can produce stable individual differences in behaviour. It is important that theories of temperament consider the child's behaviour in a social context and not in isolation.

5.5 Research and clinical practice

Each approach has its own strengths and weaknesses and some approaches are more wide ranging than others. The researcher's task is to obtain accurate, precise measures on well-validated dimensions of behaviour and to be able reliably to identify possible differences in the temperaments being measured in large groups of children. The paediatrician's task is to obtain an accurate picture of the behaviour of a particular child, in a way that does justice to the complexity and uniqueness that parents see in their child's behaviour.

Figure 9 Expressions of temperament depend on the situation.

The paediatrician also needs to make judgements about likely continuities in the child's behaviour and the extent to which parents' beliefs and behaviour may be influencing the child. Can one specific theory suit both research and clinical practice? Are there certain approaches that are simply not relevant to one or the other?

Activity 4   *Questionnaire assessments of temperament*

Allow about
20 minutes

This activity will help you to evaluate the effectiveness of temperament questionnaires.

The assessment of the nine dimensions of the Thomas and Chess framework is often based on the use of the Carey Questionnaires. Table 3 shows an example of ten items from the Toddler Temperament Scale (TTS) (Fullard *et al.*, 1978) which is designed for parents to complete on 1–3-year-old children.

- The complete questionnaire comprises 97 items in total. Can you think of ways in which the questions could be improved?

- A study by Vaughn, *et al.* (1987) suggested that this assessment of temperament was heavily influenced by rater bias – why do you think this bias happens?

- In Activity 3 you used the EAS scale in Table 2. What do you consider to be the comparative strengths and weaknesses of these two temperament questionnaires?

Table 3 An extract from The Toddler Temperament Scale

Using the scale shown below, please circle the figure that tells how often the child's recent and current behaviour has been like the behaviour described by each item.

		Almost never	Rarely	Usually does not	Usually does	Frequently	Almost always
1	The child gets sleepy at about the same time each evening (within half hour)	1	2	3	4	5	6
2	The child fidgets during quiet activities (story telling, looking at pictures)	1	2	3	4	5	6
3	The child takes feedings quietly with mild expression of likes and dislikes	1	2	3	4	5	6
4	The child is pleasant (smiles, laughs) when first arriving in unfamiliar places	1	2	3	4	5	6
5	A child's initial reaction to seeing the doctor is acceptance	1	2	3	4	5	6
6	The child pays attention to game with parent for only a minute or so	1	2	3	4	5	6
7	The child's bowel movements come at different times from day to day (over one hour difference)	1	2	3	4	5	6
8	The child is fussy on waking up (frowns, complains, cries)	1	2	3	4	5	6
9	The child's initial reaction to a new baby sitter is rejection (crying, clinging to mother, etc.)	1	2	3	4	5	6
10	The child reacts to a disliked food even if it is mixed with a preferred one	1	2	3	4	5	6

Source: Fullard et al., 1978.

Comment

You may have felt that many of the items in the scales are open to a range of interpretation. For example, what does 'somewhat emotional' mean in item 6 of the EAS in Table 2? Or, 'mild expression of likes and dislikes' in the Toddler Temperament Scale (TTS) in Table 3? This could mean that a parent's interpretation of an item might affect their child's score. Another reaction, particularly to the TTS, might be that many of the behaviours are affected by the context. For example, how long a child may pay attention to a game might depend very much on what game it is and the extent to which the parent effectively encourages the child's engagement with it. Both of these issues suggest that children's scores on these scales do not only reflect something intrinsic to them, but are also affected by parents' views and the sorts of environments that they are in.

Summary of Section 5

- Thomas and Chess produced the first systematic theory of temperament.
- The nine dimensions of the Thomas and Chess framework may not be independent, so a less complex theory might be preferred.
- 'Difficult temperament' is a useful category to identify some children who are at risk of later behaviour problems.
- Buss and Plomin's three dimensional framework (Emotionality, Activity and Sociability) has the advantage of being simpler than that of Thomas and Chess and of being related to a theory of adult personality.
- Kagan has identified behavioural inhibition to unfamiliarity as one of the most stable temperament dimensions.
- Dunn and Kendrick provide examples of how temperament and social context both influence the child's behavioural responses to the arrival of a new sibling.

6 Influence of temperament on development

Here we will consider whether temperamental differences are related to other aspects of children's development. Again it must be emphasized that temperament is concerned with individual differences and therefore the impact of temperament on development centres on associations between temperament and variations in children's cognitive and social development. There are several ways in which this can occur and these will be considered in turn.

6.1 Direct effect of temperament on development

A child with a short attention span and who is very impulsive is likely to experience difficulties in learning situations either at home or at pre-school groups (Tizard and Hughes, 1984). This example shows that temperamental differences may have a pervasive effect on children's cognitive and social development through their impact on behavioural control and responsivity. In older children Keogh (1982) has identified a three-factor model of temperament that is related to behaviour in school and which has implications for learning. The factors are Task Orientation, Personal–Social Flexibility and Reactivity. Clearly factors such as task orientation will have a direct impact on the child's ability to gain from learning experiences. Other temperamental influences will have more indirect effects on academic attainment. For example, reactivity is more likely to influence pupil–teacher and pupil–pupil interaction and thereby the social context within which learning takes place.

6.2 Direct effect of child temperament on parents

One of the central concepts in current thinking about child development is that of the child influencing its own development, that is, not just being a passive receiver of externally determined experiences. Bell (1968), and Sameroff and Chandler (1975) are widely recognized as bringing this *transactional* model to the fore. Under this model, the child plays a significant role in producing its own experiences both directly by its own selection of activities but, more importantly for the young child, by the influence its behaviour has upon caretakers (Sameroff and Fiese, 1990).

6.3 Indirect effect via 'goodness of fit'

There has been a strand of thinking linked with the study of temperament that has emphasized that the significance of individual differences in temperament has to be considered in relation to specific environments. A child who is very low on adaptability and very high on rhythmicity using the Thomas and Chess framework will have a more aversive experience if cared for by parents who are very erratic in their pattern of child care. The same child will be well suited to parents who are more regular in their routines of eating and sleeping. This suggests that the impact of temperament on development has to be analysed as an interaction between the child's characteristics and features of the environment including parenting.

There have been several temperament theorists including Thomas and Chess who have taken this position. One of the most extensive research studies with this goodness of fit orientation is that of Lerner and colleagues:

> The goodness of fit concept emphasizes the need to consider both the characteristics of individuality of the person and the demands of the social environment, as indexed for instance by expectations or attitudes of key significant others with whom the person interacts (e.g. parents, peers or teachers). If a person's characteristics of individuality match, or fit, the demands of a particular social context then positive interactions and adjustment are expected. In contrast, negative adjustment is expected to occur when there is a poor fit between the demands of a particular social context and the person's characteristics of individuality.
>
> (Lerner *et al.*, 1989, p. 510)

As an illustration of this notion of the goodness of fit between the child's temperament and other people's behaviour towards them, Lerner *et al.* (1989) discussed some of the evidence concerning temperament and maternal employment outside the home. A wide variety of social and economic pressures will be influencing the decision to work outside the home. However, in addition they suggest that there could be two plausible routes whereby difficult temperament could influence mothers' decisions on whether to work outside the home. The first could be that mothers find the problems of rearing the child with difficult temperament too aversive and therefore opt to go out to work to avoid the hassles of daily childcare. The second route could be that the difficult child is so unpredictable in its eating and sleeping habits and protests intensely when left with unfamiliar people that the mother feels constrained not to go out to work because the child cannot fit in with the externally required constraints of the mother attending the work place at fixed times for fixed periods.

Figure 10   A child's difficult temperament may affect the mother's work performance.

The goodness of fit approach suggests that which of these processes operates will depend on the fit between the child's temperament and the mother's tolerance. It will not be possible to predict the consequences of difficult temperament on the mother's decision to return to work with knowledge of her attitudes towards child-rearing and towards time keeping at work.

Using data from the NYLS, Lerner and Galambos (1985) found that mothers of children with difficult temperament tended to have more restricted work histories than other children. One problem with this finding is that mothers' reports on their infants' 'difficulty' may be biased by factors that also affect work performance, such as depression. Hyde *et al.* (2004) examined this possibility in a study which found that the consensus infant temperament judgements of fathers and mothers were still a good predictor of mothers' work outcomes. This study also found evidence that a mediating factor between infant temperament and maternal work outcome is maternal mood: difficult infants are likely to make mothers more depressed and diminish their sense of competence, thus affecting their work performance. The Lerner and Galambos (1985) study also found that it seemed to be harder for parents to make satisfactory daycare arrangements for difficult infants.

6.4 Indirect effect via susceptibility to psychosocial adversity

Temperament may also be related to differences in vulnerability to stress. Not all children are adversely affected by the experience of specific stresses, such as admission to hospital. Pre-school children repeatedly hospitalized are at risk for later educational and behavioural difficulties but only if they come from socially disadvantaged backgrounds (Quinton and Rutter, 1976).

It has proved more difficult to establish whether temperament does influence children's risk of being affected by adverse experiences. Dunn and Kendrick (1982b) have shown that an older child's response to the arrival of a new sibling is systematically related to their temperament as measured while their mother was pregnant. Most children respond to this event with some upsurge of behavioural disturbance, such as an increase in demands for parental attention or in crying. Which behavioural response is shown is related to prior temperament. Unfortunately their data do not suggest any clear pattern of any one aspect of temperament being more significant than any other. However, there were indications that increases in fears, worries and 'ritual' behaviours were associated with a high degree of temperamental Intensity and Negative Mood measured before the arrival of the second child.

6.5 Indirect effect on range of experiences

An important aspect of the transactional model of development is that as children become older they increasingly come to influence the range of environments they encounter and the experiences these create. During infancy, children with different temperament styles evoke different responses from the people they encounter, for example, active, smiling infants are more likely to be smiled at and played with than passive unresponsive infants. As children become more mobile and more independent they are able to select for themselves between alternative experiences, for example, a shy, behaviourally-inhibited child may avoid social encounters. This may accentuate temperamental characteristics: the avoidance of meeting other people prevents the child from becoming socially skilled and therefore more reluctant to engage in social behaviour in the future. This may have a wider impact on their development. For example, Rutter (1982) has demonstrated the way impulsive, active children are more likely to experience accidents, presumably as a result of their selecting more risky environments to play in.

These alternative mechanisms for the impact of temperament on the environments the child experiences can be classified into three types of gene–

environment correlation, following Scarr and McCartney (1983) who have suggested that children's genetic make-up comes to influence the environments they experience through three routes. These can be illustrated for temperament. One is *passive* gene–environment correlations which are produced when the child is being cared for by parents who share similar temperaments to the child. A child with a high intensity of reaction is more likely than other children to be cared for by a parent who has a similarly high intensity of reaction. Such parent–child pairs are likely to be creating experiences for the child which will be eliciting much aversive stimulation for the child. *Evocative* gene–environment correlations are created when the child's behaviour evokes specific types of responses from carers. This was illustrated in the earlier example of sociable children evoking more social stimulation from carers. The third type is *active* gene–environment correlation which arises from the child actively seeking environments that suit its behavioural predispositions. Children with a low threshold of responsiveness are likely to seek less extreme and more predictable environments.

An important feature of the Scarr and McCartney theory is that they propose that as the child becomes older the mix of these correlations will change. Initially the passive and evocative correlations will dominate. The evocative effects will remain fairly constant. The significance of passive effects declines in importance as the child encounters a wider range of people than just primarily the parents. Clearly active gene–environment effects are likely to become dominant as the child has greater and greater freedom to select its own activities.

6.6 Attachment and temperament

An important aspect of children's early development is the quality of their attachment to their caregiver. A widely used, standardized way of assessing this is a laboratory procedure called the 'Strange Situation Test' (SST; Ainsworth *et al.*, 1978), consisting of a series of separations and reunions of child, caregiver and a stranger. Depending on how children behave during these episodes, their attachment is classified as either 'secure' or 'insecure'. Insecure classifications are further subdivided into 'avoidant' or 'ambivalent' categories.

These different attachment styles are seen as important because they are associated with variations in children's subsequent development; secure attachment is generally associated with more positive outcomes. Since the formation of attachment is bound up with how an infant behaves towards the caregiver during the first year of life it would seem likely that infant temperament is a significant element. It is surprising, then, that although some research has found that infant irritability and negative emotionality are linked with the avoidant type of insecure attachment, numerous studies have found no evidence that infant temperamental differences are associated directly with secure versus insecure attachment classifications in typical development (Goldsmith and Alansky, 1987).

One feature of caregiver behaviour during the child's first year that has been widely found to influence attachment quality is 'sensitivity' (De Wolff and Van IJzendoorn, 1997), namely, the extent to which the caregiver is attentive to the infant's state, behaviour and communication, and responds appropriately. It might be expected that caregiver personality differences would thus be found to be associated with infant attachment security, but here again few direct effects have been found (Egeland and Farber, 1984).

What has been found, however, is that the *combination* of child and caregiver individual characteristics does predict attachment security (Belsky and Isabella, 1988; Notaro and Volling, 1999) lending support to a transactional model of the process. The following research summary gives one example of this.

Figure 11   Attachment shows combined effects of both maternal and child characteristics.

RESEARCH SUMMARY 4

Infant attachment

Mangelsdorf *et al.* (2000) studied 102 mother–infant dyads in Michigan, USA, to examine the contributions of maternal and infant characteristics to infant attachment. When the infants were 8 months old, their temperaments were assessed in a laboratory-based set of tasks, their mothers completed personality questionnaires (MPQ) for themselves and temperament questionnaires on their infants, and then completed a brief teaching task with their infants. At twelve months of age, each infant's attachment security was assessed in the strange situation.

Neither mothers' nor infants' characteristics, taken alone, were good predictors of infants' attachment classification. However, when the joint effects of both mother and infant factors were examined, it was found that infants were classed as securely attached if they showed more positive emotions and fewer fearful reactions in the temperament assessments, but only if their mothers also showed more positive emotionality. These secure infants were also rated low on activity level and the amount of distress they showed to novelty but, again, only if their mothers also rated high on Constraint (self-control, conventionality) in the MPQ.

The researchers comment on these findings that:

> The results of this investigation suggest that any individual characteristic of either child or mother may be less important than the relationship context within which that characteristic occurs.
>
> (Mangelsdorf *et al.*, 2000, p. 188)

Summary of Section 6

- Temperament can directly influence other aspects of development, for example, attentional variation has an impact on cognitive development.
- Temperamental variation influences the parent's response to the child.
- The goodness of fit between a child's temperament and parental style can have an impact on the child's attachment and long-term social adjustment.
- A child's vulnerability to the adverse effects of life events can be influenced by temperament.
- Temperament can have a marked effect on the type and range of experiences to which the child is exposed.

7   Conclusion

What conclusions can we draw about temperamental individuality in infancy? First, infant behaviour shows systematic characteristics and regularities. Infants show a co-ordination and adaptation in their behaviour which is consistent with there being systems regulating behaviour from a very early age. But temperament is not primarily concerned with the organization of behaviour itself but rather with broad *differences* in the way behaviour is organized in different individuals. The range and scope of these temperamental differences has not yet been agreed upon but all schemes include at least some aspects of the Emotionality, Activity and Sociability framework put forward by Buss and Plomin, plus possible attentional ability variations as suggested by Bates.

These temperament differences may be in part influenced by genetic differences between children but then so are many other behavioural characteristics. Equally there are biological effects on temperament that are not influenced by genetic differences, for example, the possibly medium-term effects of illness and the effects of prematurity and low birth weight. Temperamental characteristics can be identified during the first 2 years of life but stabilities into even middle childhood are only modest.

Temperamental differences do affect the child's development, partly through their impact on the response of caregivers towards the child. In this sense they may play an important part in the child's influence on their own development, a transactional process. Temperament's role in influencing the child's response to stressful events and a broader range of experiences is an ongoing topic for research.

References

Ainsworth, M. D. S., Blehar, M. C., Waters, E. and Wall, S. (1978) *Patterns of Attachment*, Hillsdale, NJ, Lawrence Erlbaum.

Auerbach, J. G., Faroy, M., Ebstein, R., Kahana, M. and Levine, J. (2001) 'The association of the dopamine D4 receptor gene (DRD4) and serotonin transporter promoter gene (5-HTTLPR) with temperament in 12-month-old infants', *Journal of Child Psychology and Psychiatry*, vol. 42, pp. 777–83.

Bates, J. E. (1989a) 'Concepts and measures of temperament', in Kohnstamm, G. A., Bates, J. E. and Rothbart, M. K. (eds) *Temperament in Childhood*, pp. 3–26, Chichester, John Wiley.

Bates, J. E. (1989b) 'Applications of temperament concepts', in Kohnstamm, G. A., Bates, J. E. and Rothbart, M. K. (eds) *Temperament in Childhood*, pp. 321–56, Chichester, John Wiley.

Bates, J. E. and Bales, K. (1988) 'The role of attachment in the development of behaviour problems', in Belsky, J. and Nezworski, T. (eds) *Clinical Implications of Attachment*, pp. 253–99, New York, Lawrence Erlbaum.

Bell, R. Q. (1968) 'A reinterpretation of the direction of effects in studies of socialisation', *Psychology Review*, vol. 75, pp. 81–95.

Belsky, J. and Isabella, R. (1988) 'Maternal, infant and social-contextual determinants of attachment security', in Belsky, J. and Nezworski, T. (eds) *Clinical Implications of Attachment*, pp. 253–99, New York, Lawrence Erlbaum.

Benet-Martinez, V. and John, O. P. (1998) 'Los cincos grandes across cultures and ethnic groups; multitrait multimethod analyses of the Big Five in Spanish and English', *Journal of Personality and Social Psychology*, vol. 75, pp. 729–50.

Briggs Myers, I. and Myers, P. B. (1995) *Gifts Differing: understanding personality type*, Palo Alto, California, Consulting Psychologists Press.

Buss, A. H. and Plomin, R. (1984) *Temperament: early developing personality traits*, Hillsdale, NJ, Lawrence Erlbaum.

Caspi, A., Harrington, H., Milne, B., Amell, J. W., Theodore, R. F. and Moffitt, T. E. (2003) 'Children's behavioural styles at age 3 are linked to their adult personality traits at age 26', *Journal of Personality*, vol. 71, pp. 495–514.

Cattell, R. B. and Kline, P. (1977) *The Scientific Analysis of Personality and Motivation*, New York, Academic Press.

Costa, P. T., Jr., and McCrae, R. R. (1997) 'Longitudinal stability of adult personality', in Hogan, R., Johnson, J. and Briggs, S. (eds), *Handbook of Personality Psychology*, pp. 269–90, San Diego, CA, Academic Press.

De Wolff, M. S. and Van IJzendoorn, M. H. (1997) 'Sensitivity and attachment: a meta-analysis on parental antecedents of infant attachment', *Child Development, vol. 68, pp. 571–91*.

Dunn, J. and Kendrick, C. (1982a) *Siblings: love, envy and understanding*, Cambridge, MA, Harvard University Press.

Dunn, J. and Kendrick, C. (1982b) 'Temperamental differences, family relationships and young children's response to change within the family', in Porter, R. and Collins, G. (eds) *Temperamental Differences in Infants and Young Children*, pp. 1–19, CIBA Foundation Symposium No. 89, London, Pitman.

Earls, F. and Jung, K. G. (1987) 'Temperament and home environment characteristics as causal factors in the early development of child psychopathology', *Journal of the American Academy of Child and Adolescent Psychiatry*, vol. 26, pp. 491–8.

Egeland, B. and Farber, E. A. (1984) 'Infant-mother attachment: factors related to its development and changes over time', *Child Development*, vol. 55, pp. 753–71.

Eysenck, H. J. (1981) *A Model for Personality*, Berlin, Springer-Verlag.

Eysenck, H. J. (1991) 'Dimensions of personality: 16, 5, or 3? Criteria for a taxonomic paradigm', *Personality and Individual Differences, vol. 12,* pp. 773–90.

Faraone, S. V., Doyle, A. E., Mick, E. and Biederman, J. (2001) 'Meta-analysis of the association between the 7-repeat allele of the dopamine D4 receptor gene and Attention Deficit Hyperactivity Disorder', *American Journal of Psychiatry*, vol. 7, pp. 1052–57.

Fullard, W., McDevitt, S. C. and Carey, W. (1978) 'Toddler temperament scale', Department of Educational Psychology, Temple University, Philadelphia.

Goldsmith, H. H. and Alansky, J. A. (1987) 'Maternal and infant temperamental predictors of attachment: a meta-analytic review', *Journal of Consulting and Clinical Psychology*, vol. 55, pp. 805–16.

Goldsmith, H. H., Buss, A. R., Plomin, R. *et al.* (1987) 'What is temperament? Four approaches', *Child Development*, vol. 58, pp. 505–29.

Hagekull, B., Bohlin, G. and Lindhagen, K. (1984) 'Validity of parental reports', *Infant Behaviour and Development*, vol. 7, pp. 77–92.

Hinde, R. A. (1989) 'Temperament as an intervening variable' in Kohnstamm, G. A., Bates, J. E. and Rothbart, M. K. (eds) *Temperament in Childhood*, pp. 27–33, Chichester, John Wiley.

Hinde, R. A. and Tobin, C. (1986) 'Temperament at home and behaviour at preschool' in Kohnstamm, G. A. (ed.) *Temperament Discussed*, Liss, Swets and Zeitlinger.

Hubert, N. C., Wachs, T. D., Peters-Martin, P. and Gandour, M. J. (1982) 'The study of early temperament: measurement and conceptual issues', *Child Development*, vol. 53, pp. 571–600.

Hyde, J. H., Else-Quest, N. M., Goldsmith, H. H. and Biesanz, J. C. (2004) 'Children's temperament and behaviour problems predict their employed mothers' work functioning', *Child Development*, vol. 75, pp. 580–94.

Kagan, J. (1988) 'Temperamental contributions to social behaviour', *American Psychologist*, vol. 44, pp. 668–74.

Keogh, B. K. (1982) 'Children's temperament and teachers' decisions', in Porter, R. and Collins, G. (eds) *Temperamental Differences in Infants and Young Children*, pp. 269–85, CIBA Foundation Symposium No. 89, London, Pitman.

Jones, C. J. and Meredith, W. (1996) 'Patterns of personality change across the life span', *Psychology and Aging*, vol. 11, pp. 57–65.

Lerner, J. V. and Galambos, N. L. (1985) 'Maternal role satisfaction, mother–infant interaction and child temperament', *Developmental Psychology*, vol. 21, pp. 1157–64.

Lerner, J. V., Nitz, K., Talwar, R. and Lerner, R. M. (1989) 'On the functional significance of temperamental individuality: a developmental contextural view of the concept of goodness of fit', in Kohnstamm, G. A., Bates, J. E. and Rothbart, M. K. (eds) *Temperament in Childhood*, pp. 509–22, Chichester, John Wiley.

Maziade, M., Cote, R., Thiverge, J., Boutin, P. and Berner, H. (1989) 'Significance of extreme temperament in infancy for clinical status in preschool years, I. Value of extreme temperament at 4–8 months for predicting diagnosis at 7 years', *British Journal of Psychiatry*, vol. 154, pp. 535–43.

Mangelsdorf, S. C., McHale, J. L., Diener, M., Goldstein, L. H. and Lehn, L. (2000) 'Infant attachment; contributions of infant temperament and maternal characteristics', *Infant Behaviour and Development*, vol. 23, pp. 175–196.

Maslow, A. (1973) *The Farther Reaches of Human Nature*, Harmondsworth, Penguin.

Neale, M. and Stevenson, J. (1989) 'Rater bias in temperament ratings: a twin study', *Journal of Personality and Social Psychology*, vol. 56, pp. 446–55.

Newson, J. and Newson, E. (1970) *Four Years Old in an Urban Community*, Harmondsworth, Penguin.

Notaro, P. C. and Volling, B. L. (1999) 'Parental responsiveness and infant–parent attachment: a replication study with fathers and mothers', *Infant Behaviour and Development*, vol. 22, pp. 345–52.

Pauli-Pott, U., Mertesacker, B., Bade, U., Haverkock, A. and Beckmann, D. (2003) 'Parental perceptions and infant temperament development', *Infant Behavior and Development*, vol. 26, pp. 27–48.

Plomin, R., De Fries, J. C. and Fulker, D. W. (1988) *Nature and Nurture During Infancy and Early Childhood*, Cambridge, Cambridge University Press.

Quinton, D. and Rutter, M. (1976) 'Early hospital admissions and later disturbances of behaviour: an attempted replication of Douglas's findings', *Developmental Medicine and Child Neurology*, vol. 18, pp. 447–59.

Rothbart, M. K. (1989) 'Temperament and development', in Kohnstamm, G. A., Bates, J. E. and Rothbart, M. K. (eds) *Temperament in Childhood*, pp. 187–248, Chichester, John Wiley.

Rutter, M. (1982) 'Temperament: concepts, issues and problems', in Porter, R. and Collins, G. (eds) *Temperamental Differences in Infants and Young Children*, pp. 1–19, CIBA Foundation Symposium No. 89, London, Pitman.

Rutter, M. (1987) 'Temperament, personality and personality disorder', *British Journal of Psychiatry*, vol. 150, pp. 443–58.

Sameroff, A. J. and Chandler, M. J. (1975) 'Reproductive risk and the continuum of caretaking casualty', in Harrowitz, F. D., Scarr-Salapatek, S. and Siegel, G. (eds) *Review of Child Development Research*, pp. 187–24, Vol. 4, Chicago, University of Chicago Press.

Sameroff, A. and Fiese, B. H. (1990) 'Transactional regulation and early intervention', in Meisels S. J. and Shonkoff J. P. (eds) *Handbook of Early Childhood Intervention*, pp. 119–49, New York, Cambridge University Press.

Scarr, S. and McCartney, K. (1983) 'How people make their own environments: a theory of genotype–environment effects', *Child Development*, vol. 54, pp. 424–35.

Schmidt, L. A., Fox, N. A., Perez-Edgar, K., Hu, S. and Hamer, D. H. (2001) 'Association of DRD4 with attention problems in normal childhood development', *Psychiatric Genetics*, vol. 11, pp. 25–9.

Schmidt, L. A., Fox, N. A., Rubin, K. H., Hu, S. and Hamer, D. H. (2002) 'Molecular genetics of shyness and aggression in preschoolers', *Personality and Individual Differences*, vol. 2, pp. 227–38.

Tellegen, A. (1982) *Brief manual for the Multidimensional Personality Questionnaire*, Minneapolis, University of Minnesota.

Thomas, A. and Chess, S. (1977) *Temperament and Development*, New York, Brunner/Mazel.

Thomas, A., Chess, S. and Birch, H. G. (1968) *Temperament and Behaviour Disorders in Children*, New York, New York University Press.

Tizard, B. and Hughes, M. (1984) *Young Children Learning: talking and thinking at home and at school*, London, Fontana.

Vaughn, B. E., Bradley, C. F., Joffe, L. S., Seifer, R. and Barglow, P. (1987) 'Maternal characteristics measured prenatally are predictive of ratings of temperamental "difficulty" on the Carey Infant Temperament Questionnaire', *Developmental Psychology*, vol. 23, pp. 152–61.

Wilson, R. S. (1983) 'The Louisville Twin Study: developmental synchronies in behaviour', *Child Development*, vol. 54, pp. 298–316.

Chapter 6
Origins of development

Mark Norrish and Nigel Wilson

Contents

Learning outcomes

After you have studied this chapter you should be able to:

1 provide an overview of the way in which the interaction between genes and the environment contributes to our understanding of human behaviour;
2 describe how genes work and explain how they are involved in influencing human development, with examples;
3 explain why an understanding of evolutionary psychology is important to an understanding of development;
4 discuss the ways in which genetic, environmental and evolutionary explanations of behaviour combine to give us an integrated understanding of human development.

1   Introduction

In this chapter we describe both genetic and evolutionary perspectives on child development. However, we would like to start by highlighting the relation between these two approaches to child development and the supposed debate between 'nature' and 'nurture'. For example, it is often stated, in the scientific literature as well as in the media, that a gene has been discovered *for* a particular aspect of human behaviour. For example, in 1999 *The New York Times* printed an article entitled 'Scientists find the first gene for dyslexia' (Reuters, 1999). The very wording suggests that the old dichotomy between nature (genes) and nurture (the environment) persists. In fact, these two sets of factors are far from independent. Height, for example, is usually thought of as a characteristic 'determined' by genes. However, this would only be true if environmental conditions were the same for everyone. So, if two people have very different diets this 'environmental' factor may be more important in determining their height than their genes. This chapter will therefore highlight the need for an *integrated* approach to the understanding of human development; one that incorporates the interactions between genes *and* environment, as well as the influence of evolutionary adaptations. We will also emphasize that these are *influences* on development, not factors predetermining an outcome.

  The sections that follow discuss a variety of genetic influences on behaviour and some of the interactions that exist between behaviour and genes and the environment, the study of which has become known as behavioural genetics. We then turn our attention to evolutionary psychology, which can be thought of as the inverse of behavioural genetics. That is, while behavioural genetics seeks to understand the impact of genes on behaviour, evolutionary psychology is an exploration of the effects that 'historic' human behaviour has had on the genes that are present today. These interactions and the relationship between behavioural genetics and evolutionary psychology are represented schematically in Figure 1.

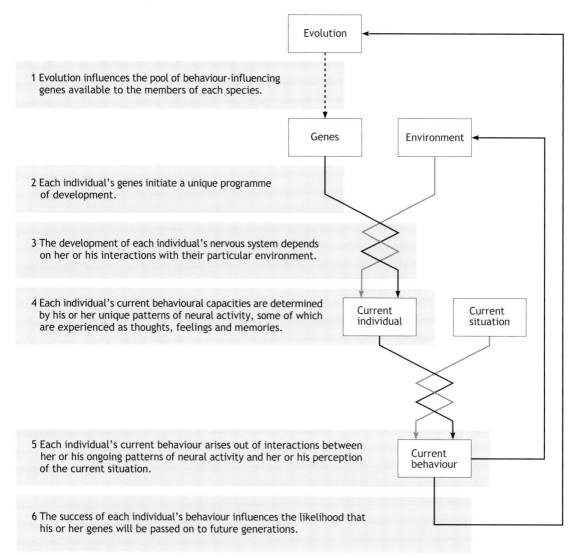

Figure 1   The contribution that genes, the environment and evolutionary history make to human behaviour (adapted from Pinel, 2003, p. 24).

One aim of psychology is to answer questions relating to why humans behave in particular ways. For most 'why' questions there are several possible answers. The temptation therefore is to test each possible answer to find out which one is correct, or at least which is the most probable. This approach can be misleading if the question can be answered simultaneously in more than one way. Genetic and evolutionary approaches to behaviour often provide explanations that are on a different 'level' to other psychological explanations, and this has led to both misunderstandings and unnecessary controversy. To understand what psychologists mean by 'levels of explanation', try Activity 1.

Activity 1   Levels of explanation

Allow about
10 minutes

This activity will illustrate how it is possible to have multiple, complementary explanations for a particular behaviour.

Imagine a little girl is throwing a tantrum in a supermarket. What reasons can you think of to explain why she is behaving in this way? Think of as many reasons as you can, including things to do with both the child and the situation.

Comment

There are lots of answers you could have generated to this question. The explanations you came up with can be seen as relating to different 'levels' of explanation – each level centres on the type of factor that may be influencing the child's behaviour. The different levels of explanation are illustrated below by some of the answers we came up with.

(a) Her mother may have bought the 'wrong' cereal instead of the one that was the little girl's favourite. This is a *proximate* level of explanation – proximate referring to some *immediate* aspect of the environment that acts as a trigger for the given behaviour (in this case, her mother not buying what she wants). Proximate explanations are, however, unable to explain why the child has learned to throw tantrums in the first place.

(b) She may have seen other children throwing tantrums and then getting what they want. This is a *developmental* level explanation. That is, she has learned to do this *through her own experience*, by watching others. However, the developmental level of explanation does not explain why children who have had similar experiences might differ in their tantrum-throwing behaviour.

(c) She might be genetically predisposed to throw tantrums! Although there is no direct genetic basis for tantrum throwing (that we are aware of) it is a recognized behavioural characteristic of several rare 'genetic' disorders. This is a *genetic* level of explanation. Such an explanation is helpful in establishing possible biological origins of the behaviour.

(d) She may be throwing the tantrum because it is a feature of juvenile behaviour that can be seen across species. For example, tantrum-throwing is common to many birds and mammals (e.g. pelicans, zebras, chimpanzees) and usually coincides with the weaning period as the mother ceases to be the only source of food and the young animal starts to fend for itself. This type of explanation is at the *comparative* level – as it is based on comparing behaviour across species.

(e) She may be throwing the tantrum because tantrum-throwing in young children has been selected for through the process of evolution. This is referred to as a *functional* explanation as, in evolutionary terms, individuals who throw tantrums will secure more parental attention than individuals who do not throw tantrums and they will therefore increase their chances of survival. Over evolutionary history, tantrum-throwing will have become a common feature of early childhood behaviour. The functional explanation is concerned with the motivating forces (albeit unconscious ones) behind the behaviour.

Look back at your answers – can you work out which levels of explanation your answers relate to?

This activity illustrates how it is possible to have multiple, equally valid explanations for an instance of behaviour, because each one offers a different *level* of explanation and the different levels of explanation are complementary, each one focusing on a different type of factor. As a result, you can see that genetic and functional (evolutionary) levels of explanation are making different, complementary contributions to more traditional psychological explanations of child development.

2   What is behavioural genetics?

Genetics is the study of how organisms store, replicate, transmit and use information via the transfer of genes in order to develop, grow, reproduce and survive in their environments (Hartwell *et al.*, 2004). Allied to this, *behavioural genetics* attempts to explain how genes influence behaviour and provides important information about how genes and the environment interact in development to modify behaviour. It takes strategies which have been developed to unravel what genes do and applies these to the study of behaviour. Within behavioural genetics, genes are seen as contributing to *differences between individuals*, whereas shared environments contribute to the *similarity between individuals*.

The key message of behavioural geneticists is that genetic effects play a major role in the development and expression of behaviour. However, this does not mean that genetic effects should be viewed as the answer to all behavioural riddles. There is a complex relationship between genetic and environmental influences such that different outcomes can occur in spite of individuals having the same genes. For example, consider identical (monozygotic – MZ) twins.

Monozygotic (MZ)
Developed from a single fertilized egg cell.

Although such individuals are genetically identical, they do not necessarily show the same personalities or behaviours. Similarly, different sets of genes can underlie identical developmental outcomes.

The view that development is based on information beyond that provided in genes is known as epigenesis.

Epigenesis
Development as a consequence of the interactions between genes and environment.

In an epigenetic system, development occurs as a result of the interaction between genes and their environment. Genes always interact with the environment at some level. Even identical twins differ in body tissues and some cell components (Malcolm and Goodship, 2001) and their fingerprints and iris patterns differ. These differences presumably reflect different epigenetic pathways being followed by each twin and challenge the view that genes absolutely determine development and behaviour.

2.1   The laws of heredity

To help you understand behavioural genetics, we outline the basic mechanisms of genetics and the terms used in genetic research in the following sections (Sections 2.2–2.4). Genetic research started with the discovery of the basic mechanisms of inheritance that were described by the Austrian monk Gregor Mendel in 1866. Mendel described the inheritance of traits in pea plants (such as purple versus white flowers or green versus yellow seeds). By studying when these traits appeared and disappeared across different generations, he was able to establish laws that enabled accurate predictions about the expression of traits across generations. Mendel proposed that observable traits were created by units of inheritance too small to be seen by the naked eye. We now call these units of inheritance *genes*. Mendel described two basic laws of heredity.

The law of segregation

Mendel concluded that two copies of the units of inheritance (genes) were present in the parents, but that these separate ('segregate') before being passed on to offspring. The offspring then receive one copy from each parent. These two separate copies are alternative forms of the same gene and one form can dominate the other. These alternative forms of a gene are now called *alleles* and an allele can be *dominant* or *recessive*. A dominant allele is so-called, because it tends to 'dominate' if it is paired with a recessive allele, resulting in its associated physical characteristic being expressed. A recessive characteristic will only occur if both inherited alleles are recessive.

An observable characteristic (such as Mendel's white or purple pea flowers, or eye colour or behaviour in humans) is called a phenotype.

The combination of alleles present in an individual is known as the genotype.

This distinction is made, in part, because different genotypes can lead to the same phenotype. Imagine, for example, that the gene for brown eyes was dominant over the gene for blue eyes (note that in reality eye colour genetics is more complicated than this). A child with brown eyes might have two dominant 'brown' alleles or he or she could have one brown allele and one blue allele. In both cases the phenotype (observed characteristic) would be brown eyes but the genotype would be different.

If the two alleles are either both recessive or both dominant the genotype is called homozygous.

So a child with two brown eye alleles would be homozygous for the eye colour gene. If they are different then the genotype is described as heterozygous.

So, if a child had one brown eye allele and one blue eye allele they would be heterozygous for the eye colour gene. He or she would still have a phenotype of brown eye colour but as a carrier of the blue eye colour allele, meaning that it may re-emerge in future generations.

Recessive allele effects are seen, for example, in the disease cystic fibrosis, which causes severe respiratory and digestive malfunction. In 1989, a cystic fibrosis gene was identified. Affected individuals were found to have two recessive alleles of this gene, that is they were homozygous for the recessive allele of the cystic fibrosis gene. The resulting recessive trait is that cells retain water and a thick mucus builds up outside the cells, causing the respiratory problems of cystic fibrosis. The unaffected parents are heterozygous carriers, in that they have both the dominant and recessive allele, but the dominant allele masks the effects of the recessive abnormal allele.

Phenotype
The observable characteristics of an individual. The phenotype results from the interaction of the genotype with non-genetic factors.

Genotype
The complete set of genes present in an individual. The genotype is determined at fertilization when genetic information from the egg and sperm is combined.

Homozygous
The state of having two identical alleles for a particular gene or trait.

Heterozygous
The state of having two different alleles for a particular gene or trait.

The law of independent assortment

Mendel speculated about what would happen if different characteristics were passed on to offspring. In his case he was interested in whether the inheritance of seed colour might also affect the inheritance of seed shape. A human example might be to consider whether someone's height affects their eye colour. Through systematic experimentation, Mendel determined that the inheritance of one gene was not affected by the inheritance of another. Thus, our height (or any other inherited trait) does not affect the colour of our eyes (or any other inherited trait). This point might seem rather obvious, but other inherited characteristics do tend to co-occur and it would be easy to assume that they do so because of a genetic association. The fact that the alleles for a particular characteristic are inherited independently of each other is known as the law of independent assortment.

Let us recap at this point. Genes are the basic units of inheritance. Genes for the same characteristic come in different forms known as alleles. Individuals inherit two alleles for a trait; one from each parent. Alleles may be dominant or recessive, so that if a dominant allele is present the observable characteristic (phenotype) is that produced by the dominant allele, regardless of whether or not the genotype contains a recessive allele. If both alleles are the same this is a homozygous genotype. If they are different then it is heterozygous.

Activity 2   *Genetic terms*

Allow about
10 minutes

This activity allows you to check your understanding of terminology used so far.

Match the terms on the left to the descriptions on the right.

(1) Gene	(a) Having two identical alleles for a particular gene
(2) Phenotype	(b) An allele that is only expressed in the phenotype if its partner allele is also recessive
(3) Genotype	(c) The basic unit of inheritance
(4) Allele	(d) An allele that is expressed in the phenotype
(5) Dominant	(e) Having two different alleles for a particular gene
(6) Recessive	(f) The alleles present in an individual
(7) Heterozygous	(g) The observable characteristics resulting from the genotype
(8) Homozygous	(h) One form of a gene

Turn to the end of the chapter to find out the answers.

2.2 How are genes organized?

Deoxyribonucleic acid (DNA) molecules form the basis of genetic information and do so for virtually every living organism. DNA is present in every cell of the body and is composed of four sub-units or *bases* (represented by the letters A, G, C and T).

DNA bases
The four sub-units of DNA: adenine (A), guanine (G), cytosine (C) and thymine (T). These are also known as nucleotides.

These bases may follow one another in any order but are 'read' in groups of three, known as *triplets*. Each triplet specifies an amino acid and combinations of amino acids make proteins. Although the 'language' of heredity is based on only four letters, the possible combinations of these letters allow the production of 20 amino acids. Various combinations of the amino acids allow for thousands of different proteins to be built.

Think of it like this. The 'language' of DNA is based on four letters (bases). These letters form words (triplets) that are three letters long. Just as many different sentences can be formed by combining words in different sequences, so too can many different proteins be formed by differing sequences of amino acids. However, only a small proportion of DNA is translated in this way. Many DNA sequences seem to be redundant or at least have no known function (so called *junk DNA*). Only regions of DNA that do have an identified function are known as genes (the 'sentences' in our analogy).

DNA molecules are assembled into *chromosomes*, long thread-like structures inside every cell of the body that package and manage the storage, duplication, expression and evolution of DNA. Chromosomes contain thousands of genes along with junk DNA. Each gene occurs at a specific region of a chromosome known as the gene *locus*. Continuing the language analogy from above, chromosomes organize the words of the genetic alphabet into chapters and the complete set of chromosomes forms the human genetic 'book'.

Humans have 46 chromosomes which are organized into 23 pairs. Each locus for a particular gene occurs at the same place on each of the two matching chromosomes. The combination of the pair of alleles at a gene locus determines the phenotype.

Figure 2 illustrates the relationships among DNA, genes and chromosomes. Twenty-two of the pairs of chromosomes are matching. The twenty-third pair, however, differs between males and females, with females having a matching pair (known as XX) and males having a non-matching pair (known as XY) in which one of the chromosomes (Y) is shorter. Because of this difference between males and females, these chromosomes are known as the 'sex chromosomes', and the presence of the Y chromosome (inherited from the father) determines the development of a foetus as a male. This difference also explains why some conditions are more likely to affect males than females. For example, red–green colour blindness occurs due to a recessive allele carried on the X chromosome. If a female inherits the allele on one of her X chromosomes, it is still possible that she will inherit a dominant allele on the other one that will prevent her from developing colour-blindness. However, as males only have one X chromosome in this pair, if the colour blindness allele is present the male will be colour blind.

Traits like these that are influenced by genes on the sex chromosomes are known as *sex-linked traits*.

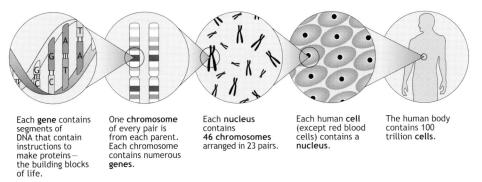

Each **gene** contains segments of DNA that contain instructions to make proteins — the building blocks of life.

One **chromosome** of every pair is from each parent. Each chromosome contains numerous **genes**.

Each **nucleus** contains **46 chromosomes** arranged in 23 pairs.

Each human **cell** (except red blood cells) contains a **nucleus**.

The human body contains 100 trillion **cells**.

Figure 2   The relationships among DNA, genes and chromosomes (adapted from Passer and Smith, 2004, p. 69).

One complete set of 23 chromosomes is inherited from each parent during conception resulting in a novel combination of genes in the new individual but a combination that is obviously influenced by the genetics of the parents. The different chromosomes that people carry are known as the *human genome* and this has now been mapped (see Box 1).

BOX 1

The Human Genome Project

The Human Genome Project, mapping the entire sequence of DNA that codes for humans, was completed in 2003, after draft sequences were released publicly in 2001. The entire sequence is some 3 billion base pairs long but contains surprisingly few genes. Researchers have only identified about 30,000 genes that code for proteins, although this number may increase as techniques for identifying very small or very big genes are improved. Nevertheless, this leaves a large portion of the genome that is thought to be active in some way but not specifically coding for proteins.

The mapping of the genome is an incredible achievement and it is suggested that this will allow researchers to understand the relationship between genes and behaviour more quickly. But there is a note of caution. Consider the nature of epigenetic development that has been described in this chapter in Section 2.2. Genes and gene products do not operate independently but as part of complex interactions with each other and with the environment. Knowing the catalogue of genes that go towards creating a human, including developmental aspects, is only a first step. It is a book in which we do not know the meaning of many of the words or how they interact to form sentences, and which does not have an index. These limitations are recognized by genomic researchers. Nevertheless, one of the defined challenges in genomic research is to 'understand the consequences of uncovering the genomic contributions to human traits and behaviours' and 'to provide a sound understanding of the contributions and interactions between genes and environment in ... complex phenotypes' (Collins *et al.*, 2003, p. 844).

Evolutionary pressures have created the genome we have today. Another challenge for genomic researchers is the study of interspecies DNA sequence comparisons. These comparisons enable the identification of functional elements of the genome but also allow mutation of processes to be studied. These mutations drive long-term evolutionary change, and studying the genome may 'yield new insights into the dynamic nature of genomes in a broader evolutionary framework' (Collins *et al.*, 2003, p. 839).

2.3 What do genes do?

Genes carry the codes for the production of proteins in the body. Proteins are the essential building blocks of the body. They are involved in building structural elements of the body (such as the cell membranes) including the nervous system. They are also involved in neurotransmitter functioning.

Neuro-transmitters Chemicals involved in the transmission of information through the nervous system.

In short, proteins are essential to the functioning of the body. By affecting the structures and activity of the nervous system through protein production genes affect behaviour. Moreover, genes do not produce constant amounts of protein. The activity of genes alters dynamically so that protein levels adjust to changing situations and this can happen rapidly.

Genes also have another important function. Many genes, rather than producing proteins, are involved in regulating the function of other genes in response to changes in internal and external environments and it is thought that more DNA may be involved in these regulatory processes than in producing proteins (Lawrence, 1992). The key point here is that gene expression is not fixed. For example, although identical twins have identical regulatory genes, the expression of those genes, and their effects on other genes, can differ depending on the environment (Plomin *et al.*, 2001).

2.4 Genetic variation

Mendel outlined the mechanisms by which genes are passed on to offspring, but it is important to note that children are never identical to their parents. There are many sources of genetic variation. For example, mutations (new DNA differences) occur when mistakes occur in copying DNA. Mutations can result in new alleles, leading to variation. If the mutations occur in either the egg cells produced by females or the sperm cells produced by males, they can then be passed on to the offspring. Where a mutation is not perpetuated in the population this may be because the change led to fatal consequences or provided some evolutionary disadvantage across generations. There are also several exceptions to Mendel's laws of inheritance, a few of which are outlined here.

Normally an egg or sperm carries just one half of the normal pair of chromosomes. However, during the production of an egg or sperm sometimes it receives both copies of a chromosome pair and the individual then inherits an extra chromosome. This extra genetic material can result in conditions such as Down syndrome.

Mendel looked at traits for which there were two alleles, but many traits have multiple alleles. For example, the ABO blood types are determined by three alleles of one gene (see Figure 3). Alleles may not be completely recessive or dominant, such that a combination of characteristics is expressed. This is seen, for example, in roan cattle where incomplete dominance of an allele for red coat colour, over an allele for white coat colour, results in a pinkish coat. Alleles may be *co-dominant*. This is shown in sickle-cell anaemia. People with two copies of the sickle cell allele have the disease. However, people with one of the sickle cell alleles also have both normal and sickle cell proteins in their red blood cells, although they are generally healthy. In this case the characteristics of both normal and sickle cells are expressed at a molecular level (co-dominance) but in terms of the whole organism the normal allele is dominant for overall health.

Another example of an exception to Mendel's laws is *genomic imprinting*. This is when the expression of a gene depends on whether it is inherited from the mother or the father.

Finally, many complex traits such as cognitive ability are influenced by many genes at once (i.e. the trait is polygenic or influenced by multiple alleles).

Polygenic
Involving more than one gene.

Thus, although Mendel's laws hold true in many situations there are also exceptions to these laws that add to the rich complexity of development.

Genotypes	AA	Ao	BB	Bo	AB	oo
Phenotypes	A		B		AB	O

Figure 3   Multiple alleles result in the ABO blood types. The alleles are represented here by A, B and o. The A and B alleles are co-dominant and so are both expressed in the phenotype. The 'o' allele is recessive to both A and B and so is only expressed for the homologous 'oo' genotype. Thus, six genotypes produce four blood group phenotypes.

Summary of Section 2

- The unit of inheritance is the gene.
- Genes exist in different forms known as alleles.
- The combination of alleles present in an individual is the *genotype* whereas the expression of these as physical or behavioural characteristics is the *phenotype*.
- Mendel's laws of inheritance describe how genes are passed on through generations in a predictable way; however, there are many sources of genetic variation that result in differences between individuals.
- Genes influence the structure and function of the body, including the nervous system, and may also interact with each other.
- Epigenetic development is the result of the interaction between genes and their environment.

3 Investigating human behavioural genetics

3.1 Family, adoption and twin studies

Due to ethical considerations, controlled experimental genetic manipulations are not possible in human genetic research. Instead, researchers have relied on 'natural' experiments to examine the roles played by genes in development and behaviour. The classic techniques in studying human behavioural genetics are family, adoption and twin studies.

Family members vary in genetic relatedness, such that first-degree relatives are more genetically similar than, for example, cousins. Differences between relatives can be used to assess the relative contribution of the environment and genetics. However, family members often also share similar environments, and so it is difficult to separate out the potential effects of this 'shared environment' from those of genetic factors.

Adoption studies allow a better separation of genetic and environmental influences. These are instances where a child has been adopted away from his or her biological parents. Similarities between the biological parents and the child can be used to assess the genetic contribution to a trait. Similarly, the degree to which an adopted child is similar to his or her adoptive parents can be used to assess the environmental contribution.

Finally, both family and adoption studies can involve twins. Identical (monozygotic – MZ) twins are genetically identical. Non-identical, fraternal (dizygotic – DZ) twins are, on average, 50 per cent genetically similar. If a particular characteristic has a significant genetic component then there should be a greater similarity between MZ than between DZ twins for that trait. For example, Rietveld *et al.* (2004) conducted a longitudinal study of the heritability of attention problems in children aged 3–12 years. They found consistently greater similarity in maternal ratings of over-activity and attention problems for MZ than DZ twins across ages. They calculated that the heritability (see Section 3.2) of these problems was about 75 per cent (i.e. individual differences in childhood attention problems in this sample were mainly due to genetic differences).

In each of these approaches, the basic technique is to calculate a correlation between the relevant pairs of individuals. For a particular characteristic, if the correlation is higher between pairs of, for example, MZ twins than DZ twins, this is taken to indicate a genetic influence on that characteristic. Such correlations are known as *concordance rates* and individuals may be described as *concordant* (they both show a particular characteristic) or *discordant* (only one shows the characteristic). Such studies show that even complex mental disorders such as schizophrenia may be heritable. The concordance rate for schizophrenia in MZ twins is at least four times higher than that for DZ twins (Tsuang *et al.*, 1991) and adoption studies show that if an adoptee has schizophrenia, the condition is much more likely to be present in the biological parents than in the adoptive parents (Kety *et al.*, 1994). However, it should be noted that the statistical procedures used in modern twin studies are quite complex and there is ongoing controversy about the interpretation of results from such studies (Joseph, 2003).

3.2 Heritability

So far we have seen that, at an individual level, it is nonsensical to ask whether genes or the environment are more important to behaviour. However, it *is* useful to ask about the degree to which differences between individuals can be explained by the differences in their genes.

Geneticists use a statistic called *heritability* to describe the amount of genetic influence that can be detected for a given characteristic. Heritability is the percentage of observed differences that can be explained by genetic differences among individuals within a given population at a given time. Although you do not need a detailed understanding of heritability as a statistic it is useful to be aware of its meaning, as you will come across statements such as the one in Section 3.1 referring to the heritability of attention problems being about 75 per cent. Note particularly that:

- Heritability is a specific population statistic and does *not* refer to individuals. It describes the degree to which genes influence the differences between group members and not the degree to which genes influence an individual's traits. For example, Turkheimer *et al.* (2003) studied the heritability of children's IQ in impoverished and affluent families. In the impoverished families, heritability estimates were close to zero suggesting little genetic influence on individual differences. However, in affluent families the results showed much greater genetic influence.

- Heritability does not tell us how much a specific characteristic is fixed or modifiable. Heritability statistics are valid only for the environment(s) in which data were collected. A particular trait might be highly heritable in some environments but hardly at all in others.

- Heritability changes across the lifespan. For example, longitudinal studies suggest that the heritability of IQ is higher in adulthood than in childhood. Correlations for general cognitive ability between parents and children increase from infancy onwards (Plomin *et al.*, 1997) for both non-adopted children and children adopted away from their biological parents. There may be some sort of cascading effect whereby small genetic effects accumulate over time or environmental influences on a phenotype may lessen. For example, parents and others are important influences on the intellectual development of children, but such influences become less important with increasing age, allowing genetic influences to become more apparent.

Summary of Section 3

- Family, adoption and twin studies allow behavioural geneticists to examine the relative contribution of genes or the environment to expressed phenotypes for a population.
- The statistic used to describe the relative contribution of genes to phenotypic variation within a population at a particular time is called heritability.

4 The influence of genes on development

4.1 Selective breeding in animals

The results of selective breeding in animals indicate that genes have an effect on both physical and psychological characteristics. A consideration of how dog breeds differ illustrates how genes can be manipulated by selective breeding to produce particular physical and temperamental characteristics. An experimental example comes from the selective breeding of rats. Tryon (1934) provided one of the first examples of selective breeding for a behavioural trait. After training a group of rats to complete a complex maze, he selectively mated the males and females that were either best or worst at completing the maze. He continued to breed together the best pairs and the worst pairs across 21 generations. By the eighth generation there was almost no overlap in the maze-running ability of the two groups, that is, the worst members of one group at running the maze were still better than the best members of the other group. These two strains of rats were named *maze-bright* and *maze-dull*. He looked for the possible environmental effects of learning by testing maze-bright offspring that had been reared by maze-dull parents and vice versa. The adopted offspring still performed like their biological parents.

Tryon's results were initially taken to suggest that he had bred for some form of intelligence, but later studies (Searle, 1949) suggested that the rats differed on emotionality rather than intelligence; the maze-bright rats were less anxious about running the maze. As the two groups' abilities only diverged gradually over successive generations it is also likely that maze-running ability is a polygenic trait which involves many genes.

Cooper and Zubek (1958) further showed how experience could interact with genetic influences. They raised maze-bright and maze-dull rats in either an impoverished environment or an enriched environment. The impoverished environment was a bare wire cage whereas the enriched environment contained tunnels, ramps, displays and objects. At maturity, the maze-dull rats that had been raised in an enriched environment performed as well as the maze-bright rats, suggesting that the early environment interacted with and could overcome the genetic effects.

4.2 Gene defects in humans

Many studies of genetic contributions to human behaviour have considered atypical rather than typical development. With atypical development it is often easier to pinpoint some genetic change that can be linked to the observed phenotype. However, you should be cautious about the extent to which typical development can be taken to parallel atypical development. Nevertheless, some of the clearest examples of genetic effects on human development come from studying human disorders. Several disorders arise from single-gene defects such as those leading to phenylketonuria (PKU) and Huntington disease. Others, such as Williams Syndrome, arise from defects affecting multiple genes. The genetic basis of these disorders illustrates some of the many ways in which genes can influence development.

PKU is a neurological disorder characterized by learning difficulties, vomiting, seizures, hyperactivity and hyperirritably. The pattern of inheritance of PKU through families is consistent with it being transmitted by a *single gene*. As the parents of PKU children do not usually suffer from the condition it can be traced to a recessive allele, carried by the parents, but not expressed in them. PKU occurs in about 1 in 10,000 births, but 1 in 50 individuals are carriers of the recessive allele. In the 1930s the disorder was also linked to a failure to convert phenylalanine (an essential dietary amino acid) to tyrosine. The build up of phenylalanine is damaging to the normal development of neurons and consequently damages the developing brain. Figure 4 illustrates the pattern of inheritance of the recessive allele from two parent carriers. In this diagram P represents the dominant allele and p represents the recessive allele (it is common in genetic notation to represent dominant alleles by uppercase letters and recessive alleles by lower case letters). When considering this diagram remember that alleles for this characteristic come in pairs: hence the parents have both the dominant and recessive allele represented by Pp. They produce eggs or sperm that contain one of the alleles. The alleles from one parent may potentially recombine with either of the alleles from the other parent. The final, shaded line of the diagram shows these potential crosses and the proportion of offspring likely to be affected or unaffected. Note that, as this is a recessive allele, only 25 per cent of offspring are likely to be affected (with the allele combination pp).

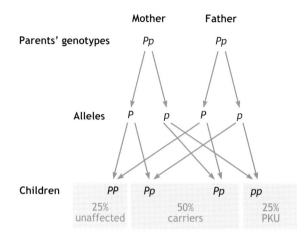

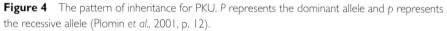

Figure 4 The pattern of inheritance for PKU. *P* represents the dominant allele and *p* represents the recessive allele (Plomin *et al.*, 2001, p. 12).

PKU is a genetic condition as the presence of the recessive allele is both necessary and sufficient for the disorder to develop. This does not mean, however, that there is no role for the environment in PKU. In the case of PKU, altering the environment is used as a treatment. Beginning a diet low in phenylalanine early in childhood reduces the amount of phenylalanine in the blood and limits the development of learning difficulties. The interactions between genes and the environment for PKU are illustrated in Figure 5.

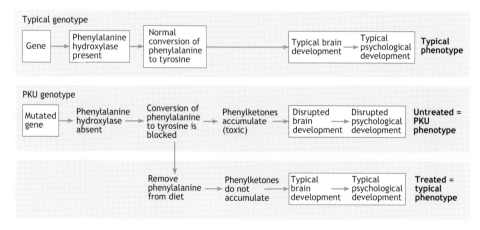

Figure 5 The identification of a genetic cause of (disrupted) development in the case of PKU, and its correction by human intervention.

Late-onset condition
A condition, such as Huntington disease or Alzheimer disease, in which the effects are not observed until relatively late in the lifespan.

Single-gene mutations can also involve dominant alleles. This is the case, for example, with Huntington disease. This is a late-onset genetic condition (usually appearing in middle age) characterized by progressive neural degeneration resulting in involuntary movements of the body, changes in personality and forgetfulness. Because the disorder involves a dominant allele, at least one parent shows the condition.

Activity 3   *Inheritance of Huntington disease*

Allow about
15 minutes

This activity tests your understanding of how alleles separate and recombine during fertilization.

Starting with parents with genotypes of *Hh* and *hh*, where *H* represents the dominant allele for Huntington disease and *h* represents the recessive allele, work out the possible pattern of inheritance for offspring of these parents. Use Figure 4 as a guide. Remember that the alleles from a parent separate and form all possible combinations with the alleles from the other parent. Remember also that Huntington disease will be present if the combination of alleles contains the dominant *H* allele.

Comment

From the possible combinations in the offspring you should find in your diagram that there is a 50 per cent chance of inheriting the condition.

The examples above illustrate the effects that just one gene can have on human development. They also show that in some cases it is possible to moderate these effects by changing the environment. Furthermore, there is a developmental aspect to the expression of some genetic disorders as individuals do not develop problems until relatively late in life.

Much more common than single-gene disorders are abnormalities involving multiple genes, extra chromosomes or deletions in parts of chromosomes. Williams Syndrome provides an example of a disorder involving multiple genes.

Williams Syndrome is a relatively rare disorder involving learning difficulties, a short stature, outgoing personality and distinctive facial features. Most cases of Williams Syndrome are associated with the deletion of at least sixteen genes on one chromosome and most cases seem to arise spontaneously. The exact number of genes that is deleted varies between individuals. Similarly, there are differences in the effects on facial features and on cognitive development. It would be tempting to relate the extent of such differences to the number of genes deleted. However, Karmiloff-Smith (1998) points out that even individuals with almost identical gene deletions can show quite different outcomes, and argues that there is no simple gene–outcome relationship. At a neurological level it is also the case that most work done on describing the brains of individuals with Williams Syndrome has been conducted with adult brains. Little research has been done with developing infant brains.

Reading

At this point you should turn to the end of this chapter and read Reading A, 'Williams syndrome: the resulting cognitive-behavioural phenotype' which is an extract from 'Development itself is the key to understanding developmental disorders' by Karmiloff-Smith (1998). This describes how apparently intact cognitive processing in Williams Syndrome individuals cannot be taken to mean that the brain processes involved are also intact. Note Karmiloff-Smith's argument in relation to these differences and how complicated the genotype–phenotype link can be.

4.3 A developmental perspective on genetic influence

One way to view epigenetic development is to think of genes as encoding behaviours in such a way that they are triggered into action at the appropriate time by environmental cues. This has been described as 'predetermined epigenesis'.

However, Karmiloff-Smith approaches the problem of how genes affect development from a different perspective. She argues that the study of genetic defects such as Williams Syndrome suggests that there are complex gene–environment interactions occurring throughout development. In this view, genes, the environment and development interact dynamically and progressively. Genes do not simply pre-specify thoughts or behaviours which are then triggered by environmental inputs. Rather, as one factor in an epigenetic system, they contribute to the likelihood of particular developmental pathways being followed. Thus the individual with Williams Syndrome has apparently unaffected (spared) language abilities but has reached this end point via a different developmental route. Such developmental plasticity is argued to be a feature of both typical and atypical development.

Developmental plasticity
The ability of the brain to reorganize neural pathways during development.

Changes to gene expression early in development will produce less specific phenotypic outcomes, in interaction with other genetic and environmental events, than those which are expressed later in development. Furthermore, specific effects can result from subtle genetic influences. For example, a single-gene mutation that affects the rigidity of fibres found in cell plasma is thought to lead to deafness. This is not because the gene directly affects hearing. Rather, because cells involved in hearing are particularly sensitive to this loss of rigidity they become dysfunctional, resulting in deafness (Lynch *et al.*, 1997). Presumably, similarly subtle general gene effects can affect typical cognitive and behavioural development.

Genes are therefore thought to provide constraints on development but they do not innately pre-specify developmental outcomes in a fixed and inflexible way. Behavioural genetics recognizes that behaviour is likely to be influenced by many genes rather than any single gene. Each of these multiple genes is likely to have a small effect, but in combination or by accumulation across the lifespan, small effects can cascade into substantial behavioural outcomes, such as schizophrenia. Each gene by itself is likely to be neither necessary nor sufficient to lead to schizophrenia, but increases the probability of the disorder developing in interaction with environmental and developmental influences.

4.4 Environmental interactions

'Environment' in this chapter, means *all* influences other than genetic inheritance. This could refer to prenatal biochemical changes, illness during childhood or family socialization. Genetic research indicates that environmental factors are as important as genetic factors in development. However, it also indicates that the environment itself can be a product of genetic influence. Factors as diverse as mother–child interactions, television viewing and life events have been shown to have significant genetic influence on them (Plomin *et al.*, 2001). In other words, we create our own environment and there are genetic influences on how we create it.

A related concept is the idea of *genotype–environment interaction*. This refers to genetic sensitivity to the environment. For example, you have already seen how children with PKU are sensitive to the amount of phenylalanine in their diet.

Another way that genetic research has influenced how the environment is viewed is by drawing attention to the difference between *shared* and *non-shared environments*. This is usually in relation to families. The influence of shared family environments may be estimated by looking at adoptive relatives, as similarities between adopted children and their unrelated siblings cannot be explained by genes. Genetically unrelated adoptive siblings nevertheless show a low but significant correlation on measures such as general cognitive ability in childhood (Plomin *et al.*, 2001) and this can only be explained by shared family environments. However, in later adolescence the same correlation is virtually zero: it would seem that shared environments become less important over time. What seems to be more important to explain differences between individuals within a family is the influence of non-shared environments. For example, on measures of personality only moderate correlations are found between identical twins in the same family. As the twins have the same genes and a similar shared environment, this suggests that most of the differences are explained by non-shared environments. In this context non-shared environment can refer to influences from outside the family such as friends or teachers but can also refer to factors within a family that impact on different children in different ways. For example, parents may interact with different children in different ways and there may be age-related differences in sibling experiences.

Technological advances arising from genetic research mean that there is now an array of tools and procedures that are available to geneticists interested in human behaviour. These advances raise some important ethical questions. A few selected examples are considered in Box 2.

BOX 2

Recent advances in genetics and questions raised

Diagnostic (DNA) markers: The Human Genome Project has paved the way for diagnostic tools that test whether a person has a specific genetic predisposition (however small) for a particular disease (e.g. Alzheimer disease, breast or colon cancer). This has enormous potential benefits in conditions where preventative solutions are available. But, soon this list may extend to include developmental disorders where prevention is not possible. Would being able to identify markers for these conditions be useful/ethical?

Gene therapy: The aim of gene therapy is to find cures for genetic defects. For example, for cystic fibrosis, the benefits of transferring non-defective copies of the gene to the lungs of young people are being tested. Along with the excitement that surrounds this type of therapy there is also some caution – especially since the death of Jesse Gelsinger in 1999 during a gene therapy trial (Stolberg, 1999).

Genetic modification/enhancement: The movie *Spider-Man* (2002) depicted the genetic merger of a human with a genetically modified spider, conferring special 'spider powers' to the character. Although this was a work of fiction its premise is firmly based within the foreseeable future of genetic engineering. So-called 'smart' mice have already been genetically engineered so that they possess an extra gene that codes for additional receptors in the brain with the hope that this will enhance cognitive functioning. As these technologies advance, the line between therapy and enhancement is likely to become increasingly blurred.

Receptors
Binding sites in
the nervous
system for
neurotransmitters.

Designer babies: Much has been written about the possibilities and implications of a designer baby culture. Fictional possibilities are now becoming a reality and the constraints are moral and ethical rather than technological. There are now several examples where children have been 'selected' to be of medical assistance to their older siblings. For example, Adam Nash was born in 2000 and was selected (from a group of fifteen embryos) on the basis of not having the same genetic condition as his elder sister and being a tissue match for her. Following a stem cell transplant from Adam's umbilical cord and bone marrow to his sister, both children are now healthy (Weiss, 2000). The public response to this case contrasted with another where a couple were refused donor selection from a sperm bank when they wanted to increase their chances of having a child who would be deaf (they themselves are both deaf and later succeeded in their aim through finding their own donor) (Mundy, 2002). On what basis should selection be allowed?

These brief examples highlight the need for very clear guidelines on the use of new technologies that arise from genetic research, especially when the focus is on factors other than treating genetic disorders. An attempt to provide guidelines comes from the Nuffield Council on Bioethics. Their report *Genetics and Human Behaviour* (2002) includes explicit consideration of potential genetic manipulation of traits such as intelligence, antisocial behaviour, personality and sexual orientation.

Summary of Section 4

- Selective breeding in animals shows that genes can influence both physical and behavioural development.
- Behavioural geneticists studying human gene disorders have demonstrated the influence that genes can have on cognitive and behavioural development. They have also illustrated how important environmental influences are to development and some of the complex interactions that occur between genetics, the environment and development.
- For some theorists, development is a process in which environmental influences trigger genes into action. For others, development itself is a key process that alters how genes and the environment interact as part of a complex dynamic system.
- The possibilities of modern genetics research raise difficult ethical and moral issues.

5 Evolutionary developmental psychology

5.1 Introduction to evolutionary psychology

So far we have been concerned with the link between the genotype and the phenotype. However, it is now the phenotype itself that is the focus of attention, since all aspects of the phenotype, including the mind and behaviour, are affected by evolutionary processes. An evolutionary perspective seeks answers to psychological questions at a *functional* level (recall Activity 1).

The theory of evolution can be characterized by the following important principles.

1   *Variation*: individuals possess different combinations of physical, mental and behavioural characteristics.
2   *Heredity*: much of the variation between individuals is heritable.
3   *Selection*: interactions between individuals and their environments result in the characteristics of some individuals being passed on to future generations while the traits of other individuals (who are not reproductively successful) are not.

Inclusive fitness
Aiding the success of other individuals who are likely to carry similar genes.

These basic principles have been significantly revised since Darwin first penned them. For example, the concept of inclusive fitness has replaced simple reproductive success.

Modern evolutionary explanations often refer to some form of *selective pressure* along the lines of Darwin's principle of natural selection. This 'pressure' is the effect of natural selection conferring a reproductive advantage on individuals who solve recurring problems in the *environment of evolutionary adaptedness* (EEA). For humans, this is thought to be the Pleistocene period dating from between 1.8 million years ago to 10,000 years ago. It is worth noting that 'civilization' has emerged since the end of this period and this has advanced far more quickly than evolution. In summary, we are adapted for an environment in which we do not live, namely the hunter-gather environment of the late Pleistocene.

Environment of evolutionary adaptedness (EEA)
The environment of our hominid ancestors that has shaped the psychological mechanisms present in modern humans through the process of selective pressure.

The central theme in evolutionary psychology is that the human mind and behaviour have been shaped through the processes of natural selection. Evolutionary psychology concentrates on the functional (adaptive) aspects of behaviour, on the premise that the recurring problems in the EEA are solved by the application of behaviour. Since behaviour is the result of psychological processes, it then follows that sets of psychological processes, sometimes referred to by psychologists as 'modules', must be the units of selection in evolution:

> The mind is organized into modules or mental organs, each with a specialized design that makes it an expert in one area of interaction with the world. The modules' basic logic is specified by our genetic program. Their operation was shaped by natural selection to solve problems of the hunting and gathering life led by our ancestors in most of our evolutionary history.

(Pinker, 1997, p. 21).

Although many of our physical adaptations and behavioural responses were designed to solve recurrent problems of adapting successfully to environmental circumstances, others are considered by-products of such adaptations. By-products serve no adaptive purpose themselves and some may have negative consequences. One example of a physical adaptation that has a negative by-product is brain size. As a species, humans have a relatively large brain, which has the consequence of increasing the size of the newborn skull. Although a large brain has advantages, the infant's skull size increases the risk of maternal death or injury during the birth as the size of the female pelvis is constrained by the requirement for being able to walk. This negative side effect is outweighed by the adaptive benefits of an enlarged brain. Few, if any adaptations provide perfect solutions to a problem and most come with associated costs. However, the balance between the benefits and the costs must have, over evolutionary history, swung in favour of the adaptations that are present in modern humans.

5.2 A developmental perspective on evolutionary psychology

Although the study of human evolutionary psychology is weighted towards an understanding of adult behaviour, aspects of child development are now being approached through *evolutionary developmental psychology*. In their landmark text for this new area, Bjorklund and Pellegrini define evolutionary developmental psychology as:

> the application of the basic principles of Darwinian evolution, particularly natural selection, to explain contemporary human development. It involves the study of the genetic and environmental mechanisms that underlie the universal development of social and cognitive competencies.

(Bjorklund and Pellegrini, 2002, p. 4)

Approaching child development from an evolutionary perspective is not new. For example, Bowlby (1969) proposed that a recurrent problem of our evolutionary past was the helplessness of young infants. The solution was to ensure that infants stay close to their mothers by the evolution of a psychological mechanism for attachment.

One critical shift of emphasis from earlier applications of the Darwinian approach to behaviour is the critical role played by environmental factors. The current approach views thought and behaviour as the products of interactions between experiential and biological factors, and these interactions are often bi-directional. Thus the view that development arises from an activation of the genetic blueprint (genetic determinism) is unsupported. The role of the environment is not merely acknowledged in evolutionary psychology, it is critical. Not only do adaptations only arise in response to environmental challenges, but they are often then very sensitive to environmental change. Since there is tremendous variation in the environments in which humans live, cognitive and behavioural flexibility is an essential adaptation.

Evolutionary psychology is a controversial topic (Rose and Rose, 2000; Kurzban, 2002) and many psychologists are sceptical about its claims. One of the reasons for this is that it is an approach that often lacks either empirical rigour or applicable outcomes. The impression is that evolutionary psychology is speculative and lacks grounding in either evolutionary or psychological science. It is therefore essential for evolutionary psychology to seek empirical verification. Since, almost by definition, it is not possible to directly test or falsify causality in the case of evolutionary psychology, it instead relies on a predictive approach for its empirical verification.

Activity 4   *Testing evolutionary psychology*

Allow about 20 minutes

This activity will help you to explore the difficulties associated with the predictive approach of evolutionary psychology.

When reading Sections 5.3 and 5.4, consider the question 'How well do evolutionary principles predict the aspects of child development in question?'. Make a note of your answers.

5.3 What is the point of childhood?

Humans have an extended juvenile period in which the period of socialization is longer than is required for physical (nutritional) dependence. Thus humans remain culturally dependent for many additional years; 'We are born big, grow fast, wean early, but mature late' (Low, 1998, p. 135). Such a long juvenile period is problematic in evolutionary terms, as it increases the risk of death before reaching the age of reproduction. It has therefore been suggested that a prolonged childhood can have only evolved if it also conferred benefits to us that outweigh this drawback (Greary and Bjorklund, 2000).

Development during childhood involves preparation for adulthood such that it will increase inclusive fitness. One of the most frequently cited reasons for the extended childhood in humans is that it is required for children to master the complex social world. However, it is unlikely that all of the experiences of childhood serve to prepare the adult for survival and reproduction. Evolutionary developmental psychology suggests that natural selection has resulted in cognitive and social traits that support survival at all stages of development (Greary and Bjorklund, 2000). To illustrate this, we will introduce you to examples of adaptive behavioural mechanisms that:

Adaptation
An inherited characteristic that came about through natural selection in order to solve recurring problems in the EEA.

- have immediate functional benefits for children, but are lost before adulthood;
- demonstrate that immaturity itself can be beneficial to the developmental process;
- are a preparation for adulthood.

There is a range of postnatal behaviours that are common to all infants, and serve specific functions but which are 'lost' with advancing age. An obvious example might be the suckling reflex (enabling the infant to effectively breastfeed). One of the most obvious childhood activities is play. Play is commonly defined as behaviour that appears to have no function or that is less important than the outcome of that behaviour. This would suggest that the process of play must provide adaptive benefit for the child. Play may well have benefits that are deferred until adulthood (such as learning social structure and social dominance), but it also has immediate benefits for children. Not only does it provide physical exercise, it also provides opportunities to put multidisciplinary (social and cognitive) learning into practice.

Some views of childhood often consider it to be an inferior stage, which should be passed through as quickly and smoothly as possible. As a result, efforts have sometimes been made to speed up development through specific training. Whether it is wise to accelerate development is considered in Box 3.

BOX 3

The wisdom of accelerated development in question

If immaturity has adaptive benefits then this has clear implications for activities (passive or active) that accelerate progress through this period. One unfortunate, but all too common, effect of preterm birth is that disrupted development of the nervous system often results in physical and cognitive impairments. Als (1995) has proposed that rather than these impairments being a result of preterm birth per se (i.e. the result of less time in the womb) they may well be a result of the unexpectedly early stimulation that the brain receives during a sensitive period in brain development. This may then lead to a disruption in the 'natural' course of development (particularly in the frontal areas of the cortex). He notes that the impairments often include attentional difficulties and lowered IQ and speech problems, while there are often also concurrent and specific enhancements (e.g. in mathematics) depending on gestational age at birth. An explanation from an evolutionary perspective is that the early experiences of preterm infants do not conform to species-typical expectations of the environment.

> Social contexts evolved in the course of human phylogeny are surprisingly fine-tuned in specificity to provide good-enough environments for the human cortex to unfold, initially intrauterinely, then extrauterinely ... [medical advances now mean that] ... even very immature nervous systems exist and develop outside the womb. However, the social contexts of traditional special care nurseries bring with them less than adequate support for immature nervous systems ... leading to maladaptations and disabilities, yet also to accelerations and extraordinary abilities.
> (Als, 1995, quoted in Bjorklund and Pellegrini, 2002, pp. 187–8.)

Experimental studies in rhesus monkeys suggest that this principle extends to training during infancy in normal (not preterm) infants. Early training (beginning at 155 days) led to poorer performance for the same task as an adult, than monkeys who began their training later (Harlow, 1959). In humans the evidence is less conclusive with some studies suggesting that early learning can be detrimental to later performance and others stating that there are just no improvements. Bjorklund and Pellegrini therefore suggest that 'it is entirely possible that training can either be harmful or helpful, depending upon the nature of the training and the organism's stage of development' (Bjorklund and Pellegrini, 2000, p. 1695).

An evolutionary perspective on accelerated learning in young infants raises several questions. Furthermore, this topic provides an appropriate forum for testing whether changes on the bases of principles from evolutionary psychology have real-world benefits.

An evolutionary perspective, however, forces one to consider the benefits of an extended childhood, some of which are adaptive to children, rather than being merely a preparation for adulthood. We present here three brief examples of 'adaptive immaturity'.

Egocentric bias
The notion that young children claim more responsibility for the results of a joint action than an outside observer would attribute to them.

1   *Young children have an egocentric bias: they tend to take the credit for another child's actions.*

It has been argued that this bias is adaptively beneficial as it may result in better learning. One result of egocentric bias is that the source of action is a common one (the child) and this may lead to a more structured event memory and therefore enhanced memory retrieval. This is well illustrated by a study involving rearranging the furniture in a doll's house. Young children who displayed egocentric bias in a group condition had better event memory in comparison to a control condition involving individual play (Ratner *et al.*, 2002).

Metacognition
The ability to gain conscious insight into, and reflect on one's own knowledge and cognitive processes.

2   *It is commonly observed that many young children over-estimate their own abilities. This inaccurate self-knowledge, or poor metacognition, is actually thought to be advantageous.*

An overly optimistic view of self may allow children to engage in a wider range of activities without being put off by their poor abilities. The developmental literature alludes to this view. Bandura (1989), for example, argued that children who view their abilities optimistically would attempt more challenging tasks and persevere with them longer.

Working memory
A part of short term memory, that temporarily stores and manipulates information.

3   *The capacity of working memory in children is very much restricted.*
This is thought to have adaptive value in aiding language acquisition. One of the effects of poorer working memory may be that the complexity of the stimulation that they receive is minimized thereby making the resultant analysis more manageable (since information will be processed in smaller chunks). A similar effect was found in adults learning an artificial grammar (Kersten and Earles, 2001).

These examples illustrate how taking an evolutionary perspective on the immature psychological mechanisms that accompany childhood shows that they can be considered beneficial for the child.

Differences between men and women often take centre stage in accounts of adult evolutionary psychology. It is clear, however, that these differences do not suddenly emerge in adulthood and so childhood has often been seen as the developmental training ground for the emerging psychological mechanisms associated with the behaviour of the two sexes. There are many examples of differences in behaviour between young girls and boys, including the common observation that boys tend to be more aggressive than girls during their early childhood. Since evolutionary benefits of aggression are concerned with securing additional resources or for securing and defending a mate, it is clear that there are few immediate similar benefits for children. Rather, this form of behaviour is considered training or practice so that the child can usefully develop the skills that might be adaptively useful in later life. This assertion finds some support in the way in which rough and tumble play changes with age. Young children are more likely to engage in rough and tumble play that is co-operative and playful, whereas in early adolescence this type of play becomes more aggressive and is related to the development of social dominance (Pellegrini, 1988).

Another difference is that boys and girls, from as young as 3 years of age, tend to segregate themselves into different social groups. The evolutionary psychological literature also cites examples of play parenting (playing with dolls) and the absence of dominance-related play in girls' behaviour as providing gender-relevant preparation for adulthood/motherhood. However, few evolutionary psychologists have attempted to provide falsifiable evidence for these behaviours.

There is also support for the existence of cognitive differences in boys and girls. That is, the cognitive mechanisms that have evolved to solve different adaptive problems in males and females should be observable in children too. Consistent with this, boys tend to perform better in tests of spatial cognition whereas girls outperform boys on memory tasks involving the locations of objects (Eals and Silverman, 1994; Silverman *et al.*, 2000). These differences in spatial cognition are thought to reflect the differential division of labour in ancient hunter-gatherer societies, with males' spatial cognition being selected for the type of navigation over large areas that may be required for hunting, whereas females' spatial cognition may have been selected for foraging-related skills, such as finding and selecting appropriate wild-growing foods.

5.4 Evolved psychological mechanisms

The adaptations resulting from natural selection are often referred to as domain-specific adaptations, in that they provide solutions to a specific adaptive problem in the EEA.

Although these domain-specific adaptations take the foreground in almost all discussions of evolutionary psychology, there are also thought to be a range of domain-general adaptations.

These domain-general adaptations must provide benefits to a wide range of adaptive solutions. In this section we will consider both domain-specific and domain-general psychological mechanisms as they relate to social and cognitive aspects of child development.

With respect to social development, comparative studies show that the length of childhood is related to the complexity of a species' social world (Joffe, 1997). The extended juvenile period in humans is therefore thought to provide a useful forum in which to examine adapted social mechanisms. As there are many aspects to social development, we will limit our discussion to children's friendships. Psychologists argue that successful social integration involves the ability to understand the needs of others. Reciprocity and symmetry are two of the characteristics that are central to friendship formation in children.

Reciprocity and symmetry are also themes central to an evolutionary understanding of behaviour. Infants and toddlers can be seen to engage in

Domain specific
Relating to a specific context.

Domain general
Applicable across different contexts.

Reciprocity
The principle of equality within a relationship, such as in terms of commitment, time, generosity, etc.

Symmetry
In this context, symmetry relates to equality of status between people. A relationship between two people of unequal status would be referred to as 'asymmetrical'.

positive social interactions that involve reciprocity, such as sharing and turn-taking. The 'meaning' of these social exchanges develops such that older children often regard reciprocity and symmetry as indicators of friendship.

One outcome that would be predicted from this type of reciprocity-dependent friendship is that children should interact and form friends with those individuals to whom they are phenotypically most similar (this has clear parallels with mate selection principles in adults). The literature on friendship formation supports this prediction: children who engage in rough and tumble play invariably have similar 'rank' in the dominance hierarchy and aggressive children form groups with other aggressive children and are nominated as 'best friends' by other aggressive children (Humphreys and Smith, 1987). This principle has been shown to extend to a range of attitudes, interests and personality characteristics, with closer friends tending to be more similar than casual friends (Berndt and Ladd, 1989).

Perhaps the clearest example of a domain-general adaptation is the g factor of general intelligence.

g factor
A generalized factor of intelligence that is common to all intellectual tasks.

This g factor is thought to have evolved in order to solve a wide-range of non-recurrent problems, rather than any specific recurrent problem in the EEA. Some theoreticians propose that one of the defining characteristics of humans, as distinct from the other great apes, is the emergence of one domain-general cognitive mechanism – 'special' intelligence (Parker and McKinney, 1999).

One further distinction is useful when considering the development of cognitive skills: *biologically primary abilities* are useful in all human environments (e.g. language, simple mathematics) whereas *biologically secondary abilities* solve problems that are specific to only some cultures (e.g. reading). This distinction has been found to be useful in educational settings. As a biologically primary ability, language should 'come naturally' to children whereas there should be no 'innate' motivation to read, since reading is a relatively recent cultural phenomenon. Pinker expresses this difference in terms of the cognitive learning resources involved: 'children are wired for sound, but print is an optional accessory that must be painstakingly bolted on' (Pinker, 1997, p. ix).

Reading

At this point you should turn to the end of this chapter and read Reading B, 'An extract from "Child development and evolutionary psychology"' (Bjorklund and Pellegrini, 2000). This provides an evolutionary perspective on social and cognitive development, focusing on theory of mind. It also emphasizes the modular nature of children's social functioning.

SG

We have already noted that adaptations provide solutions to recurring problems in the EEA. However, the present environment is markedly different from the EEA, and so the original problems may no longer be relevant. This discrepancy should reveal mechanisms that are non-adaptive in contemporary environments. Humans must also have evolved to expect particular inputs from the environment. What happens if these environmental expectations are not met? Or more relevant here – how does the ancient brain hinder the modern child? The differences in the mechanisms and resources involved in language versus reading (mentioned above) are one example and emphasize that much of what is taught in schools is 'unnatural', as far as our brains are concerned.

Another example is the *Westermarck effect*, which describes the lack of sexual interest that develops between individuals who were raised together as children. Although it has clear benefits in reducing inbreeding, it is an example of an adaptation that may result in maladaptive behaviour when the environmental conditions have changed substantially from the EAA (Tooby and Cosmides, 1990). The adaptation leading to the Westermarck effect, and the avoidance of incest, can be thought of as a mechanism that judges relatedness on the basis of the extent and duration of intimate exposure during the first years of life, and uses this judgement to reduce sexual interest. Although a useful adaptation in its original environmental context, it is maladaptive for a situation in which non-relatives grow up together, for example in a kibbutz crèche.

5.5 The role of culture

One criticism of evolutionary psychology is that it suggests that there are biological causes for certain behaviours despite evidence that they are learned behaviours. This view, however, implies that learning and psychological adaptations are contradictory, when most evolutionary psychologists view these as interrelated explanations 'learning is not a surrounding gas or force field, and it does not happen by magic. It is made possible by innate machinery designed to do the learning' (Pinker, 1997, p. 33).

One of the distinguishing features of human evolution is that we have evolved the skills that are necessary for the transmission of information (knowledge) from one generation to the next. This transmission of information exists in *addition* to the transference of genetic information through the generations that is the mainstay of evolutionary theory, and it has resulted in the creation of an elaborate human culture. The interrelation of cultural and genetic evolution is illustrated in Box 4 which considers the 'evolution' of the teddy bear.

BOX 4

The evolution of the teddy bear

Cultural change may be driven by adaptation to an existing genetic predisposition. One example of this is ... the evolution of the teddy bear. When bears were first invented during the early 1900s, they were very bearlike with pronounced snouts and low foreheads. However, Hinde and Barden (1985) have shown that, as the century progressed, their design became increasingly babylike, with foreshortened snouts and higher foreheads ... [see Figures 6a and 6b].

The concept of a teddy bear is clearly not a genetically inherited trait, so we can be reasonably sure that ... this is a cultural trait. However, it is a cultural trait that seems to be ... [guided by a] ... genetic trait, namely the cues that attract us to babies (high foreheads and small faces). A likely explanation is that the designers of teddy bears respond to their customers' past buying patterns when designing the next season's bears. The designs that sell better are copied and adapted more often the following year than the more bearlike ones that remain unsold on the shelves.

Morris et al. (1995) used a forced-choice paradigm to assess 4–8-year-old children's preferences for bears with contrasting features. They found that, while there was an increasing tendency for more babylike bears to be preferred with age, younger children did not exhibit a preference for babylike features. They therefore concluded that it must be adults' preferences that are reflected in Figure 6.

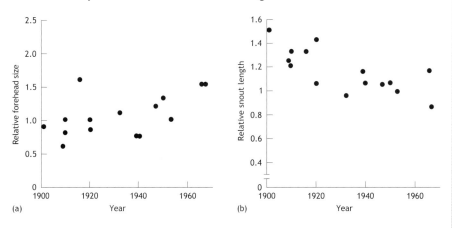

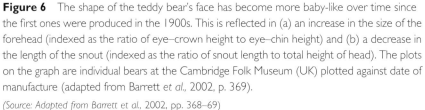

Figure 6   The shape of the teddy bear's face has become more baby-like over time since the first ones were produced in the 1900s. This is reflected in (a) an increase in the size of the forehead (indexed as the ratio of eye–crown height to eye–chin height) and (b) a decrease in the length of the snout (indexed as the ratio of snout length to total height of head). The plots on the graph are individual bears at the Cambridge Folk Museum (UK) plotted against date of manufacture (adapted from Barrett *et al.*, 2002, p. 369).

(Source: Adapted from Barrett et al., 2002, pp. 368–69)

In Activity 4 you were asked to 'test' the predictive value of evolutionary principles as you read through the preceding sections. You should have noticed that although some of the examples were accompanied by empirical evidence, others remain speculative. A second test for the evolutionary approach to child development is the amount of novel applications that have arisen as a result of the approach. One example, suggested by Greary (1998), involves changing the classroom teaching of mathematics (and other problem-based disciplines) on the basis of differences between boys and girls: boys being more competitive while girls prefer collaboration. Greary suggests that teaching should reflect these sex-biased dispositions. More examples of this type will allow the applicability of an evolutionary approach to be tested.

Summary of Section 5

- Evolutionary developmental psychology is an emerging discipline and it will take time for consensus to form on the best investigative approaches and the core principles.
- An evolutionary approach to child development highlights the importance of childhood rather than it being just a necessary stage of immaturity on the way to adulthood.

- There are several areas of social and cognitive development to which evolutionary psychology can be applied.
- More empirical evidence in support of evolutionary predictions is needed, and this evidence must also be subjected to alternative explanations in order for it to be considered persuasive.

6   Conclusion

At the beginning of this chapter, Figure 1 was used to represent the important interactions between the genetic, environmental and evolutionary influences on our behaviour. Having provided an overview of both behavioural genetics and evolutionary psychology, and the contributions that they make to an understanding of development, we now return to this figure (see Figure 7) to explain how various aspects of the chapter relate to it.

Figure 7

An update to Figure 1, annotated to illustrate how the content of this chapter evidences the contribution genes, the environment and evolutionary history make to human behaviour (adapted from Pinel, 2003).

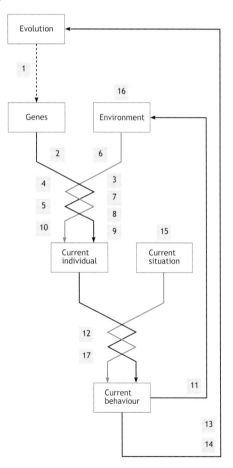

1 The genes that we have are the result of natural selection conferring a reproductive advantage on individuals who solved recurring problems in the EEA (Section 5.1).

2 The relative contributions of genes and environment are investigated through studies of shared versus non-shared environments (Section 3.1).

3 Monozygotic twins differ (Section 2).

4 Different genes can lead to the same outcome (Section 2.1).

5 Having the genetic basis for a condition does not inevitably mean that you will develop the condition (Section 4).

6 Development occurs as a result of the interaction between genes and the environment (epigenesis) (Section 2).

7 An 'enriched' environment overcomes the effects of selective breeding in rats (Section 4.1).

8 The expression of genes depends on the environment (Section 2.3).

9 Manipulation of the environment can overcome a genetic disorder (e.g. PKU) (Section 4.2).

10 There is an interaction between genotype and phenotype (Section 4.3).

11 There is a correlation between genotype and the environment because we 'select' our own environment (Section 4.4).

12 Situations vary greatly, requiring a degree of behavioural (phenotype) plasticity (Section

13 Natural selection occurs based on 'inclusive fitness' (Section 5.1).

14 Childhood involves preparation for adulthood to improve inclusive fitness, but also confers immediate advantages on children (adaptive immaturity)

15 Over time the 'current situation' may be a 'recurring problem in the EEA' (Section 5.1).

16 The 'environment' refers to all factors other than inheritance (Section 4.4).

17 A possible mismatch between the EEA and the current situation means that humans are not primarily adapted for the modern environment e.g. language versus reading (Section 5.4).

As you can see, Figure 7 is a replication of Figure 1, but this time it is annotated to illustrate many of the salient points that have been made in the previous sections and how they relate to this model of gene and evolutionary processes. As with most models this figure also has several limitations. The changing contributions of the environment and genetics during development are not fully represented in the diagram. There may also be a need for additional links, for example, it is possible that the environment directly mediates the activity of genes to suit the situation. If evidence supports this, then a direct link would be required from environmental to genetic influences.

There are many examples in the literature that provide evidence for a genetic and/or environmental contribution to a variety of behavioural characteristics. This figure provides a useful conceptual framework that allows a broad overview of these influences, and importantly it also shows how evoluationary psychology has added to the genetic and environmental influences that are more commonly considered. However, like much of the literature it does not identify the specific manner by which these factors are combined to 'produce' behaviour. Recent advances in genetic science and progress within the emerging discipline of evolutionary developmental psychology will hopefully provide not only additional evidence but they may also elucidate the way in which these factors actually produce behaviour.

Answers to Activity 2

1 (c), 2 (g), 3 (f), 4 (h), 5 (d), 6 (b), 7 (e), 8 (a).

References

Als, H. (1995) 'The preterm infant: a model for the study of fetal brain expectation', in Lecanuet, J.-P., Krasnegor, W. P., Krasnegor, N. A. and Smotherman, W. P. (eds) *Fetal Development: a psychobiological perspective,* pp. 439–71, Hillsdale, NJ, Erlbaum.

Bandura, A. (1989) 'Social cognitive theory', in Vasta, R. (ed.) *Annals of Child Development,* pp. 1–60, Greenwich, CT and London, JAI Press.

Barrett, L., Dunbar, R. and Lycett, J. (2002) *Human Evolutionary Psychology,* New York, Palgrave.

Berndt, T. J. and Ladd, G. (eds) (1989) *Peer Relationships in Child Development,* New York, Wiley.

Bjorklund, D. F. and Pellegrini, A. D. (2000) 'Child development and evolutionary psychology', *Child Development,* vol. 71, pp. 1687–1708.

Bjorklund, D. F. and Pellegrini, A. D. (2002) *The Origins of Human Nature: evolutionary developmental psychology*, Washington, DC, American Psychological Association.

Bowlby, J. (1969) *Attachment and Loss: vol. I: attachment*, London, Hogarth Press and the Institute of Psychoanalysis.

Collins, F. S., Green, E. D., Guttmacher, A. E. and Guyer, M. S. (2003) 'A vision for genomics research', *Nature,* vol. 422, pp. 835–47.

Cooper, R. M. and Zubek, J. P. (1958) 'Effects of enriched and restricted early environments on the learning ability of bright and dull rats', *Canadian Journal of Psychology,* vol. 12, pp. 159–64.

Eals, M. and Silverman, I. (1994) 'The hunter-gatherer theory of spatial sex differences: proximate factors mediating the female advantage in recall of object arrays', *Ethology and Sociobiology,* vol. 15, pp. 95–105.

Greary, D. C. (1998) *Male, Female: the evolution of human sex differences,* Washington, DC, American Psychological Association.

Greary, D. C. and Bjorklund, D. F. (2000) 'Evolutionary developmental psychology', *Child Development,* vol. 71, pp. 57–65.

Harlow, H. (1959) 'The development of learning in the rhesus monkey', *American Scientist,* December*,* pp. 459–79.

Hartwell, L. H., Hood, L., Goldberg, M. L., Reynolds, A. E., Silver, L. M. and Veres, R. C. (2004) *Genetics: from genes to genomes,* Boston, MA., McGraw-Hill.

Hinde, H. A. and Barden, L. A. (1985) 'The evolution of the teddy bear', *Animal Behaviour,* vol. 33, pp. 1371–3.

Humphreys, A. P. and Smith, P. K. (1987) 'Rough and tumble, friendship, and dominance in school children: evidence for continuity and change with age', *Child Development,* vol. 58, pp. 201–12.

Joffe, T. H. (1997) 'Social pressures have selected for an extended juvenile period in primates', *Journal of Human Evolution,* vol. 32, pp. 593–605.

Joseph, J. (2003) *The Gene Illusion: genetic research in psychiatry and psychology under the microscope*, Ross-on-Wye, PCCS Books.

Karmiloff-Smith, A. (1998) 'Development itself is the key to understanding developmental disorders', *Trends in Cognitive Sciences,* vol. 2, pp. 389–98.

Kersten, A.W. and Earles, J. L. (2001) 'Less really is more for adults learning a miniature artificial language', *Journal of Memory and Language,* vol. 44, pp. 250–73.

Kety, S. S., Wender, P. H., Jacobsen, B. *et al.* (1994) 'Mental illness in the biological and adoptive relatives of schizophrenic adoptees: replication of the Copenhagen study in the rest of Denmark', *Archives of General Psychiatry,* vol. 51, pp. 442–55.

Kurzban, R. (2002) 'Alas poor evolutionary psychology: unfairly accused, unjustly condemned', *Human Nature Review,* vol. 2, pp. 99–109.

Lawrence, P. A. (1992) *The Making of a Fly: the genes of animal design,* Oxford, Blackwell.

Low, B. S. (1998) 'The evolution of human life histories', in Crawford, C. B. and Krebs, D. L. (eds) *Handbook of Evolutionary Psychology: ideas, issues and applications,* Mahwah, NJ, Lawrence Erlbaum Associates.

Lynch, E. D., Lee, M. K., Morrow, J. E., Welcsh, P. L., León, P. E. and King, M. -C. (1997) 'Nonsyndromic deafness DFNA1 associated with mutation of a human homolog of the Drosophila gene diaphanous', *Science,* vol. 278, pp. 1315–18.

Malcolm, S. and Goodship, J. (2001, 2nd edn) *Genotype to Phenotype,* Oxford, BIOS Scientific Publishers Ltd.

Morris, P. H., Reddy, V. and Bunting, R. C. (1995) 'The survival of the cutest: who's responsible for the evolution of the teddy bear?', *Animal Behaviour,* vol. 50, pp. 1697–1700.

Mundy, L. 'A world of their own', *The Washington Post,* 31 March, 2002.

Nuffield Council on Bioethics (2002) *Genetics and Human Behaviour: the ethical context,* London, The Nuffield Council on Bioethics. Available from: http://www.nuffieldbioethics.org [Accessed 25 June, 2004].

Parker, S. T. and McKinney, M. L. (1999) *Origins of Intelligence: the evolution of cognitive development in monkeys, apes, and humans,* Baltimore, The Johns Hopkins University Press.

Passer, M. W. and Smith, R. E. (2004) *Psychology: the science of mind and behaviour,* Boston, MA., McGraw-Hill.

Pellegrini, A. D. (1988) 'Elementary-school children's rough and tumble play and social competence', *Developmental Psychology,* vol. 24, pp. 802–6.

Pinel, J. P. J. (2003, 5th edn) *Biopsychology,* Boston, MA., Allyn and Bacon.

Pinker, S. (1997) *How the Mind Works,* New York, Norton.

Plomin, R., Defries, J. C., McClearn, G. E. and McGuffin, P. (2001, 4th edn) *Behavioral Genetics,* New York, Worth Publishers.

Plomin, R., Fulker, D. W., Corley, R. and DeFries, J. C. (1997) 'Nature, nurture and cognitive development from 1 to 16 years: a parent-offspring adoption study', *Psychological Science,* vol. 8, pp. 442–7.

Ratner, H. H., Foley, M. A. and Gimpert, N. (2002) 'The role of collaborative planning in children's source-monitoring errors and learning', *Journal of Experimental Child Psychology,* vol. 81, pp. 44–73.

Reuters (1999) 'Scientists find the first gene for dyslexia', *The New York Times,* 7 September, p. 7.

Rietveld, M. J. H., Hudziak, J. J., Bartels, M., van Beijsterveldt, C. E. M. and Boomsma, D. I. (2004) 'Heritability of attention problems in children: longitudinal results from a study of twins, age 3 to 12', *Journal of Child Psychology and Psychiatry,* vol. 45, pp. 577–88.

Rose, H. and Rose, S. (2000) *Alas Poor Darwin: arguments against evolutionary psychology*, New York, Harmony Books.

Searle, L. V. (1949) 'The organisation of hereditary maze-brightness and maze-dullness', *Genetic Psychology Monographs,* vol. 39, pp. 279–325.

Silverman, I., Choi, J., MacKewn, A., Fisher, M., Moro, J. and Olshansky, E. (2000) 'Evolved mechanisms underlying wayfinding: Further studies on the hunter-gatherer theory of spatial sex differences', *Evolution and Human Behavior,* vol. 21, pp. 201–13.

Spider-Man, film, directed by Sam Raimi. USA, Sony Pictures, 2002.

Stolberg, S. G. (1999) 'The biotech death of Jesse Gelsinger', *The New York Times Sunday Magazine,* 20 November.

Tooby, J. and Cosmides, L. (1990) 'On the universality of human nature and the uniqueness of the individual: the role of genetics and adaptation', *Journal of Personality,* vol. 58, pp. 17–67.

Tryon, R. C. (1934) 'Individual differences', in Moss, F. A. (ed.), *Comparative Psychology*, pp. 409–48, New York, Prentice Hall.

Tsuang, M. T., Gilbertson, M. W. and Farone, S. V. (1991) 'The genetics of schizophrenia: Current knowledge and future directions', *Schizophrenia Research,* vol. 4, pp. 157–71.

Turkheimer, E., Haley, A., Waldron, M., D'Onofrio, B. and Gottesman, I. I. (2003) 'Socioeconomic status modifies heritability of IQ in young children', *Psychological Science,* vol. 14, pp. 623–8.

Weiss, R. (2000) 'Test-tube baby born to save ill sister', *The Washington Post,* 3 October, 2000.

Readings

Reading A: Williams syndrome: the resulting cognitive-behavioural phenotype

Annette Karmiloff-Smith

Classic Williams syndrome (WS) has been characterized along the following lines (for more details, see Refs a–c):

- IQs mainly in the 50s (range: 45–87)
- serious deficits in spatio-constructive skills, but spatio-perceptual skills as would be predicted by Mental Age
- serious deficits in numerical cognition
- serious deficits in problem solving and planning
- intact syntactic capacities alongside aberrant semantics
- intact face processing capacities
- relatively spared social cognition skills.

The above conclusions stemmed mainly from standardized tests used to assess intact and impaired functions, an approach inspired theoretically by the adult neuropsychological model of deficit. However, even in cases where behavioural scores are equivalent to chronologically matched controls, it is essential to go beyond behavioural success and study the underlying cognitive processes in detail (d, e). For example, our study of face-processing capacities of people with WS (Ref. e) showed that, although their scores were equivalent to normal controls, the way in which they solved the task was different. Whereas normal controls used predominantly configural (holistic) processing, the subjects with WS reached their good scores by using predominantly componential (feature-by-feature) processing. In other words, different *cognitive* processes led to similar *behavioural* outcomes. The notion that WS displays a normal, intact face-processing module is thereby challenged. None the less, the neuroconstructivist view could accept that people with WS might have developed a face-processing module. However, it would be argued that, rather than simply being triggered, such a module – like the normal face-processing module – is the result of a developmental process of modularization, but emerging in this case from an atypical ontogenetic pathway.

A similar story obtains for WS language acquisition. Several studies now suggest that neither syntax nor semantics is entirely normal in WS, despite earlier claims to the contrary. First, there is a discrepancy between vocabulary Mental Age (MA) and syntactic MA, the former being considerably higher (f). Second, high vocabulary scores in WS patients camouflage the fact that they learn the lexicon in a somewhat different way from normally developing children (g). Third, they show dissociations within syntax itself, with problems in forming agreement between elements in phrase structure, difficulties in processing embedded relative clauses and subcategorization frames (the distinction between transitive and intransitive verbs), and so forth (f, h, i). Furthermore, even when language is fluent, Williams syndrome cannot be used to claim, as some have (j), that syntax develops independently of cognition. The use of IQ scores is very misleading in this respect. To state that a person has fluent language but an IQ of 51 indeed appears theoretically surprising and could lead to the conclusion that syntax develops in isolation from the rest of the brain. But to state that the same person has fluent language and an MA of 7 yrs changes the conclusion. In other words, those people with WS who have relatively fluent language might indeed have low IQs, but their MAs in non-verbal cognition, although seriously behind their chronological age, are usually well over 5, the age at which most language has been acquired in normally developing children.

In sum, not only are brain anatomy, brain chemistry, and temporal brain processes atypical, but Williams syndrome also displays an abnormal cognitive phenotype in which, even where behavioural scores are equivalent to those of normal controls, the cognitive processes by which such proficiency is achieved are different.

Our ongoing longitudinal behavioural and brain-imaging studies of atypical infants (with Janice Brown, Sarah Paterson, Marisa Gsödl, Michelle de Haan, Mark Johnson and others) already point to important differences in the initial state of WS patients compared with controls. The atypical groups' patterns are not one of juxtaposition of intact and impaired functions, as different end states might suggest. Interestingly, too, although WS linguistic performance ends up resembling normal language far more than Down syndrome performance, our preliminary results with infants show how important it is to distinguish the cognitive level from the behavioural level [...]. Fluent linguistic behaviour might stem from different processes at the cognitive level of description. Our initial results suggest that Down syndrome language comprehension has a delayed but relatively normal developmental pathway in infancy, whereas WS language development seems to be deviant from the outset. It is only by focusing studies of developmental disorders at their roots in early infancy that we will ultimately be able to chart longitudinally the varying developmental pathways that progressively lead to different phenotypical outcomes.

References for Reading A

a Udwin, O. Yule. W. (1991) A cognitive and behavioural phenotype in Williams syndrome *J. Clin. Exp. Neuropsychol.* 13, 232–244

b Bellugi, U., Wang, P. and Jernigan, T. L. (1994) Williams syndrome: an unusual neuropsychological profile, in *Atypical Cognitive Deficits in Developmental Disorders: Implications for Brain Function* (Broman, S. and Grafman, J., eds), pp. 23–56, Erlbaum

c Mervis, C.B. *et al.* Williams syndrome: findings from an integrated program of research, in *Neurodevelopmental Disorders: Contributions to a New Framework from the Cognitive Neurosciences* (Tager-Flusberg, H., ed.), MIT Press (in press)

d Pennington, B. (1997) Using genetics to dissect cognition *Am. J. Hum. Genet.* 60, 13–16 e Karmiloff-Smith, A. (1997) Crucial differences between developmental cognitive neuroscience and adult neuropsychology *Dev. Neuropsychol.* 13, 513–524

f Karmiloff-Smith, A. *et. al.* (1997) Language and Williams syndrome: how intact is 'intact'? *Child Dev.* 68, 246–262

g Stevens, T. and Karmiloff-Smith, A. (1997) Word learning in a special population: do individuals with Williams syndrome obey lexical constraints? *J. Child Lang.* 24, 737–765

h Karmiloff-Smith, A. *et al.* (1998) Linguistic dissociations in Williams syndrome: evaluating receptive syntax in on-line and off-line tasks *Neuropsychologia* 6, 342–351

i Volterra, V. *et al.* (1996) Linguistic abilities in Italian children with Williams syndrome *Cortex* 32, 67–83

j Bickerton, D. (1997) Constructivism, nativism and explanatory adequacy *Behav. Brain Sci.* 20, 557–558.

(Source: Karmiloff-Smith, A. (1998) 'Development itself is the key to understanding developmental disorders', *Trends in Cognitive Sciences*, vol. 2, pp. 389–98.

Reading B: An extract from 'Child development and evolutionary psychology'

David F. Bjorklund and Anthony D. Pellegrini

[...]

Aspects of children's understanding of social functioning has been hypothesized to be modular in nature (e.g., Baron-Cohen, 1995; Leslie, 1994). For example, by age 4, most children understand that other people have beliefs and desires, sometimes different from their own, that motivate their behavior. This knowledge that people's behavior is motivated by their beliefs and desires (belief-desire reasoning; Wellman, 1990) has been referred to as a *theory of mind,* and it is difficult to imagine how any person could survive in human culture without such a theory. Being able to think about others' thoughts is crucial to detecting deception and other social strategies that might handicap individuals. Although social intelligence, broadly defined, continues to develop into adulthood, most children by the age of 4 have developed a belief-desire theory of mind. Most children much younger than 4 years of age, however, seem to lack the requisite knowledge or conceptual ability characteristic of belief-desire reasoning.

Theory of mind is illustrated by false-belief tasks. In the standard false-belief task (e.g., Wimmer & Perner, 1983), children watch as a treat is hidden in a specific location (in a box, for example). Another person (Maxi) is present when the treat is hidden but then leaves the room, at which time the treat is moved to a new location. Children are then asked where Maxi will look for the treat when he returns. Most 4-year-old children can solve the problem, stating that Maxi will look where the treat was originally hidden, whereas most younger children state that Maxi will look for the treat in the new hiding place, apparently not realizing that Maxi's knowledge is different from their own.

Having a belief-desire theory of mind is required for everyday exchanges of resources between two people. For instance, in research by Peskin (1992), 3-year-old children play a game with 'mean monkey,' who always wants the toy that the child wants most. When children are asked to tell 'mean monkey' which of several toys they 'really' want and which one they 'really don't want,' 'mean monkey' (a hand puppet controlled by the experimenter) always takes the most desired toy, leaving the child with the least desired one. Four-year-old children catch on very quickly to the trick to deceive 'mean monkey' by pretending that the least-wanted toy is really their favorite, thus foiling 'mean monkey's' evil plan. Most 3-year-olds, in contrast, never catch on and spend the entire game being honest with 'mean monkey' and never getting the toys they most desire. They fail either to monitor their own thinking or to realize that 'mean monkey' has a different goal in mind than they do.

[...]

Consistent with an evolutionary developmental psychological perspective, research has indicated that this ability may be composed of a small set of modular-like skills. For example, Baron-Cohen (1995) has proposed four separate, interacting modules involved in mindreading that develop over infancy and early childhood. The earliest developing module is the *Intentionality Detector*

(ID), which interprets moving objects as having some volition or intention. For example, an object that is moving toward an individual may be perceived as an agent with some intention toward that individual (for instance, it wishes to harm me, to be near me). This is a very primitive skill, likely possessed by all animals with a nervous system. The second module is the Eye-Direction Detector (EDD), which has three related functions: It detects the presence of eyes or eye-like stimuli, determines whether the eyes are looking toward it or toward something else, and infers that if an organism's eyes are looking at something then that organism sees that thing. In other words, this module is responsible for our belief that knowledge is gained through the eyes (both ours and the eyes of others). According to Baron-Cohen, these first two modules develop between birth and 9 months of age. The third module is the Shared-Attention Mechanisms (SAM). Whereas the ID and EDD involve only two objects/individuals (that is, dyadic interactions/representations), the SAM involves triadic interactions/ representations. For example, if person A is looking at object B, and person C can see the eyes of person A and can see object B, person C can come to the conclusion that 'You (person A) and I (person C) are looking at the same thing.' This module develops between 9 and 18 months. Finally, the *Theory-Of-Mind Module (TOMM)* is roughly equivalent to the belief-desire reasoning described earlier and is reflected by passing false-belief tasks. This module develops between the ages of about 18 to 48 months.

[...]

Evidence for the modularity of the various components of Baron-Cohen's model comes from studies of children with autism. Baron-Cohen (1995) reviewed research from his laboratory and those of other scientists suggesting that the more advanced forms of mind reading (SAM and TOMM) are typically absent in children with autism. Autistic children (and later adults) often seem to be in a world of their own and have a difficult time in most forms of social interaction. Baron-Cohen claims that the primary deficit of these children is an inability to read minds, or what he calls *mindblindness*. Evidence for this conclusion comes from studies in which autistic children are presented with false-belief and other theory-of-mind tasks and consistently fail them, despite performing well on other, nonsocial tasks (e.g., Baron-Cohen, 1989; Baron-Cohen, Leslie, & Frith, 1985; Perner, Frith, Leslie, & Leekam, 1989). This is in contrast to children with mental retardation, such as Down syndrome, who perform theory-of-mind tasks easily, despite often doing poorly on other tasks that assess more general intelligence (e.g., Baron-Cohen *et al.*, 1985). Most autistic children are able to perform well on the simpler tasks requiring the ID or EDD modules, but fail tasks involving the SAM and especially the TOMM modules. According to Baron-Cohen, autistic children are unable to understand other people's different beliefs, even those children who are functioning at a relatively high intellectual level.

Acknowledgements

The authors thank six anonymous reviewers and Barbara R. Bjorklund for helpful comments on earlier drafts of this manuscript. They also acknowledge the W. T. Grant and Spencer Foundations for their support of this work.

Addresses and affiliations

Corresponding author: David F. Bjorklund, Department of Psychology, Florida Atlantic University, Boca Raton, FL 33431; e-mail: dbjorklund@fau.edu. Anthony D. Pellegrini is at the University of Minnesota at Minneapolis.

References for Reading B

Baron-Cohen, S. (1989). The autistic child's theory of mind: A case of specific developmental delay, *Journal of Child Psychology and Psychiatry, 30*, 285–298.

Baron-Cohen, S. (1995). *Mindblindness: An essay on autism and theory of mind.* Cambridge, MA: MIT Press.

Baron-Cohen, S., Leslie, A., & Frith, U. (1985). Does the autistic child have a "theory of mind"? *Cognition, 21*, 37–46.

Leslie, A. (1994). ToMM, ToBY, and agency: Core architecture and domain specificity. In L. Hirschfeld & S. Gelman (Eds.), *Mapping the mind: Domain specificity in cognition and culture* (pp. 119–148). Cambridge, U.K.: Cambridge University Press.

Perner, J., Frith, U., Leslie, A., & Leekam, S. (1989). Exploration of the autistic child's theory of mind: Knowledge, belief, and communication. *Child Development, 60*, 689–700.

Peskin, J. (1992). Ruse and representations: On children's ability to conceal information. *Developmental Psychology, 28*, 84–89.

Wellman, H. M. (1990). *The child's theory of mind.* Cambridge, MA: MIT Press.

Wimmer, H., & Perner, J. (1983). Beliefs about beliefs: Representation and constraining function of wrong beliefs in young children's understanding of deception. *Cognition, 13*, 103–128.

(Source: Bjorklund, D. F. and Pellegrini, A. D. (2000) 'Child development and evolutionary psychology', *Child Development*, vol. 71, pp. 1687–1708.)

Chapter 7
First relationships

John Oates

Contents

Learning outcomes

After you have studied this chapter you should be able to:

1 describe some of the psychological processes that are involved in relationships between people;

2 describe the special features of relationships between infants and their caregivers;

3 describe some aspects of the development of infants' relationships during the first year of life;

4 critically discuss concepts of psychological processes in infants' relationships and identify their theoretical origins in psychoanalysis and elsewhere;

5 appreciate the complexity of describing and theorizing about infants' relationships.

1 Introduction

Babies *have* to depend on other people for their sheer physical survival, for their primary needs of warmth, shelter and food. In this very basic sense, babies can only exist as part of a social system in which more mature, less dependent people take the time to meet their needs. But it seems that babies require more than just these bodily needs to be met – even to develop physically. Babies whose basic physical needs are met may still 'fail to thrive' if this care is given by a succession of different people with whom they do not have the opportunity to form relationships with. Many historical studies of babies raised in orphanages, where attention was paid only to physical care, attest to this fact (Rutter, 1981).

1.1 Babies' attention and behaviour towards other people

Relatedness
The special quality of contact between human beings that involves 'person-to-person' mutuality.

Babies come into the world with their perceptual systems already seemingly 'tuned-in' to such features as faces and voices, and biological motion, that direct their attention towards other human beings (Reddy *et al.*, 1997). Hobson (1993, 2002) has argued that babies also come into the world with a readiness for entering into and experiencing 'relatedness' with others.

Figure 1
A mother and baby playing.

RESEARCH SUMMARY 1

A readiness to relate?

Developmentalists such as Colwyn Trevarthen and Daniel Stern (Stern, 1985; Trevarthen, 1979) have long been energetic in drawing attention to the finely-tuned patterns of co-ordinated face-to-face interchange that occur between caregivers and their infants in the early months of a baby's life. In fact, the most dramatic demonstrations of such interpersonal meshing have emerged as a result of systematic interventions to disrupt the flow of this dyadic to-and-fro. Following up early reports of infants' responses to still-faced mothers (Carpenter, Tecce, Stechler and Friedman, 1970; Tronick, Als, Adamson, Wise and Brazelton, 1978), Jeffrey Cohn and Edward Tronick (1983) instructed mothers of three-month-old infants to interact with depressed expressions during three-minute periods of face-to-face interaction. The effect was that the infants became negative and showed protest and wariness, continuing in this way for a short while after the mothers returned to a style of normal interaction. [...]

We can see how young infants showed organised expressions of affect and attention when the form and timing of their mothers' natural style of engagement were disrupted. The person-with-person configurations of mutual gaze and of facial, vocal and gestural interchange seem to involve not merely the co-ordination of behaviour between infant and mother, but also some kind of psychological linkage which when established – or when broken – has emotional consequences for both participants. There is a sense in which the infant (or some 'mechanism' within the infant) seems to expect appropriate forms of dynamic, bodily expressive response from another person.

Source: Hobson, 1993, pp. 34–7.

If we accept that evolution has produced babies:

*   who are biologically designed to learn, and particularly to learn socially;
*   who are predisposed to direct their interest towards other humans, and to behave in special ways towards them; and
*   that development involves extended transactions between babies and their social environment

then the formation of enduring relationships, or 'attachments', between babies and caregivers can be seen as a basic starting-point for human psychological development.

Making use of the social transmission of knowledge (in the broad sense of knowing *how to do* things as well as knowing *about* things) gives human beings a great advantage in their flexibility and adaptability. Advances and changes in socio-cultural knowledge allow a much more rapid response to changing environmental conditions (including those brought about by socio-cultural processes themselves) than can be achieved through evolutionary processes.

1.2 Cultural framing of relationships with babies

There is a widely portrayed image of the biological mother being the pre-eminent and sole ideal figure for the infant's first attachment, and indeed this image is consonant also with infant-rearing practice for many babies in many cultures. However, this image, and the practice of mothers being babies' prime caregivers, is by no means universal. Many cultures pattern childcare differently and the web of relationships that form around a newborn infant can take many different forms.

Babies can be looked after by grandparents, older siblings, fathers, others sharing the same household, by nannies or childminders, as well as by biological mothers. In some cultures, the mother's role is seen in a very different way, and the practice of a mother spending most of her time caring for her new baby, in relative seclusion from the social and economic life of the community, would seem strange and alien. However, a virtually universal feature, both across and within cultures, is the establishment of either one or a small number of ongoing, caring relationships between baby and carer(s). Although this issue of cultural relativism will be returned to at points, the focus of this chapter is on these so-called 'dyadic' (two-person) relationships.

1.3 Concepts and theories

Many of the concepts underlying developmental psychologists' theories and research concerning babies' relationships with others have roots in psychoanalytic theory. This originated with Sigmund Freud's work and has since continued to be modified and elaborated, not as a single theory, but as a set of theories with different foci and indeed with certain important differences in points of view. In general, though, psychoanalytic theories have always placed the period of early childhood at centre stage as a formative influence on the development of adult personality. Although Freud himself concentrated on the relationships of the child with the parents around what he called the Oedipal phase (3–5 years of age), other psychoanalytic theorists, notably Anna Freud (Sigmund Freud's daughter) and Melanie Klein, as well as others building on their ideas, have developed views on infant development and the role of relationships from the time of birth.

There is an important distinction between psychoanalysis and psychoanalytic theory. Psychoanalysis is the treatment of mental disorders through techniques such as regular talking sessions in which the analyst's aims include uncovering unconscious conflicts and resolving them through the medium of the client–analyst relationship. There is also a somewhat distinct body of theory to do with how these conflicts arise, which is pre-eminently developmental. Psychoanalytic theory is about how personality difficulties arise in development, and it is also about how conflicts arise and may be resolved in everyday life, not just in therapy. Freud himself, and others who have worked with his ideas, saw this aspect of theory as applicable to the development of all children.

There has always been a degree of tension between developmental psychology and psychoanalytic research. The two disciplines share a common interest in the significance of infancy, yet have some fundamental differences of view on what counts as evidence in theory development. Psychologists interested in language, personality, cognition and emotion, in fact virtually every facet of mental life, have looked to the behaviour of infants with their caregivers for sources and precursors of abilities that are seen to emerge and develop later on in childhood. Their approach has been dominated by a view that researchers' subjective interpretations of the phenomena of interest are inadequate, even inadmissible, as evidence. In contrast to this approach, psychoanalytic researchers see these sorts of interpretations as being important sources. Nevertheless, much contemporary research on infants' relationships in developmental psychology is informed by psychoanalytic ideas, and psychoanalytic theory itself is influenced by progress in developmental psychology.

This chapter does not attempt to give a complete picture of 'the psychology of relationships with infants', but rather to focus on some important developmental aspects. In part it covers a range of social abilities that develop in children, but it also has the main aim of elaborating some key concepts and the theoretical positions that underlie them.

Summary of Section 1

- Although there is much cultural variation, caregiver–infant dyads are universal.
- Many developmental psychologists argue that infants' abilities are 'pre-tuned' for social interactions.
- Social interactions can be seen as providing the basis for psychological development.
- Psychoanalytic theory has provided a basis for much of the research into early relationships.

2 Describing relationships

Most adults would agree that our relationships with others are vitally important to our psychological life. Building a psychological understanding of how relationships operate and how they develop is a complex and difficult task. For example, relationships can be examined at the level of moment-to-moment interchange, in terms of how eye contact and other aspects of body language allow people to interact, or they can be examined at the level of how they change over years. They can be looked at in terms of what image each person in the relationship has of each other and how these images match up, or in terms of the language that flows between them. In a sense, each of us already has a vast amount of knowledge about relationships, from our experiences in them, but this knowledge may often not be thought about or expressed.

Activity 1

Allow about 20 minutes

What is a 'good' relationship?

This activity will help you to think about the richness of personal relationships.

Think about your image of a 'good' relationship with another person, for example a close friend or partner, and write down as much as you can to define what you understand by the term. Draw up a checklist of features. You might feel the need to differentiate different sorts of relationship; does your list of features help you to do this?

Comment

The following list of features is one that has been drawn up from looking at what various psychologists have suggested are important factors in relationships:

Duration: a relationship is something that is ongoing and has a history – it takes time for relationships to be formed, and they tend to go on.

Proximity-seeking: one of the qualities of a relationship is that the two people in it seek each other's company.

Rewards: the two participants find positive rewards in being together.

Intimacy: a relationship involves sharing things about oneself that are to some extent private.

Commitment: both people feel an investment in each other that continues into the future.

Conversation: the two people talk together and exchange points of view.

Meshing: both individuals feel 'comfortable' together and each experiences a 'fit' with the other's behaviour.

Empathy: each person can make correct judgements about the other's state of mind and can share in it.

Concern: each individual shows interest in the other's emotional state and any difficulties they have, and will offer help/advice if it is perceived to be needed.

Warmth: each person communicates to the other positive feelings about being with the other.

Knowledge: the two people know a significant amount about each other and their lives.

This is not an exhaustive list, and the above elements are obviously linked in various ways: for example, warmth and rewards can be seen as two aspects of the same thing. Also, even the best relationships vary in the extent to which these factors are present. You might like to modify your own list on the basis of the above and draw linking lines between different features to further explore the possible linkages between them.

This activity should have made you more aware of the richness and complexity of your own knowledge and feelings about relationships. It also highlights the difficulty in pinning down in simple terms what it is that develops in children and takes them towards adult ways of relating to others.

At this point, I would like to introduce the idea that relationships between people usually depend on some form of mental representation, or 'mental model' of the other. Your answers to the previous activity almost certainly contained some element of this. For example, you may have included 'concern for the other', 'understanding the other', or similar features. By this idea of a mental model I do not necessarily mean just a representation of the other that is solely based on what the other says and does, in other words, a simple 'taking in' of the qualities of the other. What will become clearer as you progress through this chapter is the argument that a representation of the other may include (and perhaps necessarily includes) elements of our *own* thoughts and feelings which are felt as located in this internal model of the other. To give an example of this, a young child who is very demanding of attention at times when we wish to get on with other things may be represented, in our internal model of this child, as persecutory, as trying to interfere with us and prevent us doing what we want to do, and our reactions may as a result have an angry, rejecting content. However, looked at from the child's point of view, if their model of us does not include a representation of our own wishes, their demanding behaviour is simply and straightforwardly a wish for attention, not a wish to upset us by interfering with what we want to do.

This process, of emotions that are actually in us being

Figure 2   Getting to know each other.

experienced in part as emanating from, or being located in another person, has been encapsulated in the psychoanalytic concept of *projection*. This describes a way of handling feelings that are actually our own, but instead are felt as being partially or wholly located in others. Our models of others play a central role in affecting what we say and do in relationships: our thoughts and feelings about others' motives, wishes and needs (contained in our internal models of them) affect how we behave towards them.

Although caring for infants involves looking after their bodily needs and ensuring that they are warm, well-fed, clean and healthy, it is the development of personal relationships with infants that tends to bring the greatest rewards. The first smile from a baby is for most parents a highly significant experience that can make all the efforts of childcare seem worthwhile:

> Being a mother is very special. I feel that having a baby changes your life completely. You are no longer a person, as you have someone else who depends on you totally. Being a mother is very tiring, especially in the first few months when you are up in the night feeding. It is also very rewarding when your baby smiles at you for the first time and starts to recognize you.

> She smiled at both her father and me, this morning. It made getting up at 5 a.m. to feed her worthwhile. Her whole face lit up, it was wonderful.

(Extracts from mothers' diaries)

A great deal is usually made of this experience: when this first intimation of the baby having a model of their carer as a person is experienced, it opens up the possibility for a major elaboration of the adult's model of their baby.

Activity 2   The importance of the adult's model of their baby

Allow about
10 minutes

This activity should help you to clarify the idea of a 'mental model'.

Reflect on the implications of an adult seeing their baby as recognizing them as a person for the first time. How can their model of the baby now change and grow? What might be projected into this model? If you have had children of your own, consider whether the concept of projection helps you to understand your feelings towards your children, particularly when they were babies.

Comment

Once a baby's smile allows us to feel that the baby recognizes us as a person, it is possible also to believe that they feel pleasure at our presence, as the source of all the things that we do to care for them. This allows our model of the baby now to include the ability of the baby to reward, to show gratitude. This in turn can enhance our motivation to continue to give, supported by the idea that the baby is now able to give back and acknowledge all that we do for them.

Our need to have all our caring recognized and affirmed can now be projected into the baby as the baby wanting to 'give thanks' for what is being done for them. This enhancement of our model of the baby allows the relationship to develop at a new level of reciprocity.

For many mothers who experience depression or other negative feelings in the period after their baby's birth, the experience of the baby's first smile can mark a turning point in the developing relationship.

▲

This section has stressed particularly the development of the carer's mental model of the baby as an individual who can have motives, thoughts and feelings, because these attributions frame and shape much of the carer's behaviour and feelings towards the baby. This gives the baby the experience of having a place as a person within the relationship. Much of the carer's behaviour towards their baby in this very early period can have a strong 'as-if' quality; for example, the carer talking to the baby 'as if' they understand the words.

The carer's mental model of their baby is not just based on the actualities of what the baby does, but can also contain 'potentials' of what the baby might come to be able to do and be.

2.1 Idealization of the mother—infant dyad

Winnicott once said 'There is no such thing as a baby ... if you set out to describe a baby; you will find that you are describing a *baby and someone*. A baby cannot exist alone, but is essentially part of a relationship' (Winnicott, 1964, p. 88). By saying this he was referring to the essentiality of some other person or persons who can provide for the baby's needs, without whom the baby would simply be unable to survive. Even to supply the most basic human needs of nourishment and warmth, there has to be at least a rudimentary relationship with a 'carer' (or 'carers'). For a majority of babies, this carer is in fact the biological mother, although the contribution she makes, and the extent to which this is shared with others, is highly variable in its qualities and quantity. There are many babies who are cared for by persons (male or female) other than the biological mother, and it seems that there is nothing unique about what the biological mother brings to the relationship with her baby that cannot in principle be provided by some other person. What does seem to be important is that this care is provided by a person or persons in a reasonably consistent and continuing way. So, in this chapter, the word 'mother' is being used as shorthand for any person who is providing ongoing care for the baby, who provides the baby with the opportunity to form a relationship with them.

Nevertheless, using this word 'mother' remains somewhat problematic, particularly since much theory and research in this area is based more or less explicitly on an assumption of care devoted to the baby by the biological mother. This tends to produce data based on samples of mothers and infants that conform more or less to this ideal image.

Figure 3 Shared parenting.

Another possible bias that can arise in a reading of research studies of babies is the idealization of the baby's experience. Infancy may appear to be an innocent 'golden age', without upset or strife. Babies become portrayed as, for example, 'pure cognitive systems' (Norman, 1980), having no connection with emotions, either positive or negative. This issue will be discussed in detail later in the chapter. However, here it is worth noting how the 'controlled' nature of many experiments with babies and their mothers is specifically designed to minimize the involvement of emotions other than those that support babies' engagement in the tasks that the experimenters set them. Of course, any mother knows that caring for a baby is to some extent a struggle, but the insidious effect of the 'perfect baby' image, and the assumption of this being supported by the 'perfect mother' can do little to help the self-confidence of the mother.

Winnicott also introduced the idea of the 'good enough mother', a concept that suggests perfection in caring is not something to be striven for, but rather that caring which is sufficient for the baby's needs could be a more attainable goal.

Summary of Section 2

- Many psychologists believe that relationships between infants and their caregivers are crucial for development.
- Relationships between adults and infants can be described on many levels and are based on a complex set of psychological processes.
- The psychoanalytic concept of projection can be used to describe some important aspects of relationships with infants.
- The word 'mother' can be used as shorthand for any adult who cares for

a baby: fathers and other people can also form close and significant relationships with babies.

- It is important not to idealize mother–infant relationships, nor to ignore that there are both positive and negative emotions involved in infant care.

3   Meshing

This section examines how an adult's and an infant's behaviours commonly fit in, or 'mesh', with each other during social interaction.

One of the key features of relationships is that when two people 'get on well' together, their interactions tend to be smoothly integrated, with each person's contribution to the interaction fitting in with the other's. Perhaps the most striking situation in which this meshing can be evident is where two people are having a conversation. When a conversation runs smoothly, turn-taking is well managed by both participants: one waits until the other has finished speaking, picks up the signals that the other has finished, and then makes their input, while their conversational partner in turn takes the listening role, waiting for their turn to come round again, and so on.

Activity 3   Meshing

Allow about 15 minutes

This activity should help you to be clearer about how people's behaviour fits together in conversations.

(a) Observe two people in conversation. (You could usefully do this using a video recording of a conversation, taken from a television programme, for example: this would allow you to look at the interaction more closely.)

(b) Note how much turn-taking is involved: pay particular attention to the points at which speaking shifts from one person to the other. Look also for non-verbal behaviours that go along with turns.

(c) Look out also for segments where there is not turn-taking, but where both people are doing something, like laughing.

Comment

From this activity, you should have noticed that a simple view of conversation as turn-taking is appropriate up to a point, but that a lot of 'mutual action' happens as well, often connected with expressions of emotion. Trevarthen (1993) has suggested that 'co-regulation' is a useful term to describe these two aspects of turn-taking and synchronizing.

All this is orchestrated not only through the speech that each utters, but also in their non-verbal behaviour: the nods, eye-contacts, body movements and so forth that signal ongoing attention. This is undoubtedly a complex skill that can be analysed at a number of levels and has often been seen as having its origins in the interactions between babies and their caregivers. In the 1970s developmental psychologists started looking closely at film recordings of mothers with their infants, and documented the ways in which the interaction of the two partners can have a very 'conversation-like' quality.

Proto-conversation
A type of interaction, usually mother–infant, that has the form of a conversation but without meaningful speech. Often seen as a developmental precursor to conversations proper.

Observations of these 'proto-conversations' often show, quite strikingly, that both the baby's and the adult's behaviour are closely meshed. However, it is by no means essential for both partners in the interaction to be skilled at the sort of management of their behaviour that goes on in conversations between older children and/or adults. It may simply be that the adult fits their behaviour around the natural ebb and flow of their baby's behaviour so that a conversation-*like* interaction is sustained, but with little or no adjustment or use of social skill on the baby's part. In effect, this would mean that these early mother–infant interactions, which can look just like true dialogues, may in fact be 'pseudo-dialogues'. In these interactions the mother fits her behaviour so subtly into the infant's behaviour that the lack of adaptation on the infant's part is not evident.

Research summary 2 below offers some evidence that suggests that although this second interpretation may have some truth in it, it is not the whole story. Probably the most important consequence of meshed interactions between mother and infant is that they can give the infant the *experience* of taking part in a dialogue. This experience is unique to interactions that the infant has with other human beings and provides the first experiences of relatedness. No other 'objects' in the infant's world can give this experience: an adult or older child who is interacting with an infant in this very special way is giving many aspects of the infant's behaviour quite new and rich meanings. Infants can experience their actions producing results with other parts of their environment, for example, by a turn of the head bringing a new scene into view, or an arm movement meeting resistance when the arm hits the side of the cot. However, the animation and richness of adults' responsiveness, tuned finely to ongoing changes in infant behaviour, can provide a sense of being closely *engaged* with something very responsive and attuned. The significant feature here is that the other's behaviour is contingent on the infant's. This provides an opportunity for the infant to begin to form not only a representation of the other but also a representation of how the infant's own behaviour has meaning in being responded to in consistent ways by the other.

RESEARCH SUMMARY 2

'Conversations' with babies

Figures 4 to 6 are graphs drawn from mother–infant interaction periods. Time is measured along the horizontal axis; the number of behaviors, along the vertical axis. Curves drawn above the horizontal axis indicate that the individual whose behavior the curve represents was looking at his or her partner. Curves drawn below the axis indicate that he or she was looking away. Solid lines represent the mother's behavior; broken lines, the baby's. Thus, a deep, broken line below the horizontal axis indicates that the baby was looking away while engaging in several behaviors.

Figure 4

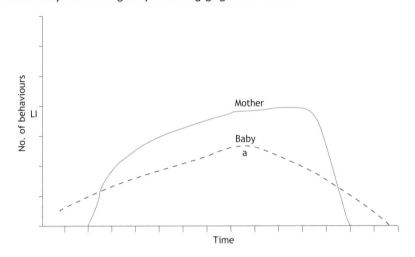

As reflected by Figure 4 (16-second interaction), the mother looks at the baby after the baby turns to her. As they look at each other, she adds behaviors – smiling, vocalizing, touching baby's hand, holding baby's leg – to accelerate their interaction. The baby responds by increasing the number of his or her own behaviors (smiling, vocalizing, and cycling arms and legs) until the peak at point (a). At this point, the baby begins to decrease his or her behaviors and gradually cuts down on them toward the end of their interaction. The mother follows the baby's lead by decreasing her behaviors more rapidly, and she ends her part of the cycle by looking away just before the baby does.

Figure 5 (5-second interaction) shows a baby starting a cycle by looking at the mother. She follows by looking at the baby and adding four more behaviors in rapid succession – touching, smiling, talking and nodding her head. The baby watches her, vocalizes, smiles back, cycles briefly, and then begins to decrease his or her responses and turns away at point (a). The mother stops smiling as the baby begins to turn away but rapidly adds facial gestures to try to recapture the baby's interest. She continues to talk, touch, nod her head, and make facial gestures until point (b). At this point, she stops the gestures but begins to pat the baby. At (c), she stops talking briefly and stops nodding. At (d), she makes hand gestures in addition to her facial grimaces but stops them both thereafter. At point (e), she stops vocalizing, and the baby begins to look at her again. He or she vocalizes briefly and then looks away again when her activity continues.

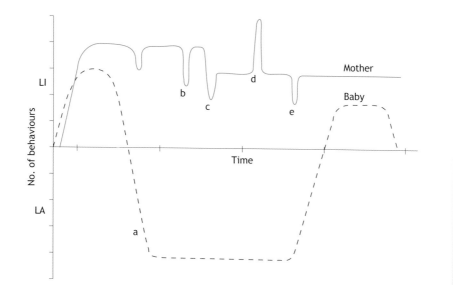

Figure 5

In Figure 6 (also a 5-second period), the mother and baby are looking at each other, smiling, and vocalizing together. The baby begins to cycle and reach out to her. At point (a), the baby begins to turn away from the mother. She responds by looking down at her hands, and she stops her activity briefly. This brings the baby back to look at her at point (c). Her smiling, vocalizing and leaning toward the baby bring a smiling response. In addition, the baby's arms and legs cycle, and he or she coos contentedly while watching her. As the baby turns away, the mother first adds another behavior and gestures. The baby, however, adds activities – ignoring her reminders – and turns away from her. She gradually cuts out all her activity and by point (e), she looks away from her baby. Immediately afterward, the baby begins to look back to her, and the cycle of looking at each other begins again at point (f).

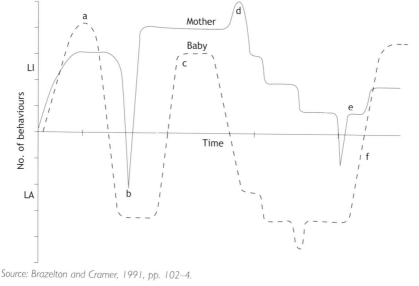

Figure 6

Source: Brazelton and Cramer, 1991, pp. 102–4.

As you saw in Research summary 1, evidence that infants aged 2–3 months are sensitive to their mothers' responsiveness has come from several studies that have artificially disrupted the pattern of mothers' behaviour towards their infants in one way or another. For example, infants who are interacting with their mother through a video link, where each is seeing and hearing the other on a television screen and loudspeaker, show clear signs of distress if the live link with the mother is replaced either by a delay in the circuit or a replay of a recording of the mother made in the same situation a few minutes previously (Murray and Trevarthen, 1985).

Also, many babies show quite striking reactions if their mothers are asked to make their faces expressionless while face-to-face with their infants; so-called 'still face' studies (Tronick *et al.*, 1978).

3.1 The development of turn-taking in feeding

For a mother to be able to mesh her behaviour with her infant's, there has to be some structure in the infant's behaviour that provides 'spaces' for the mother's contributions. Infant feeding, from breast or bottle, has received particular attention from developmental psychologists because of the pronounced rhythmic nature of the infant's behaviour. Uniquely among mammals, human infants feed with a 'burst–pause' rhythm, in which they suck for a while, and then pause for a varying few seconds before starting to suck again. This rhythm is one around which mothers usually start to fit their own behaviour from the very first feed: when they speak to their baby during a feed they usually do so in a pause rather than while the baby is feeding. They also tend to gently shake, or 'jiggle', their baby during a pause.

Mothers typically say that jiggling 'wakes up' their baby and helps to keep them sucking. Kaye and Brazelton (1971) came up with the surprising finding that jiggling actually seems to *lengthen* the pauses, in that babies do not suck while the mother is jiggling, even if the jiggling lasts for longer than a baby's pause would normally last. However, when the mother stops jiggling, then the baby is more likely to start a new burst of sucking. A mother tends to synchronize her behaviour with her baby's by jiggling in a pause shortly after a sucking burst and the baby is similarly likely to respond with a burst at the end of a jiggle. The inhibition of sucking by the baby during a jiggle, and the mother fitting her jiggles into the baby's pauses, together produce a very 'conversation-like' interaction between the two during feeding.

It is not only during feeding that mothers adjust their behaviour, but also in the way they interact with their babies at other times, when they are engaged in 'face-to-face play', as described in Research summary 3.

Turn-taking in face-to-face interactions

Kaye and Fogel (1980) examined the development of interactions between 52 mothers and their infants over the first 6 months after infants' births, at ages 6, 13 and 26 weeks. They looked at videotapes of 5-minute play periods to analyse how the mothers' and infants' behaviour and patterns of interaction developed. Infants were on their mothers' laps, and mothers were asked to 'Try to get their attention and play with them as you normally do'. At 6 weeks of age, infants did not show any evidence of controlling their smiles, vocalizations and mouthing expressions (which the researchers called 'greetings') which were randomly distributed and just as frequent when babies were looking away from the mothers as when they were looking at them. By 13 weeks, however, these behaviours were beginning to occur in 'packages', that is, more like the burst–pause rhythm of sucking. By 26 weeks these behaviours were clearly clustered and also much more likely to be seen when the baby was attending to the mother.

Babies' 'greetings' were divided into two categories:

(a) Reactive: those that occurred closely following the mother having smiled, vocalized or mouthed; and

(b) Proactive: those that occurred closely following the baby directing their attention to the mother.

When the proportions of these two types of infant behaviour were compared at the three different ages, a striking pattern was found. At 6 weeks, babies' greetings were almost entirely reactive, occurring only in response to mothers' greetings, and they were not very frequent. At 13 weeks, babies' greetings were more than twice as frequent overall and although the majority were still reactive, a larger proportion of greetings were proactive (that is, initiated by the baby). By 26 weeks, babies were producing equal numbers of proactive and reactive greetings: an indication that the babies had developed a progressively more active, initiating role.

Turning to the mothers' greetings, it was found that these did not change significantly in frequency over the 6 months. What changed was the way that mothers fitted them into the babies' behaviours. Although babies tended to spend less time attending to their mothers as they got older, their mothers also became much better at giving their 'greetings' when their babies were actively attending to them. It was also found that mothers' greetings were not very effective at drawing their babies' attention, particularly at 6 and 13 weeks; by 26 weeks, mothers rarely greeted when babies were not attending, suggesting that their babies' lack of response to such greetings had modified their behaviour.

Framing
Giving a broader meaning to a piece of behaviour; e.g. 'that's naughty'.

Overall, looking at both feeding and face-to-face play, the picture is one of mothers progressively allowing their babies to take over a more active role in interaction, and both mothers' and babies' behaviour developing to sustain and enhance the reciprocity of interaction. The role of the mother can be seen as one of 'framing' the baby's behaviour with actions on her part that fit in with the baby's at first unadapting behaviour to give the 'feel' of being in a dialogue. Initially, this is a 'pseudo-dialogue' in that the baby plays little or no active part in sustaining it, other than their behaviour having a rhythmic quality that gives the mother natural points for interjection. Babies then become progressively more able to drive the interaction with their own active, appropriately timed inputs. So, pseudo-dialogue gradually metamorphoses into 'proto-dialogue', still without the meaningful language content that will come later, but with a clearly defined turn-taking frame which is more truly interactive.

3.2 Features of the mother's adjustments to her baby

You have seen above how a mother can play a dominant part in allowing the baby to get the feel of being in a relationship, by being very responsive to the baby's fluctuating state and behaviour. But her adjustments go far beyond simply this responsiveness: the qualities of what she does in interaction are quite strikingly different from what she will do with an older child or another adult. This is particularly noticeable in her use of language towards her baby.

Adults who are attuned to babies tend to talk to them in quite distinctive ways, using a lot of repetition, with simplified short utterances, raised pitch and exaggerated expression. This special form of speech has been called 'baby-talk' (Snow and Ferguson, 1977). Other terms for it are 'motherese' or 'infant-directed speech'.

Table I **Some features of the adaptation of adults' speech to children in comparison with speech to other adults**

Phonological characteristics	**Semantic characteristics**
Higher pitch	Limited range of vocabulary
Exaggerated and more varied intonation	'Baby-talk' words
Lengthened vowels	More words with concrete referents
Clear enunciation	
Slower speech	
Longer pauses	**Pragmatic characteristics**
Syntactic characteristics	More directives
Shorter utterance length	More questions
Sentences well-formed	More attention devices
Fewer subordinate clauses	Repetitions of child's utterances
Fewer embeddings	More deictic utterances (i.e. referring to things present; I, you, it, that, etc.)
Fewer verbs	

Source: Schaffer, 1984, p. 146.

The following extract is a good illustration of some of the features listed in Table 1, taken from a recording of a mother talking to her 13-week-old baby.

Baby-talk

Are you going to give me a smile?

Or going to be a bastard.

Come on Alan.

Come on.

You can give Mommy a smile.

Come on.

You give Mommy a smile.

Come on.

Come on.

Come on.

Can you give me a smile?

Can you give me a smile, sweetheart?

Come on.

ARRRRRRRR.

ARRRRRRRR.

Can you give me a smile?

Can you give me a smile?

Yeah.

Come on.

You can give me a smile.

Come on.

Come on.

Oh, what you going to do, Al?

What you going to do?

Come on.

Come here.

Come on.

Give me a smile.

Hey, Alan.

Hey.

Come on. [...]

Source: Kaye, 1982, p. 191.

Some of the features of baby-talk that are not evident in the above extract, the exaggerated intonation and the raised pitch, make sense as adaptations to babies' developing sensory abilities. But these adaptations are not solely made by mothers (which is why the term 'motherese' is not wholly appropriate): women who have not had children (Snow, 1972), fathers (Berko Gleason, 1973) and even 4-year-old children (Shatz and Gelman, 1973), show similar speech towards babies. Baby-talk is very widespread, having been identified in cultures as widely separated as the !Kung Bushmen of the Kalahari, forest-dwellers in the Cameroons, the Yanomami of the Amazon Basin and the Eipo of New Guinea (Fernald *et al.*, 1989).

The simplification and repetition of baby-talk, however, may have much more to do with what the baby can learn than just with what they can perceive. These repeated experiences of very similar short 'bouts' of interaction, where the mother provides consistent 'verbal accompaniment' along with responsive framing provide the infant with a rich social environment, with simple consistencies. In this way speech can be appreciated as part and parcel of a much broader range of behaviours that go together to make up social interaction.

Summary of Section 3

- Close study of mother–infant interaction reveals 'conversation-like exchanges' that may form the basis of the development of conversation proper.
- The way mothers interact with their babies during feeding shows some of the key elements of turn-taking.
- Adults and even young children tend to use a special form of speech when interacting with babies.

4 Imitation

This section reconsiders the controversial issue of infants' imitations of the facial gestures of adults, which was raised in Chapter 4. There, we were looking at imitation primarily for what it might tell us about the abilities of infants to represent another's facial gestures, in other words, their cognitive abilities. The studies reported in Chapter 4 were laboratory studies, and the facial gestures were to some extent 'lifted' from the natural context in which purported imitations occur: 'conversations' between mothers and infants. Imitations can also be seen in a different light; as a basic building block of the interactive sequences that make up 'pseudo-dialogues'.

The actions studied in the imitation studies are very similar to those that occur both in 'pre-speech' (Trevarthen's term) and in 'greetings' (Kaye's term), namely:

Figure 7 A baby and mother imitating.

tongue protrusion, mouth opening, lip widening and pouting (Meltzoff and Moore, 1977). This is probably far from accidental – it may reflect a partial appreciation of the significance of these behaviours in natural interactions. So, babies already produce them as part of their ongoing behaviour, and mothers make great use of them in responding to their babies. For example, in a study by Moran *et al.* (1987) with 1 year olds and their mothers, mothers were found to imitate their babies much more than their babies imitated them. This study also found that babies were slightly more likely to produce imitations when the mothers were themselves imitating. It was suggested that mothers may be sensitive enough to the patterns of their babies' behaviour to anticipate with some accuracy what they will do next, and precede it with what could be called an 'anticipatory imitation'.

Pawlby (1977), in a longitudinal study of 'imitative sequences' between mothers and their infants aged from 4 to 10 months, also found that across this age range mothers did a lot more imitating of their babies than the other way round. Interestingly, she also found that these facial units of imitation were a dominant focus when the babies were 4–6 months old, with hand movements and sounds only accompanying them with any regularity from 6 months onwards. By 8 months old, the imitation of actions with objects (rattles, and so forth) began to dominate.

These studies confirm what most carers know at some level: that babies do produce these 'units' of behaviour without any specific stimulus as a matter of course, and that they are ideal behaviours around which to frame interaction sequences. Indeed, they are often seized upon by the interacting mother as the focus for *her* imitations. For the mother, they are aspects of the baby's behaviour that can be given particular meanings by being responded to *as if* they had communicative intent. What can the baby learn from this repetitive and hence predictable response from the mother? First, the baby can learn, through the repeated experience of these units leading to predictable responses from the mother, that these units are *effective*, that they are part and parcel of these early pseudo-dialogues. Second, they allow the baby to begin to represent the mother as offering a predictable responsiveness to, and elaboration of, these units. This is arguably one of the foundations of the sense of relatedness and of an embryonic 'theory of mind' in the baby.

Theory of mind
The ability of one person to understand what is going on in another person's mind.

Just as was shown for both feeding and face-to-face play, over the first 6 months, the way that interaction develops can be seen as the mother's framing function (which at first is driven almost entirely by her fitting into the baby's rhythms) gradually being taken over by the baby. There is evidence suggesting that infant imitation definitely increases in frequency and accuracy over the first year of an infant's life (Kaye and Marcus, 1981).

So, although imitation may be important when viewed as a rather solitary achievement of the baby, it makes a much richer sense when viewed as being at the centre of the development of the natural interactions between infant and mother. The units of imitation are just those behaviours that the mother chooses as foci for showing the baby that their behaviour can make sense within an interaction, as elements in a dynamic interchange. This sense, this learning of what can be meaningful between people, can then be taken in by the baby and become in turn part of the baby's repertoire of social actions.

During the first 6 months or so of babies' lives, the 'topics' of interactions are very much 'of the moment', to do with what is actually happening between the mother and baby at the time. Each is responding to the other, and what are being commented on by both baby and mother are primarily 'interpersonal events' such as the units of imitation discussed above. Trevarthen coined the term *primary intersubjectivity* to describe this type of interaction and phase of development, highlighting a belief that the function of these interchanges was primarily the development of a sensitivity in the baby to the subjective experience of the mother. This sensitivity is coupled with an awareness that the mother can also be sensitive to the subjective experience of the baby; effectively a 'meeting of minds'.

Inter-subjectivity
A sharing of experience between two people which is more than a simple interaction.

But a new development enters the interpersonal arena when the mother–infant interaction is sufficiently advanced to allow the involvement of other things – objects such as rattles and squeaky toys. The interaction can then begin to extend its topics to include joint action, and joint attention, directed to things other than the interaction itself. What this development makes possible is a dawning realization by the baby that events and objects in the world (and actions that affect these) can be shared in the experience of two people. Recognizing the significance of this step forward, Trevarthen (1979) described it as marking an entry into *secondary intersubjectivity*.

Summary of Section 4

- Imitations, by mothers as much as by infants, are an important feature of early relationships.
- The development of intersubjectivity is a key feature of early relationships.

5 Scaffolding

During the primary phase of their relationship, it could be said that the mother is helping the baby to come to an understanding that interactions with others can be predictable. The baby can play an active part within the relationship and certain 'units' of inter-personal behaviour can carry meaning. These achievements are reached through joint attention and sharing in the interactions and, as you have seen, the mother is in a sense tutoring the baby in the 'rules of the game'. Once this foundation is firm enough, the breakthrough to joint attention elsewhere allows the mother to begin to tutor the baby in *things they can do together, with objects.*

Bruner is a psychologist who has done much to elaborate our understanding of how such joint action may provide an essential basis for the development of language proper (and hence of dialogue proper, rather than pseudo-dialogue). By involving the baby in what Bruner has called *joint-action formats*, the mother creates simplified and stereotyped sequences of actions with objects. These sequences are repeated over and over so that the baby can learn them as potent intersubjective topics, and also, through their own involvement in them, as potentially 'do-able' alone. Bruner has argued (e.g. Bruner, 1975) that these then become capable of being talked about and hence lay the foundation for the first steps in true language.

Before language emerges in the infant, mothers can structure interactions with their infant, involving other objects, such that knowledge about what can be done, and how to do it, can be transmitted. Bruner has used the term *scaffolding* to describe a particular way of interacting with an infant (or child). In this type of interaction the adult controls some elements of the situation sufficiently to allow the infant to make progress and to achieve results in a way that they would be unable to do alone.

In Box 2 you will see how a mother controls the interaction with her infant concerning the use of a book as an object and topic of interaction. This shows what Bruner means by the term scaffolding and also points up clear parallels with the processes operating during the primary phase, before the use of objects.

BOX 2

The 'book-reading' action format

As for mother's role in 'book-reading', she (like all mothers we have observed) drastically limits her speech in the format and maintains a steady regularity. In her dialogues with Richard in 'book-reading' she uses four utterance types in her speech and in a strikingly fixed order. First, to get his attention, she says 'Look'. Second, with a distinctly rising inflection, she asks 'What's that?' Third, she gives the picture a label, 'It's an X'. And finally, in response to his actions, she says 'That's right'. Each of these utterance types is highly contingent on Richard's behaviour. She only says 'What's that?' when he has given some responsive gesture of vocalization to 'Look!'

In each case, a single verbal token accounts for from nearly half to more than 90 per cent of the utterance types. The way Richard's mother uses the four speech constituents is closely linked to what her son says or does, as noted. When she varies her response, it is with good reason. Thus, if *he* initiates a cycle by pointing and vocalizing, then *she* responds invariably and at the appropriate point in the cycle rather than at the beginning.

Her fine tuning is fine indeed. For example, if after her query Richard labels the picture correctly, she will virtually always skip the label and jump to the response 'Yes'. Like the other mothers we have studied, she is following ordinary, polite rules for adult dialogue.

Source: Bruner, 1981, pp. 48–9.

Figure 8   Book reading.

Scaffolding infant visual behaviour

In practice, most mothers are apparently very skilled in sustaining the interest and attention of their babies, both towards themselves and towards significant objects and events which are encountered in the course of everyday life. Mothers also often act as mediators between the baby and outside events. They tend to provide, quite unselfconsciously, forms of feedback which are dramatically attention-compelling because they are contingently geared – in a very delicately timed way – to actions which are spontaneously made by the infant himself. Even in the most straightforward adult-and-baby encounters with objects, the adult's visual monitoring of the baby's activity may be highly critical. Note how, in practice, one is able to elicit simple visual following behaviour in a supine four-week-old infant using a dangling ring. In this superficially simple task, the test demonstrator will carefully attend, not just to the general state of arousal of the infant, but to his precise focus and line of regard. Having 'hooked' the attention of the infant upon the ring, one then begins gingerly to move it across his field of vision in such a way that the infant's eyes continue to hold the object with successive fixations until eventually the head follows the eyes in that coordinated overall movement pattern which denotes successful tracking. If the test object is moved too suddenly, or is left static too long, the visual attention of the infant will flag and the attempt will have to begin all over again from scratch. In this instance, what is in fact happening is a highly skilled monitoring by the adult and a consequent adjustment of the dangling object moment by moment, depending on the feedback which is being obtained from the spontaneous actions of the infant. It might even be argued that one is dragging from the infant a complex response which he would be unlikely to give to an object which was moved by mechanical means across his visual field. The resulting sequence of the infant is therefore a combination of his own activity and an *intelligent manipulation of that activity by the much more sophisticated adult partner.* The adult, by being contingently responsive to the infant in a way which only another human being could be, manages both to hold the infant's attention and to shape the course of his ongoing activity pattern; and, incidentally, the infant is provided with a sustained looking experience which might not otherwise have occurred.

Source: Newson and Newson, 1976, pp. 91–2.

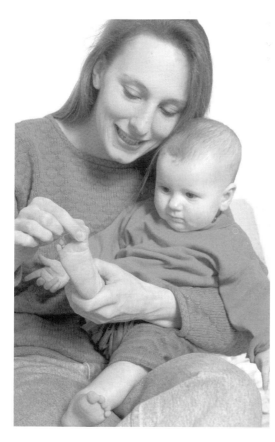

Figure 9 Joint attention.

A mother or a psychologist testing a baby needs to be very sensitive to the baby's behaviour in order to get the baby to track an object visually. Box 3 shows scaffolding in action with even a very young baby.

Also supporting this process are the mother's *modelling, cueing* and *'raising the ante'* (Wood *et al.*, 1976). In *modelling*, the mother shows what can be done, providing a model for what can be achieved. In *cueing*, the mother indicates to their infant that a particular format is appropriate to the situation and, finally, in *raising the ante* the mother encourages the child to elaborate their formats, perhaps by joining different formats together, to achieve more complex goals.

Clearly, then, there are striking parallels between what mothers do with infants prior to the involvement of objects in their interactions together, and what they do in joint-action formats. Having overviewed, then, the development of interactions from birth up to the emergence of language, this chapter shows how important the *social* world can be for the development of what will become *individual*, that is, within the child. Vygotsky (1962) (see Chapter 2) argued strongly for this *social constructivist* view of cognitive development, proposing that all thought arises first in actions between people and only then becomes internalized. Vygotsky also used the term *zone of proximal development* (ZPD) to describe the area within which the sort of effective tutoring referred to above can take place. It is defined as the area that the child is capable of working within, given the support of a more able other person; an area which is 'reachable' given help and, ultimately, reachable alone.

Summary of Section 5

- The joint-action format concept is a useful way of describing simplified and stereotyped interaction patterns between mothers and babies.
- Scaffolding is a particular way in which adults use various techniques to enable infants to elaborate on their behaviour.
- Caregivers can help to foster their infants' development by creating a 'zone of proximal development' (ZPD), as described by Vygotsky.

6   Containing

So far this chapter has taken rather a narrow and 'rose-coloured' view of mother–infant relations, as if they are always comfortable, with engaging feeding situations and lively, mutually rewarding interactions. This picture pervades much experimental work with babies, and the 'down side' of caring for an infant rarely gets mentioned. For example, it is a common experience for researchers working with young babies to fail to get data from up to 50 per cent of their participants because of fretting, falling asleep, burps and all the other vicissitudes of infant life

(Oates, 1998). Indeed, the 'quiet, alert' state in which conversations with the mother can be sustained and experiments successfully completed is a relatively small proportion of the baby's day. In many ways this takes up a rather unrepresentative 'peak' of the baby's ability to organize their behaviour and attend to events in the outside world.

There is general agreement that babies' states can be fairly clearly delineated, as outlined in Table 2.

Table 2 **Babies' states of attention**

State 1	Deep sleep
State 2	Light sleep: eyes closed, but irregular breathing and small movements
State 3	Quiet, alert: eyes open and baby still and attentive
State 4	Active awake: vigorous movement
State 5	Crying or fretting

The proportion of the day that a baby is in these different states varies a great deal from baby to baby, and also to some extent from day to day, and week to week as well as changing as the baby gets older. It is difficult to say quite what the differences between babies are caused by, because mothers can obviously make a difference, at least some of the time, by shifting babies' states (e.g. from State 5 to State 3 by comforting and pacifying). Hence, there will clearly be an interaction between any differences in the babies' and the mothers' behaviours. There are also many other environmental factors that affect proportions of time in the different states: temperature, amount of clothing, ambient noise levels and feeding schedule (to name just a few) can all play a role. It is also a matter of the infant's temperament as well; babies do seem to have consistent, individual differences in how they respond to stimulation, how active they are and how easily they are soothed when upset.

On average, young babies spend between 1½ and 3 hours each day in State 5, this being between a quarter and a half of their total awake time (Bradley, 1989). So, a large proportion of the baby's early experience is basically distressful.

A major task for many mothers is to alleviate their babies' distress, as much as it is to engage in pseudo-dialogues or conversation-like feeding sessions. For many mothers the stresses and strains of this, compounded with the many other pressures of having a new baby, can cause quite severe reactions. Table 3 gives some indication of the prevalence of negative feelings in mothers with a young baby.

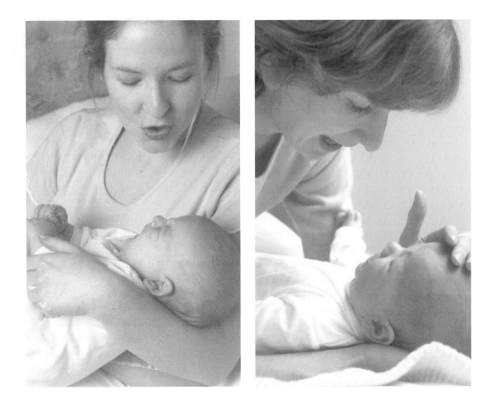

Figure 10   Positive and negative emotions.

Table 3   **Loss versus gain in early maternal care**

Mothers' reactions	% of sample
Not interested in the baby at birth	70
Disappointed with baby's sex	25
Babycare harder work than expected	77
Felt angry/violent towards baby	70
Cannot get enough sleep	100
Feeding problems	73
Felt very anxious about baby	45

$N = 55$

Source: Oakley, 1980, p. 255.

To understand more fully the development of relationships between mothers and infants it is important to take account of how negative feelings in one or both partners, as well as more positive emotions, are dealt with and experienced. Studies of infants' perceptions of emotional facial and vocal displays have shown that babies aged under 1 month are able to tell apart happy, angry, surprised and sad expressions, although other emotions, such as fear, are not reliably discriminated (Walker-Andrews, 1986). Babies can also appear to express a range of emotions through different cries and patterns of facial and bodily movement (Haviland and Lelwica, 1987). Whether babies actually experience these basic emotions themselves in the same way as adults is of course impossible to fully verify, but perhaps the most important point about infant emotional experience is that the mother treats these different expressions of the baby as if they indicate distinct emotional experiences. Babies' cries can have a very powerful emotional effect on mothers, and it can often be a struggle to deal with the strong feelings evoked by a crying infant, especially if attempts to pacify are not immediately successful.

If a mother is to be empathic towards her baby, she has to be open to her baby's emotional experience. But empathy involves actually experiencing the same feelings as another person, a baby who is really crying intensely and inconsolably can stir up a mother to a degree that can be very difficult for her to cope with. The successful handling of such situations by the mother can provide the infant with the experience of strong, overpowering emotions being 'contained' and not catastrophic (Sorensen, 1997), just as the scaffolding of pseudo-dialogues by the mother allows the infant to experience 'being in a dialogue'.

6.1 People and objects

All the various processes that you have been looking at so far in this chapter clearly give a young infant the opportunity to experience repeated episodes of particular sorts of relatedness with the mother. A central question which attracts the attention of many psychologists, is 'What does the baby learn from these repeated experiences?'. This is a question of special interest because many theorists believe that what babies make of these early experiences is connected to the whole course of the development of their personalities. The basic idea is that babies construct an inner model or mental representation of this first relationship and because of its potency and centrality to their lives, this becomes a foundation for future relationships with others. This is a very pervasive notion that underlies much psychological and psychiatric practice as well as theory.

Mental model
A structure in the mind that represents some object or process in the outside world; e.g. a memory of a happy event.

The construction of this mental model is seen as being a necessary key part of the formation of an emotional *attachment* to the mother. A dominant view of this mental model has its origins in the theoretical ideas developed by Melanie Klein, a psychoanalyst, who made some striking and controversial suggestions about the nature of a baby's inner world and how it comes to be populated with 'objects' based on the experiences arising in the baby's relationship with their mother. Kleinian theory has formed the basis for a dominant way of thinking about adult emotional life and its development from infancy that has come to be known as 'object-relations theory' and informs therapeutic and research work with adults and with children.

There are four starting-points for this theory:

1   What is built up in the baby's mind is not just some sort of copy or abstraction of the mother herself, but rather something that is based on an amalgam of the baby's own experiences with what the baby perceives of the mother, through all the senses.

2   Babies do not at first differentiate clearly between themselves and their mothers.

3   A dominance of emotion in experience is paralleled by a relatively primitive ability in the baby to separate the emotions evoked by something from the thing itself.

4   Babies do not at first recognize that an object that gives a good experience at one time is nevertheless the same object even if it gives a bad experience at another time.

These have some striking similarities to Piaget's descriptions of young babies' mental representations of inanimate objects. He argued that the idea of the permanence of an object, independent of one's perception of it, is not understood at all by young infants (see Chapter 4).

6.2 Object-relations theory

Klein believed that infants do not have a concept of whole objects at all in the first 2–3 months of life, but instead see the world around them as a series of quite separate experiences of parts of objects: Klein called these 'part-objects'. She saw this happening because the infant is unable to co-ordinate these moment-to-moment impressions in such a way as to construct concepts of the whole objects of which the impressions are a part. So, for example, the newborn's world might include such part-objects as 'the-nipple-giving-milk', 'the-nipple-not-giving-milk', the 'difficult-to-suck-nipple', and so forth. These part-objects would not be related to each other in any way at first: the infant would not see that they were part of the same object. The infant would also tend to associate particular part-objects with particular good or bad feelings. Further, in response to unsatisfying experiences, the infant would compensate for these unconsciously by fantasizing a part-object that was satisfying. For Klein, even the newborn baby has the ability to construct internal objects: to have unconscious fantasies. So, for example, a response to unsatisfied hunger would be to fantasize a 'nipple-that-gives-milk' part-object. An example of the sort of behaviour that suggested this idea to Klein would be a hungry infant apparently being satisfied by sucking on something that does not give milk. Thus, the infant's mind would come to contain representations of many part-objects, derived from experiences with their mother, some with associated good feelings, and some with associated bad feelings, some based on experience, some on fantasy. In the early stages of an infant's life, these would be quite separate and not seen as being different aspects of the same part-object (for example, the breast), or even as the same parts of the whole object

Figure 11   'Good' and 'bad' part-objects.

(the mother). This aspect of Kleinian theory has led to the term 'object-relations' being used to describe the approach of theorists, analysts and therapists following Kleinian principles.

Psychoanalytic theory has a special term to describe the 'taking-in' of objects or part-objects so that representations of them are built up in the mind: this process is called '*introjection*'. Introjected objects, or parts of them, enter into a person's mental life. In a way, introjection is, for psychoanalytic theory, what learning is for many other psychological theories. The opposite of introjection is what was described earlier in this chapter as projection: in this process, inner feelings are projected outwards onto outside objects. In this way, objects outside the individual come to take on, for the individual, the feelings originally felt towards the internal representations of those objects. Thus, if a child feels anger towards a person, projection would result in the child seeing the person as angry with the child.

Because of the projective and introjective processes, and because this period of development, the first 3–4 months, is characterized for Klein by the splitting of objects into good and bad part-objects, she called the dominant mode of this period the 'paranoid–schizoid position'. She used the word 'position' because she saw this way of relating to the world as one to which adults are likely to return, or regress, when under mental stress. This perspective contrasts with stage theories of development where such regressions are not believed to occur.

The depressive position

As the child comes to the discovery that many part-objects in fact belong to the same whole object, so the good and bad introjections and fantasies of the part-objects come closer together in the mind. As they do so, conflict then arises from the realization that 'wholly-good' part-objects are in reality part of the same object as the 'wholly-bad' part-objects. So, for example, the infant begins to appreciate that 'the-breast-that-satisfies' is actually the same object as 'the-breast-that-frustrates'. Similarly, at the same time all the feelings and wishes associated with the previously discrete part-objects begin to draw together and hence come into conflict.

To develop in a healthy direction, Klein believed, the infant has to cope with these disturbances by giving up the wholly-good part-objects for the more ambivalent object that is beginning to be seen as the amalgam of the split part-objects. This, according to Klein, is the infant's first major feeling of loss, and leads to sadness and grief for the lost, good part-objects. The depression this causes led Klein to call this the 'depressive position'. She saw the depressive position as being the source of good, loving relationships with other people, not just split-off parts of them: their good aspects can be accepted along with their bad aspects.

I have covered these ideas in some detail because they are challenging and interesting, and also because they have had some significant effects on developmental psychology. Among many others, John Bowlby and Donald Winnicott, who were closely associated with Klein's work, were very much influenced by Kleinian theory. But they are not without their critics. Apart from the general criticisms of psychoanalytic theory that see it as difficult to investigate empirically, two central problems have been pointed to: the nature of the infant experience (the infant's capacity to have fantasies, to feel persecution, anger and a sense of good and bad) and the idea of splitting (which hinges on the dominance of 'good' and 'bad' in mental representations). While accepting the general notion that the formation of a mental model of 'being with the mother' is indeed a critical and central task of infancy, Stern, a psychoanalytic clinician and theorist, has argued instead that splitting is a much later development since the young baby simply does not have the 'reference points' to divide experience up in this way (Stern, 1985). Instead, he argues, the subtle gradations of pleasurable through to unpleasurable experiences, happening many times each day with the mother, actually allow even a primitive mental ability to begin to pick out what is *invariant* (certain consistent perceptual qualities of the mother and the relatedness that goes with these) from what is more variable and in the baby's experience. His argument is that this can actually allow the baby to develop quite quickly a clearer idea of boundary between self and mother and also of the mother as a consistent and whole object.

Summary of Section 6

- Experimental studies of infants give only a partial picture of the various emotional states of infants' lives.
- Dealing with distress is a central part of caring for a baby.
- The way mothers deal with distress in their babies may play an important part in their babies' development.
- Object-relations theory describes how babies may form representations of other people and their relationships with them, but there are competing views on this process.

7 Transacting

As you approach the conclusion of this chapter, and also the conclusion of this book, it is appropriate to draw on ideas that have been introduced in your reading so far. This will enable you to reflect on the sorts of models of the developmental process that are needed to encompass the aspects of relationships between mothers and babies that you have looked at.

First, a model that simply views the baby as a passive reactor to how the mother behaves is clearly inadequate. At the very least the baby has to be active in rudimentary behaving and expressing feelings in order for the mother to be able to frame and give sense to these feelings and behaviours. Similarly, a model that sees development as proceeding within and originating from the baby would rule out this process of the development of mutually shared and eventually internalized joint meanings.

So, at the very least, the desired model has to have an interactive element: each partner has to be seen as influencing the other. But, as you have seen, this interaction can be described at many different levels, from the moment-to-moment of pseudo-dialogue to the repeated experience of emotions being contained. This goes beyond simple interaction, since what changes in one partner as a result of the other's behaviour then goes on to influence their behaviour and is fed back, transformed, to the other. In a very real sense, then, a baby plays a role in constructing their own social environment: it is not something 'out there', unaffected by the baby, but effectively something that is built by mother and baby together. At several points in previous chapters this idea has been discussed, and the term *transaction* has been used to express a process that extends beyond simple, one-way effects on the baby and beyond the interaction of the baby's and mother's propensities and behaviours. This transaction is partly driven by the mother 'over-interpreting' her baby's behaviour and by her behaviour offering a framework of meanings and possible actions which the baby can then gradually internalize and make their own.

Summary of Section 7

- Infants are active agents in constructing their social worlds.
- Since the behaviour of a baby and the mother affects each other, a simple cause-and-effect model cannot fully describe the complex transactional links between the mother's and the baby's behaviour: each person plays a part in determining how the other behaves and hence what happens between them.

8   Conclusion

In this chapter a model of various aspects of 'normal' interaction between mother and baby was built up as if this is a culturally universal process and a basic necessity for the first stages in the development of adult capacities to relate to others. To the extent that the specific adjustments that mothers make to their babies have been found in most cultures, this picture seems to be accurate. For example, 'baby-talk', the adjustments in speech that adults make when talking to babies, does seem virtually universal. But there are several studies of infant–mother relationships in different cultures that should cause us to doubt the absolute necessity of these processes.

Schieffelin and Ochs (1983), refer to the 'paradox of familiarity' which may mislead researchers and carers. The paradox is that although concepts such as attributing motives and interpreting behaviour can be easily applied in studying mother–infant interaction it is far harder to recognize the underlying cultural principles that give these concepts their meanings. They argue that such 'givens' as mother–infant interaction may be embedded in a much more extensive set of cultural assumptions about what it is to be a person and to communicate with others:

> Culture is not something that can be considered separately from the accounts of caregiver–child interactions; it is what organizes and gives meaning to that interaction. This is an important point, as it affects the definition and interpretation of the behaviours of caregivers and children. How caregivers and children speak and act towards one another is linked to cultural patterns that extend and have consequences beyond the specific interactions observed. For example, how caregivers speak to their children may be linked to other institutional adaptations to young children. These adaptations in turn may be linked to how members of a given society view children more generally (their 'nature', their social status and expected comportment) and to how members think children develop.
>
> (Schieffelin and Ochs, 1983, p. 116)

Schieffelin and Ochs propose that the 'developmental story' of mother–infant interaction that is told in most cultures is based on an assumption, an image of the infant, that sees the infant as a *social being* and the mother's role as being to *take the perspective of the infant*. In the following extract, they show how a very different set of assumptions, held by the Kaluli, a Papuan New Guinea culture, lead to radically different patterns of interaction. For the Kaluli, babies are seen as helpless and unable to understand anything that is said to them: mothers take care of them because they are 'sorry for them'.

> Mothers, who are primary caregivers, are attentive to their infants and physically responsive to them. Whenever an infant cries it is offered the breast. However, while nursing her infant, a mother may also be involved in other activities, such as food preparation, or she may be engaged in conversation with individuals in the household. Mothers never leave their infants alone and only rarely with other caregivers. When not holding

their infants, mothers carry them in netted bags which are suspended from their heads. When the mother is gardening, gathering wood, or just sitting with others, the baby will sleep in the netted bag next to the mother's body.

Kaluli mothers, given their belief that infants 'have no understanding', never treat their infants as partners (speaker/addressee) in dyadic communicative interactions. While they greet their infants by name and use expressive vocalizations, they rarely address other utterances to them. Furthermore, mothers and infants do not gaze into each other's eyes, an interactional pattern that is consistent with adult patterns of not gazing when vocalizing in interaction with one another. Rather than facing their babies and speaking to them, Kaluli mothers tend to face their babies outwards so that they can be seen by, and see others that are part of the social group. Older children greet and address the infant and in response to this, the mother while moving the baby, speaks in a high-pitched nasalized voice 'for' the baby.

(Schieffelin and Ochs, 1983, p. 218)

What this is suggesting is that it may be an overinterpretation of what is seen happening with mothers and babies to say that this is the only way and the essential way that mothers can interact with babies. These psychological processes of adapting and communicating with infants may be better described as cultural processes that serve the ends of producing particular sorts of individuals, who can participate in and perpetuate the sorts of social interactions that underpin many aspects of their culture.

Further reading

Bradley, B. S. (1989) *Visions of Infancy*, Cambridge, Polity Press.

Schaffer, R. (1977) *Mothering*, London, Fontana/Open Books.

Stern, D. (1985) *The Interpersonal World of the Infant*, New York, Basic Books.

References

Brazelton, T. B. and Cramer, B. G. (1991) *The Earliest Relationship: parents, infants and the drama of early attachment*, London, Karnac Books.

Berko Gleason, J. (1973) 'Code-switching in children's language', in Moore, T. E. (ed.) *Cognitive Development and the Acquisition of Language*, New York, Academic Press.

Bradley, B. S. (1989) *Visions of Infancy*, Cambridge, Polity Press.

Bruner, J. S. (1975) 'From communication to language: a psychological perspective', *Cognition*, vol. 3, pp. 255–87.

Bruner, J. S. (1981) 'Intention in the structure of action and interaction', in Lipsitt, L. P. (ed.) *Advances in Infancy Research, vol. 1*, Northwood, NJ, Ablex.

Carpenter, G. C., Tecce, J. J., Stechler, G. and Friedman, S. (1970) 'Differential visual behaviour to human and humanoid faces in early infancy', *Merrill-Palmer Quarterly of Behaviour and Development*, vol. 16, pp. 91–108.

Cohn, J. F. and Tronick, E. Z. (1983) 'Three-month-old infants' reactions to simulated maternal depression', *Child Development*, vol. 54, pp. 185–93.

Fernald, A., Taeschner, T., Dunn, J., Papousek, M., Boysson-Bardies, B. de and Fukui, I. (1989) 'A cross-language study of prosodic modifications in mothers' and fathers' speech to preverbal infants', *Journal of Child Language*, vol. 16, pp. 477–501.

Haviland, J. M. and Lelwica, M. (1987) 'The induced affect response: 10-week-old infants; responses to three emotional expressions', *Developmental Psychology*, vol. 23, pp. 97–104.

Hobson, R. P. (1993) *Autism and the Development of Mind*, Hove, Lawrence Erlbaum.

Hobson, R. P. (2002) *The Cradle of Thought*, London, Macmillan.

Kaye, K. (1982) *The Mental and Social Life of Babies: how parents create persons*, Brighton, Harvester Press.

Kaye, K. and Brazelton, T. B. (1971) 'Mother–infant interaction in the organization of sucking', paper presented to the Society for Research in Child Development, Minneapolis, March 1971.

Kaye, K. and Fogel, A. (1980) 'The temporal structure of face-to-face communication between mothers and infants', *Developmental Psychology*, vol. 16, pp. 454–64.

Kaye, K. and Marcus, J. (1981) 'Infant imitation: the sensorimotor agenda', *Developmental Psychology*, vol. 17, pp. 258–65.

Meltzoff, A. N. and Moore, M. K. (1977) 'Imitation of facial and manual gestures by human neonates', *Science*, vol. 198, pp. 75–8.

Moran, G., Krupka, A., Tutton, A. and Symons, D. (1987) 'Patterns of maternal and infant imitation during play', *Infant Behaviour and Development*, vol. 10, pp. 477–91.

Murray, L. and Trevarthen, C. (1985) 'Emotional regulation of interactions between two-month-olds and their mothers', in Field, T. M. and Fox, N. A. (eds) *Social Perception in Infants*, Northwood, NJ, Ablex.

Newson, J. and Newson, E. (1976) 'On the social origins of symbolic functioning', in Varma, V. P. and Williams, P. (eds) *Piaget, Psychology and Education*, London, Hodder and Stoughton.

Norman, D. A. (1980) 'Twelve issues for cognitive science', *Cognitive Science*, vol. 4, pp. 1–32.

Oakley, A. (1980) *Women Confined: towards a sociology of childbirth*, Oxford, Robertson.

Oates, J. (1998) 'Risk factors for infant attrition and low engagement in experiments and free-play', *Infant Behaviour and Development*, vol. 21, pp. 555–69.

Pawlby, S. (1977) 'Imitative interaction', in Schaffer, H. R. (ed.) *Studies in Mother–Infant Interaction*, London, Academic Press.

Reddy, V., Hay, D., Murray, L. and Trevarthen, C. (1997) 'Communication in infancy: mutual regulation of affect and attention', in Bremner, G., Slater, A. and Butterworth, G. (eds) *Infant Development: recent advances*, Hove, Psychology Press.

Rutter, M. (1981, 2nd edn) *Maternal Deprivation Reassessed*, Harmondsworth, Penguin.

Schaffer, H. R. (1984) *The Child's Entry into a Social World*, London, Academic Press.

Schieffelin, B. B. and Ochs, E. (1983) 'A cultural perspective on the transition from prelinguistic to linguistic communication', in Golinkoff, R. M. (ed.) *The Transition from Prelinguistic to Linguistic Communication*, Hillsdale, NJ, Erlbaum.

Shatz, M. and Gelman, R. (1973) 'The development of communication skills: modifications in the speech of young children as a function of listener', *Monographs of the Society for Research in Child Development*, vol. 38, no. 5 (serial no. 152).

Snow, C. E. (1972) 'Mothers' speech to children learning language', *Child Development*, vol. 43, pp. 549–65.

Snow, C. and Ferguson, C. (eds) (1977) *Talking to Children: language input and acquisition*, Cambridge, Cambridge University Press.

Sorensen, P. B. (1997) 'Thoughts on the containing process from the perspective of infant/mother relations', in Reid, S. (ed.) *Developments in Infant Observation: the Tavistock model*, London, Routledge.

Stern, D. (1985) *The Interpersonal World of the Infant*, New York, Basic Books.

Trevarthen, C. (1977) 'Descriptive analyses of infant communicative behaviour', in Schaffer, H. R. (ed.) *Studies in Mother–Infant Interaction*, London, Academic Press.

Trevarthen, C. (1979) 'Communication and cooperation in early infancy: a description of primary intersubjectivity', in Bullowa, M. (ed.) *Before Speech*, Cambridge, Cambridge University Press.

Trevarthen, C. (1993) 'The functions of emotions in early infant communication and development', in Nadel, J. and Camaioni, L. (eds) *New Perspectives in Early Communicative Development*, London, Routledge.

Tronick, E., Als, H., Adamson, L., Wise, S. and Brazelton, T. B. (1978) 'The infant's response to entrapment between contradictory messages in face-to-face interaction', *Journal of the American Academy of Child Psychiatry*, vol. 17, pp. 1–13.

Vygotsky, L. S. (1962) *Thought and Language*, Cambridge, MA, MIT Press.

Walker-Andrews, A. S. (1986) 'Intermodal perception of expressive behaviours: relation of eye and voice', *Developmental Psychology*, vol. 22, pp. 373–77.

Winnicott, D. W. (1964) *The Child, the Family and the Outside World*, Harmondsworth, Penguin Books.

Wood, D. J., Bruner, J. S. and Ross, G. (1976) 'The role of tutoring in problem-solving', *Journal of Child Psychology and Psychiatry*, vol. 17, pp. 89–100.

Acknowledgements

Grateful acknowledgement is made to the following sources for permission to reproduce material within this book. Every effort has been made to contact copyright holders. If any have been inadvertently overlooked the publishers will be pleased to make the necessary arrangements at the first opportunity.

Chapter 1

This chapter is based on Das Gupta, P. (1994) 'Images of childhood and theories of development' in Oates, J. (ed) *The Foundations of Child Development*, Milton Keynes, Blackwells in association with The Open University.

Text

Reading A: Miller, L., Drury, R. and Campbell R. (eds) (2002) 'Work, play and learning in the lives of young children', *Exploring Early Years Education and Care*, Granada Learning Ltd.

Figures

Figure 1 upper left: Getty images; *Figure 1 upper right*: Alamy; *Figure 1 lower*: Bubbles; *Figure 2*: Bubbles; *Figure 3*: English Heritage Photo Library; *Figure 4*: From Berk, L. (1994) *Child Development* (3rd edn), Published by Allyn & Bacon, Boston, MA. Copyright © 1994 by Pearson Education. Reprinted/adapted by permission of the publisher. Originally taken from Malina, R. M. (1975) *Growth and Development: the first twenty years in man*, p. 19, Minneapolis, Burgess Publishing Company; *Figure 5*: Shirley, M. M. (1933) 'The First Two Years – a study of twenty-five babies', *Intellectual Development*, vol. 2, University of Minnesota Press, Copyright © 1933 by University of Minnesota Press; *Figure 6*: Bubbles; *Figure 7:* Still Pictures.

Chapter 2

Text

Reading A: Keenan, M. (2004) 'Autism in Northern Ireland: the tragedy and the shame', *The Psychologist*, vol. 17 (2), The British Psychological Society; *Reading B*: Bandura, A. (1973) 'Origins of aggression', in *Aggression: a social learning analysis*, Prentice Hall, Inc., Copyright © Albert Bandura; *Reading C*: Vygotsky, L. (1986) 'Piaget's theory of the child's speech and thought', in Kozulin, A. (trans.), *Thought and Language*, The MIT Press, Copyright © 1986 by The Massachusetts Institute of Technology.

Figure

Figure 5: Copyright © Albert Bandura.

Chapter 3

Text

Reading A: Fantz, R. L. (1963) 'Pattern vision in newborn infants', *Science*, vol. 140, AAAS; *Reading B*: Pascalis, O., de Haan M. and Nelson, C. (2002) 'Is face processing species-specific during the first year of life?', *Science*, vol. 296, AAAS.

Figures

Figure 5: Maurer, D. and Maurer, C. (1998) *The World of the Newborn* (2nd edn), New York, Basic Books. Reproduced with permission from Perseus Books and The Copyright Clearance Centre; *Figure 9*: Copyright © Ian Bushell.

Chapter 4

Table

Table 1: Hood, B. and Willatts, P. (1986) 'Reaching in the dark to an object's remembered position: evidence of object permanence in 5 month old infants', *British Journal of Developmental Psychology*, by kind permission of The British Psychological Society.

Figures

Figure 4: Reprinted from Baillargeon, R., Spelke, E. S. and Wasserman, S. (1985) 'Object Performance in 5-month old infants', *Cognition*, vol. 20 (3), pp. 191–208, with permission from Elsevier; *Figure 5*: Reprinted from Baillargeon, R. Spelke, E. S. and Wasserman, S. (1985) 'Object Performance in 5-month old infants', *Cognition*, vol. 20 (3) , pp. 191–208, with permission from Elsevier; *Figure 6*: Reprinted from Baillargeon, R. (1986) 'Representing the existence and the location of hidden objects', *Cognition*, vol. 21 (1), pp. 1–94, with permission from Elsevier; *Figure 7*: Diamond, A. (1985) 'Development of the ability to use recall to guide action, as indicated by infant's performance on AB', and Melzoff, A. N. (1983) 'Newborn infants imitate adult facial gestures', *Child Development*, Blackwell Publishing Ltd.

Chapter 5

Figure

Figure 9: Alamy.

Table

Table 3: Fullard, W. *et al.* (1978) 'Toddler temperament scale', Department of Educational Psychology, Temple University, Philadelphia.

Chapter 6

Text

Reading A: Reprinted from Karmiloff-Smith, A. (1998) 'Development itself is the key to understanding developmental disorders', *Trends in Cognitive Sciences*, vol. 2, pp. 389–98, Copyright © 1998, with permission from Elsevier; *Reading B*: Bjorklund D. F. and Pellegrini, A. D. (2000) 'Child development and evolutionary psychology', *Child Development*, vol. 71 (6), pp. 1696–97, Blackwell Publishing Ltd.

Figures

Figure 1: From Pinel Biopsychology (5th edn), Published by Allyn & Bacon, Boston, MA. Copyright © 2003 by Pearson Education. Adapted by permission of the publisher; *Figure 2*: Passer, M. W. and Smith, R. E. (2004) 'Biological foundations of behaviour', in *Psychology: the science of mind and behaviour*, The McGraw-Hill Companies Inc.; *Figure 4*: Plomin, R. *et al*., (2001) 'Mendel's laws of heredity', in *Behavioral Genetics* (4th edn), Worth Publishers and W. H. Freeman and Company.

Chapter 7

Tables

Table 3: © Copyright Professor Ann Oakley.

Figures

Figure 1: Alamy; *Figure 2*: Bubbles; *Figure 3*: Bubbles; *Figure 4*: Brazelton, B. T. and Cramer, B. G. (1990) *The Earliest Relationship*, Karnac Books, Copyright © 1990 T. Berry Brazelton and Bertrand G. Cramer; *Figure 5*: Brazelton, B. T. and Cramer, B. G. (1990) *The Earliest Relationship*, Karnac Books, Copyright © 1990 T. Berry Brazelton and Bertrand G. Cramer; *Figure 6*: Brazelton, B. T. and Cramer, B. G. (1990) *The Earliest Relationship*, Karnac Books, Copyright © 1990 T. Berry Brazelton and Bertrand G. Cramer; *Figure 7*: Alamy; *Figure 8*: Alamy; *Figure 9*: Bubbles; *Figure 10a*: Bubbles; *Figure 10b*: Bubbles.

Cover photographs

© Getty Images

Name index

Subject index

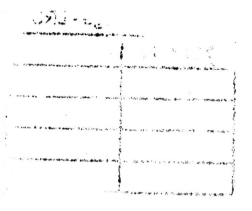